Eye for an Eye

EYE FOR AN EYE

William Ian Miller
University of Michigan

CAMBRIDGE
UNIVERSITY PRESS

CAMBRIDGE UNIVERSITY PRESS
Cambridge, New York, Melbourne, Madrid, Cape Town, Singapore, São Paulo

Cambridge University Press
40 West 20th Street, New York, NY 10011-4211, USA

www.cambridge.org
Information on this title: www.cambridge.org/9780521856805

First published 2006

Printed in the United States of America

A catalog record for this publication is available from the British Library.

Library of Congress Cataloging in Publication Data
Miller, William Ian, 1946–
Eye for an eye / William Ian Miller.
p. cm.
Includes bibliographical references and index.
ISBN 0-521-85680-9
1. Lex talionis – History. 2. Law, Ancient. 3. Law, Primitive. I. Title.
K5103.M49 2005
340.5′3–dc22 2005008077

ISBN-13 978-0-521-85680-5 hardback
ISBN-10 0-521-85680-9 hardback

For Joseph Weiler:
soldier, teacher, friend

And if any mischief follow, then thou shalt give life for life,
Eye for eye, tooth for tooth, hand for hand, foot for foot,
Burning for burning, wound for wound, stripe for stripe.

Exodus 21.23–25

Contents

Preface: A Theory of Justice?

This book is, in its peculiar way, a theory of justice, or more properly an antitheory of justice. It is an antitheory because it is not abstract. It is about eyes, teeth, hands, and lives. It is an extended gloss on the law of the talion: an eye for an eye, a tooth for a tooth, measure for measure. In its biblical formulation, the talion puts the body – lives, eyes, hands, teeth – front and center as *the* measure of value. True, the body has always provided us – until the metric system relieved it of the task – with feet to measure length, fathoms (the measure of the arms spread out from tip to tip) to measure depth, hands to measure the height of horses, ells (from elbow) to measure cloth, even pinches to measure salt.

But the talion cuts deeper than this. For what it means to do is measure and value *us*. Thus, it prices John's life as equal to Harry's. Or if Harry is a loser and his life is not quite a life, it might measure John's worth as the sum of Harry's and Pete's. The talion states the value of my eye in terms of your eye, the value of your teeth in terms of my teeth. Eyes and teeth become units of valuation. But the talion doesn't stop there. Horrifically enough, it seems to demand that eyes, teeth, and lives are also to provide the means of payment. Fork over that eye, please.

The talion (the same Latin root supplies us with *retaliate*) indicates a repayment in kind. It is not a talon – not an eagle's claw – of which I must inform my students and even remind an occasional colleague. It is easy to excuse the misunderstanding. After all, the difference between talion and talon is but the difference of an *i*. And then one has to try hard not to imagine a bird of prey or carrion-eater swooping down

ix

and leaving one looking like poor Gloucester: out vile jelly, where is thy lustre now?

This book cares about matter and the facts of the matter. It is the result of years, more than thirty now, of scholarly immersion into revenge cultures. And in some small way it is my revenge on academic discussions of justice that have painted revenge as an unnuanced Vice in a morality play. Too often these discussions have the oppressive style of complacent and predictable sermonizing: lip service to, or defenses of, various safely proper positions. Would that academics had the knowledge (and irony) of a middling singer of an heroic tale.

I care about what people thought, what they actually did, what they wrote, and the stories they told, not just yesterday, but 2,500 years ago too. My themes cannot be reduced to a single encapsulable thesis. People are too smart and too inventive, the variability of daily experience too complex, to be so easily cabined. If a characterization of the book's genre is required, it is best seen as an historical and philosophical meditation on paying back and buying back – a meditation, that is, on retaliation and redemption.

In short, the book is about settling accounts, about getting even, with all that is implied by the mercantile diction of paying, owing, and satisfying obligations. Talionic cultures tended to be honor cultures, and that meant that more was required of the talion than measuring arms and legs, eyes and teeth: honor was at stake. These were cultures that were not the least bit embarrassed at taking the full measure of a man or a woman. The entire moral and social order involved sizing people up; that's what honor was, and still is, all about. They thus developed a talent for measuring complex social and moral matters that justice, in their view, demanded be taken into account for there to be justice worthy of the name. How could such measuring be avoided when people – their bodies and parts thereof, as I will show in detail – also might have to serve as the means of payment for the debts they owed or the judgments entered against them? There are hard costs to looking at the world this way, and they knew that too.

I admire the talent for justice these people had, but as the reader will discern I am at times ambivalent about them and my own admiration for them. I stand in awe and admire, but from a safe distance; and courage permitting, I am not about to edge more than a foot or two closer. But because I may not have the moral qualities to be a completely respectable member of their kind of culture does not mean that I am about to reject their wisdom and clarity of vision. Our cowardice aside, on a higher ground, our cultural and political commitments to equal dignity for everyone are what keep most of us (and even me) from wanting to go back there. But we are hypocrites: we tolerate a lot more inequality than the garden-variety honor society would ever tolerate. They policed and maintained a rough equality among the players that were admitted to the honor game with a vengeance.

And what of those deemed not good enough to play? These were often treated to shame and aggressive contempt if they had recently been legitimate players in the game, or callously if they never had been. We pity such souls and make them the objects of our official moral and political solicitude. The concern of those who were players in the honor game, however, looked more in the other direction: up. They directed their wary and hostile gaze toward the one amongst them who was getting too good to play the game with *them* – toward the person, that is, who might soon seek to rule over them, to be their lord. Was it already too late to cut him back down to size?

Those not fit to play in the game stood on the sidelines and, you guessed it, asked God (or their gods), whom they cast first and foremost as an avenger, to take revenge for them: "O Lord, thou God of vengeance, / thou God of vengeance, shine forth" (Ps. 94.1), "for the Lord God of recompenses shall surely requite" (Jer. 51.56). The low wanted accounts settled too, and though today we talk about that demand in terms of distributive justice, it was understood by them to be a conventional claim for corrective justice, for getting even, for taking back the eyes and teeth, their respect and well-being, that had been taken from them. Those above the game watched too, from the skyboxes, and taxed, which often came in the form of claiming the right to deliver "justice" to these vengeful, feuding people of honor below; and for the justice they delivered they claimed a cut of the action and charged a pretty penny.

In Chapter 1 I start by asking how we are supposed to understand the scales of Lady Justice, and I take off from there. The scales of course are there to measure, for Justice is about meting or measuring. The words *mete* and *measure* mean the same thing. And if you will pardon the vulgar pun, much of the book is also about meat. Human meat. Shylock will thus have a chapter unto himself.

The discussion ranges widely in space and time, from Hammurabi to the biblical eye for an eye, to the early Anglo-Saxon kings who made pricing humans and their severed parts one of the organizing themes of their legislation, to the witty and tough-minded world of saga Iceland, to the Venice of Shylock and Antonio, even to the Big Whiskey, Wyoming, of Clint Eastwood's *Unforgiven*. And finally to our own day, where I may give some small offense. For in making man the measure of all things, but mostly of value itself, we must value people, price them under some circumstances, rank them so as to know how to pay back what is owed, though not as the economists do: it runs deeper than that. And this stark evaluation and ranking of human beings offends – sometimes with good reason, sometimes for no good reason at all.

The talion puts valuation at the core of justice; it is about measuring. At times it is no more exotic than our worker's comp schedules are. Body parts had their price then; they have their price now. Our tort law has as one of its commonly expressed goals to make the victim "whole" by substituting money for the body part he lost, just as the talion looks to make someone whole but sometimes in a strikingly different sense. In an honor culture you have a choice about how to be made whole: by taking some form of property transfer as we do today, or by deciding that your moral wholeness requires that the person who wronged you should again be your equal and look the way you now look. In some not-so-bizarre sense a commitment to equality might argue for such a result, if not always at the end of the day, then perhaps as a starting point for some hard bargaining. Obviously there is more to it than that, at least 250 pages more.

Really to trade an eye for an eye? A live man for three corpses? A pound of flesh for three thousand ducats? Back then? You bet. Right now? How do we measure the cost of war? In dollars? Not so that you will feel the costs. Dollars are not the proper measure of all things. It is still man (and woman) who is the measure: the body count. And in a symbolic way man is also the means of payment: the dead soldier is thus understood to have paid the ultimate price.

There is so much more to an eye for an eye than meets the eye.

I have paybacks to make too, paybacks of gratitude: Annalise Acorn, Wendy Doniger, Don Herzog, Robin West, and Stephen D. White read the whole manuscript and provided copious comments and observations that have made this work much better than it would otherwise have been. Special thanks too to Peter DiCola and Kyle Logue for the help they gave me in particular sections where I cut across domains in which I had little knowledge and no sophistication. I also owe thanks for particular observations to Elizabeth Anderson, Omri Ben-Shahar, Daniel Halberstam, Madeline Kochen, Bess Miller, Eva Miller, Doron Teichman, Yoram Shachar, and Katja Škrubej. And as always to my wife, Kathleen Koehler, who manages to clear enough of the deck of our lively household so that I can find the peace and quiet to contemplate revenge.

I have often cited readily accessible modern translations for many of the early texts I use on the assumption and with the intention that this book will appeal beyond some of the narrow disciplinary boundaries to which it will probably be confined.

ONE

Introductory Themes: Images of Evenness

The Scales of Justice

We are used to seeing Justice figured as a strong woman, bearing a sword, sometimes crowned with sprigs of a plant – laurel or grain stalks – blindfolded perhaps, and surely bearing scales. Most of us, I would bet, assume that the scales merely reproduce the message of the blindfold: that justice is impartial, not a respecter of persons, which means it is blind to the social status of the people before it. The blindfold is a late addition to the iconography of Justice. It dates from the early sixteenth century, whereas scales have been associated with Egyptian Maat, Greek Dike, and Roman Lady Aequitas for a couple of millennia longer than that.

The scales overflow with productive meanings – for starters, are they properly represented in Justice's hand as even or tipped? – but the blindfold quickly degenerates into absurdity if we think on it too closely. Do you want to blindfold someone with a sword? It may not be wise to have her unable to see what she is striking, unless you do not give a damn about how much it costs to do justice; collateral damage, though unfortunate, must be borne. Blind justice morphs into blind fury. And how is she supposed to read the scales, if she is blind? This troubled early representers of Justice; some thus gave her two faces like Janus, with the side bearing the sword prudently left unblindfolded.[1]

Blindness – or being blindfolded as in the game of blindman's bluff, where the purpose was to make you stumble around like a fool – was never an iconographic virtue before Justice made it one in the early-modern period; blindness was traditionally associated with stupidity and irrationality, as in Blind Cupid, or with lack of righteousness, as in Exodus 23.8: "And you shall take no bribe, for a bribe blinds the officials, and subverts the cause of those who are in the right." But by the late fifteenth century, blindness, at least with respect to justice, had changed its valence. It was now a virtue: it kept her from favoring the rich, the beautiful, the powerful, though it still left her to be swayed by educated accents or sexy voices, and to be repelled by those who did not smell good. Thus some early-modern depictions of her and of her judges show them with stumps instead of hands, amputated so as to be bribeproof, an image made all the more necessary because surely one of the unintended meanings of blindness was that the blind often had their hands extended begging for alms.[2] And it was standard folk wisdom that many of those blind beggars were shamming their blindness anyway. Another problem with the blindfold, as any little kid knows, is that it is seldom peekproof.

So remove the blindfold, or the "scales" from your eyes, a metaphor that I wager has at least once in your life sent you into a tizzy of confusion at just how an old bathroom scale managed to get on your eyes. But it was not that kind of scale. No one, not even in the New Testament, would walk around like that.[3] The scales that are to fall from your eyes are the crusty kind that cap softer living tissue beneath, by which are meant those disfiguring cataracts that we now seldom see in the Western world. It is the balance-beam scales I want to focus on, particularly with regard to the question I just raised. How are they to be represented in Justice's hand – even or tipped? We have competing cultural stories to draw on and different legal jobs to do.

If it is evidence that is being weighed so that a decision can be made, we want the balance tipped one way or the other, or if it is defendant's negligence being weighed against plaintiff's, the balance must be tipped against the defendant or he is off the hook, and likewise if it is sins weighed against good deeds, or sins against the soul that authored them, as in images of judgment at death or on Doomsday.[4] Holding someone to answer depends on imbalance. Tipping makes the decision.

Submitting a dispute to the judgment of scales has long been under-stood to be something of an ordeal. The scales are of an ilk with car-rying a hot iron, or plunging an arm into boiling water to extricate a stone, or flipping a coin, or pulling petals off daisies to determine whether she loves you or loves you not. Zeus resorts to an ordeal of scales more than once in the *Iliad* to tip tides now in favor, now against, Troy, using them purely as a device to make a decision independent of having to come up with reasons to justify it.[5] That is why legal historians have referred to ordeals as "irrational" modes of proof, though perhaps "a-rational" would be more apt. Ancient Indian law actually provided for a formal ordeal of the balance scale. The person obliged to undergo the ordeal got on the scale, which was then balanced by placing the appropriate weights in the other pan. Then she stepped down, had a writing placed on her head, heard exhortations about the evils of untruth, and got back on her pan. She had better weigh the same.[6]

The earliest evidence we have of scales used in judicial-like proceedings comes from ancient Egypt, in depictions of the judgment of the dead – the psychostasia – in which a person's heart or soul lies in one pan and the ostrich feather of the goddess Maat in the other. Some think that the decision goes against the soul if the heart is lighter than the feather,[7] others if it is heavier,[8] but it would seem that the idea of a feather in the balance requires the scales to be level both before and after, that the judgment point is maintaining evenness, not a tipping. The soul must be light as a feather; in effect it should weigh nothing. Hence the usual portrayals of the psychostasia in the Books of the Dead have the pans balanced.[9] In this case, as in the Indian ordeal, the scales need not require tipping to decide the outcome.

I asked my law students if they could recall whether Lady Justice's scales are tipped or even. With few exceptions, they went for tipped, their quizzical looks revealing, however, that they had no recollection whatsoever and were taking a blind stab at it. I suggested that metaphors like "tipping the balance" may have prompted their "recovered memory," such memories being little more than phantoms of suggestibility. That led to blank looks, for they had no idea that the balance in that metaphor referred to a scale to begin with, the very word *balance* meaning "two pans," "two plates." I then asked what they thought was being weighed; most looked even blanker. Some suggested "the evidence"; some said guilt or innocence, and a few, it being the case that our classrooms have uninterrupted wireless Internet access, abandoned their e-mail and porn sites to Google for an answer to present as a product of their own thoughtfulness. I told them not to waste their time, that I had already done the Googling. A casual perusal of more than a hundred representations of Justice in statuary and paintings from the sixteenth century on revealed even pans outweighing tipped by 5 to 1.[10] I asked whether they had ever thought of justice as "getting even." Nods of agreement. So it seems, said I, have most depicters of Lady Justice.

I suppose that what prevents us from recognizing the sheer obviousness of the primacy of the notion of justice as evenness is that, in the law school world at least, burdens of proof weighing on one party, and not on the other, seem less dead a metaphor than restoring or striking the balance. But mostly it is because we were raised with images of Santa, or St. Peter, or God weighing our good deeds against our bad. Unless we were culpably blind to our own faults, we knew we needed cartloads of grace to have the balance come out in our favor. Imbalance was the image that threatened to put coal in our stocking. Many of us first came to question the omniscience of Santa, God, and our parents – rather than give them credit for mercifulness – when we got our gifts no matter how bad we were.

Although the notion of "tipping the balance" as the decision point is very much with us, the more ancient and deeper notion is that justice is a matter of restoring balance, achieving equity, determining equivalence, making reparations, paying debts, taking revenge – all matters of getting back to zero, to even. Metaphors of settling accounts, in which evenness is all, run deep. If the scales are tipped we are still "at odds"; there is no end of the matter until the pans regain their equipoise. The work of justice is to reestablish right order, to restore a prior supposed equilibrium that has been disturbed by some wrongful act or some debt owed but not paid. In corrective justice, evenness, not tipping, is the end point.

We can make a compromise between depictions of tipping and balance if we understand that Justice may be required to answer two different kinds of questions with her scales. There is the question of who must pay. Here your good deeds and your bad, or competing evidence,

4

may be weighed. The question may also be decided by Zeus throwing random weights into the pans. The tipping of the scale makes a decision one way or another, pretty much a-rationally, the scales functioning mostly as an ordeal in this phase, even when we think it is evidence we are weighing.

Once the scales have singled you out as having to answer we must now reemploy them to determine *how much* you must answer for. Here the matter can be concluded only when we know the full measure of the harm you are responsible for. For this the scales need to settle finally at even, and rather than behaving irrationally they are pretending to a kind of essential rationality: the rationality of calculation and the marketplace. But the question that is answered by tipping – the question, that is, of whether to hold someone liable or whom to hold liable – is preliminary, whereas the question that is answered by evenness is the remedial question, the question of resolution, and the core justice question. And thus the iconographic and conceptual primacy of depictions of evenness.

The scales are the signature emblem of the trader, those people who are taken as the torchbearers for a particular view of rationality as economic rationality (though even they only occasionally behave as economic theory orders them to). It is a standard archaeological deduction that when scales are found among the grave goods, the skeleton they accompany was involved in trade. And in the Viking Northlands a substantial number of these skeletons are female, just like Lady Justice, Maat, Dike, and Aequitas.[11] Scales are tools of the marketplace, the stuff of everyday settling accounts. Lady Justice borrows her defining instrument from the defining instrument of precisely those people mistrusted from time immemorial as sharp practicers. But justice cannot shake its connection to measuring value, setting prices, and exchange, so borrow from the trader it must. To this day we find it hard to conceptualize corrective justice independently of the language of the marketplace, of debts incurred and accounts settled, of setting value and establishing prices, of obligations discharged in full, of paying for and paying back, and of satisfaction. In the Babylonian *suq* of 1800 B.C. the scales had to end up even or else there was no conclusion to the transaction. The same is true for remedial justice.

5

Sharp practice is not confined to market traders; it is also the great suspicion that burdens administrators of the law. Imagine an artist deciding how to represent Lady Justice's scales. Even if the story he wants to dramatize requires a tipping of the scales, he might still wish to depict them in equipoise. At what point, for instance, in the judicial process is our Lady Justice to be figured? At the beginning of the proceeding, ready to judge those who come before her? Or after she has heard the case? Do we want her there as an Idea, merely overseeing but not participating, or there doing the gritty business of judging? Don't we want to know that Justice has just scales, ones that are in balance at the beginning of the process? To represent the scales as tipped, as in the weighing of evidence or the quality of one's deeds, is to have faith that the scales were not rigged to begin with.[12] Tipped scales may surely indicate judgment, but it can also suggest corrupt judgment. Better perhaps to figure her with the scales in equipoise and the pans empty to show she at least starts out an honest lady.

Not that evenness and balance cannot fall prey to sharp practice. Evenness pretends to uniqueness and exactitude, there being an infinite number of ways a scale can be imbalanced – things can be out of whack by an inch or by a mile; but there is only one point in the universe that renders them balanced. In geometry a point has no thickness, but the balance point of the scale comes in varying thicknesses; if too many degrees of precision are demanded, justice becomes impossible, or at least impractical. Ask Shylock. There has to be some play in the joints that allows for imaginative and creative restorations of equilibrium or for dealing practically with a reality that is always more complex than even the precisest of rules can get a grip on. That useful play in the joints, though, also left space for shenanigans. It was not only a matter of how inaccurate the scales might be but also of the negotiability of exactly what was to be weighed against what. What did you put in the other pan to balance my eye, my honor, my blood?

Perfect balance may be achievable only in the symbolic mode. Or we find it a relief so to believe. For in our relativistic and uncertain moral world we have come to want to believe that the values at stake in matters of justice, in all but the simplest disputes, may be incommensurable. But let us not rush to that (lazy?) comfort so quickly. Commensuration is just what the scales hold out as the highest image of justice. And though in the end pure equivalence may not be achievable, we shall see that many a lawmaker, and many an avenger, was an expert at devising practical systems of equivalences. At times they were inspired to realize balance in sublimely fantastic and poetically powerful ways. Can't we think that much of the poetry in poetic justice is precisely a commitment to perfect balance and fitness and to the belief that justice, and the passion for it, has a powerful aesthetic as well as moral component?[13]

Difficult questions of commensuration were faced and resolved in some fashion all the time.[14] What if the societies that first used the imagery of balance, equity, evenness did not have coinage or units of account? The scales themselves suggest a lack of coinage. That is why they are necessary. If you have to weigh coins to tell how much they are worth, coins are not working as coins but as ingots.[15] The medium of payment must be weighed out, and hence standardized units of weight – shekels and pounds – end by becoming units of account before they become the names of coins. So people buying goods or getting justice had to weigh out silver, or barley, or iron, or blood, maybe even eyes and teeth and other body parts. In other words, justice is not quite separate from the story of money and its origins, of primitive money, and how to measure value – largely how to measure human value in serious cases – and thus it is also not separate from notions of honor: how to value my honor, my kin, my life, against your honor, your kin, your life.

The story to be told in this book is one of how imaginative and smart people were about measuring and meting, valuing, and getting even. We will see that people were pretty good at making trade-offs, at weighing and balancing harms, pains, suffering, benefits, favors, and human worth, at measuring eyes and teeth, arms and legs, this person's life against that person's. Although paying back, getting even, and revenge are often the subject of our most vivid fantasies, theirs was a social, political, and legal world in which getting to even was the very stuff of the practical. And I suppose lurking not very far beneath my text is a vaguely teasing suggestion that the talionic world of payback and getting even will not be unfamiliar to us, if not as an official matter writ large in public discourse, then surely in the schoolyard, the workplace, the pub, the street, on the highway, in conversation, in the bedroom, in matters of love as well as hate.

Just about Words

The story I have to tell has a lot of threads. Let us begin with the diction of evenness, both in big matters of justice and in very little matters indeed, such as the filler words we use to give rhythm or to buy time in our sentences, one step up from *um* and *ah*.

Even and *Odd*

Our word *even* is *jafn* in Old Norse; they are clearly cognate words deriving from the same Germanic root. *Jafn* lies at the core of Norse notions of justice, so that the word for justice is often rendered as evenness (*jafnað*); injustice, as unevenness (*ójafnað*). (The negative prefix *ó* corresponds to the English negative prefix *un* or *in,* and the *ð,* or *eth,* is pronounced as our *th*). A bully, a man who shows no justice or equity in his dealings, is an "unevenman" (*ójafnaðarmaðr*) (*maðr* = man in the nominative case). A just man, on the other hand, is even, of even temper and fair in his dealings (*jafnaðarmaðr*). Of one such unevenman it is said that "no one got any justice from him, he fought many duels and refused to pay compensation for the men he killed and no one got payment for the wrongs that he did."[16] It is not that the unevenman in question kills that makes him unjust, but that he kills and then refuses to pay for the damage. Behaving justly means paying for the people you kill, the harms you inflict. Literally paying. Then you are no longer unjust, for you have restored the balance. An even man evens things out. I do not wish to overstate the case. A rich person could not go around killing for the hell of it and then pay compensation and be excused from being blamed for his unevenness, his arrogance, or his bullying. He still had to kill under some reasonable claim of right.

But who gets to set the going price of a corpse? Does our killer give what he thinks is fair? Do the victim's kin get to name their price? How does the balance get struck? How do we know we are even? Sometimes societies have laws that tell us how much a man of a certain status is worth; they provide a fixed *wergeld*, or man-price, that measures his legal rank and indicates how much you have to pay his kin if you kill him. This was the case in the Wessex of King Alfred in the ninth century, or the Kent of King Æthelberht in the seventh. In other places, such as saga Iceland, the price is set on a case-by-case basis but the prices actually assessed tended to cluster around certain customary amounts. Arbitrators set the value, or the parties themselves negotiated an appropriate payment.

In this light consider the word *odd*. The English word *odd* is borrowed from Old Norse. *Odd(i)* is Norse for a point, for a triangle, for a spit of land, and for an arrowhead or spearhead; in other words, *odd* indicates the effect of adding a third point outside the line formed by the two points that determine the line: the odd point makes of a line a triangle, an arrowhead, a spearpoint. They also used *odd* to indicate odd numbers, numbers that were not *jafn*. Now the plot thickens. One of the words they used to designate the person who cast a deciding vote in an arbitration panel was *oddman* (*oddamaðr*).[17] For us, "being at odds" means we are in the midst of a quarrel, and it meant that in Old Norse too; to resolve that quarrel you needed to get back to even.[18] To do that you often had to bring in an oddman, a *third* party, to declare when the balance was even again if the law did not so provide or the parties could not agree among themselves as to how to strike it. You needed odd to get even or you would forever be at odds.[19]

With two parties – an even number – the fear was that what you got was what the Greeks called *stasis*, gridlock, a kind of civil war, in which each side overvalues the harms it suffers and undervalues the harms it imposes on others, who think, as many of us do, that *getting even* means obliterating the other side.[20] You needed an oddman to undo stasis, not so much to break the tie as to convince each side that they were in fact tied. Or more imaginatively, as any parent with more than one child knows, to convince each child that he actually got the better deal.[21] It was the oddman's job to prevent getting even from getting out of hand by selling both parties on a plausible conception of evenness.

In the interest of nuance, there exists also, however, a countermovement to the tendency to exaggerate our own injuries and understate the harms we inflict. The honor game might lead people to downplay the wrongs done them (You think you hurt me? Didn't even feel it) and to play up the harms they inflicted if there was some doubt that they had the capacity or character to get even (I clobbered the guy). Playing down the harms done you was a much cheaper way of dealing with insult and injury than having a thin skin that exposed you to the dangers of taking frequent revenge. And if you could effectively sell others that the downplaying of the harms done you was not motivated by cowardice but by real toughness, you preserved your honor on the cheap without looking cheap.

Do not dismiss all this as merely the warped theory of justice of a bunch of axe-wielding Vikings. Aristotle too made justice a matter of price-setting and related it to notions of reciprocity and balance.[22] Anne Pippin Burnett, a student of Greek tragedy, reminds us that for the Greeks "revenge was not a problem but a solution. It was a form of necessary repayment."[23] The pre-Socratics were even clearer that justice meant getting back to even; they conceived the entire cosmic order to be a matter of payback and revenge. Thus winter gets even with summer, summer with winter, hot with cold, and so on. And as Gregory Vlastos has noted, "To obtain justice was literally to 'get back the equal [or to even].' The underlying principle is that of an exchange: equal value rendered for value taken. The same words apply to the closure of a commercial transaction...and to the satisfaction of justice."[24] Early Greek cosmology's commitment to balance, evenness, equality, and giving as good as you get was forcefully reaffirmed more than two millennia later in Newton's third law of motion, as succinct a principle of getting even as there is, so that the horse's hoof that strikes the earth is paid back in kind by the earth, which hits the hoof no less forcefully.

As the Teutons and Greeks, so too the Latins.[25] Take our word *umpire*: it used to begin with an *n*. In Middle English it was *noumpere* when we borrowed it from French. But the *n* got detached from the beginning of *noumpere* and reattached itself to the indefinite article, so he became *an* umpire, as, analogously, a nadder, the snake, became an adder; and a napron became an apron, but napkin stayed napkin and nappie. (And compare the reverse migration of *n* when "an other" becomes "a whole nother" in our daily speech; or when Lear is addressed as "nuncle" by the Fool.) So what is a *noumpere*? He is a nonpeer, that is, a nonequal. He is in short an oddman; the very same notion of unevenness, of a third man being necessary when a decision must be rendered, arising in the Romance world as in the Germanic.

Just, Even, Quite, and *Mere*

It does not end there. Take our casual use of the word *just*, as in "It was just as I said," or "just now," or "just a little while ago," or "just awful," or "As I was just going to say." The word *just* in these instances functions as what linguists call a discourse particle or a discourse marker. Discourse particles are exceedingly hard to get a grip on. Often it is not quite clear just what meaning they bear or whether they bear meaning at all rather than serve rhythmic or grammatical functions.[26] Really knowing how to speak a language means getting the feel for discourse markers, such as *like, oh, y'know, well, of course, um*, and *really*. Words like these in other languages seem to be the last barrier separating you from fluency. When learning another language you can memorize vocabulary lists, even learn to put together grammatical sentences on most topics, but forever be off key, because the *auchs, wohls*, and *dochs* remain elusive.

Even *even* functions as a discourse particle at times (as *jafn* does in Norse),[27] more among Brits than among Americans, and more in the sixteenth century than in the twenty-first, but when *even* does play that role it is usually doing much the same work as *just* does; in fact *even* is synonymous with *just* through significant ranges of *just*'s terrain.[28] The King James Bible and Shakespeare preferred *even* to *just*: "My father, in his habit as he liv'd! / Look where he goes even now out at the portal." "He was a mighty hunter before the Lord: wherefore it is said, Even as Nimrod the mighty hunter before the Lord."[29] And why is it that *just* and *even* do this kind of work?

That *just* and *even* should share such significant overlap bears eerie witness to how deeply embedded, in English speakers at least, is the notion of justice as getting even. That deep idea saturates the most routine of conversations. Just see how many times a day you say *just* or *even*.[30] (We might also note, *right* now, that another juristic term

that also functions as a discourse particle plays a similar role, *right?*[31])
At the core is a root sense of exactness and precision, but exactness
as imaged by getting a balance-beam scale to rest at its equilibrium
position, at the point were the pans are even, just, right, and straight.[32]
These *justs* and *evens* make no sense if the end result of meting and
measuring is to tip the balance rather than to get it to even.

Certain tics characterize my writing. Some I am aware of, others
not. I start too many sentences with *but* and then try to vary them by
changing some of them to *still* or *yet*. And these *buts, stills, yets* work
less as conjunctions than as discourse particles. But actually get rid of
them and structure my writing so as to avoid them? Impossible. I just
can't find a way to do it. I also get anxious that I am using too many
justs and *evens,* and indeed I do. I undertake global searches to see
whether I can eliminate some of them. I manage to exchange a couple of
them for an *only* or a *mere,* but then I fear my *onlys* and *meres* are starting to get ticlike. A tough-minded editor would strike out maybe half
of these *justs* and *evens* because they often do not affect the core sense
of the proposition. But I cannot get myself to cut more than one or
two because they add an indescribable justness, either just enough of
a hedge or just enough emphasis, to situate my level of commitment
to my own statements with significantly more precision than if I were
to eliminate them. In fact, so crucial are they to my psychological
orientation to my own written expression that I actually get a small
feeling of vertigo when I eliminate one. Right at the moment I am
about to strike it out, a bit of dizziness intervenes to save the *just* I
was just about to delete. Nuts, you say? But it is as if I were excising
a part of me. Incredible that words that mean virtually nothing mean
so much.

Incredible too is that these little words often work in contrary or
divergent directions. For instance, one of the functions the particle *just*
serves is to emphasize a claim. That something is awful or appalling
is one thing, but that it is just awful or just appalling is another.
Just thus works as an intensifier; it invokes feelings and registers
them in a way that a mere dispassionate statement of the view does
not. "I can't bear him" is pretty strong, but "I just can't bear him"
is more than just stronger. The former can be uttered in a cold and

rational tone, as a pure matter of fact, but add the *just* and you add passion to the utterance. And by adding passion you also add possible grounds for excusing your statement as being exaggerated if later you are called to account. So it works as a hedge too.

Aggressively hedgelike at times: thus collocations like "I was just wondering" or "I just wanted to know," in which *just* deemphasizes or downtones the core sense of the utterance by limiting its range to precisely drawn modest limits. It provides a way of not intruding your statement too directly on another by revealing a certain hesitancy of your own right to utter it. (Notice that *certain* does the same to *hesitancy* in the preceding sentence, making the hesitancy even more uncertain than a plain old unmodified *hesitancy* would be.) In this mode *just* softens, fuzzes out; that is, it ends up doing the work of politeness by adding indirection and a note of proto-apology.

Even *just*, then, ends up chickening out, backing off from its own aggressiveness. We can, however, bring back its muscle with ease: "Just you wait and see." *Just* thus comes to be one of those words that develop antithetical senses: it means, "I really really mean it, so don't mess with me," and it means, "Well, I don't want to intrude really and so I don't really mean it, except a little maybe." And such is our linguistic competence that we are completely fluent as to just what *just* is doing; we know precisely what it is up to, for, at some deep level, getting it right is just what *just* is all about. Even *even*, to a lesser extent, shows this tendency.

Yet another legal term works as a discourse particle, and it is right on point. To *quit* or to *quiet* is to discharge a claim, to requite it, to even up accounts, and *quit/quiet* is the root of the discourse particle *quite*. Quite right. Just check your OED.[33] And notice how similar *quite's* work is to *just's*. It intensifies and then can hedge too, but in the end it is about getting one's stance toward one's own uttered judgments just right.

Let me add one further data point. The word *mere(ly)* – which can function as a synonym for *just* in some settings in which *only* also works – is also used to play both sides of an evaluative fence. We use it now to indicate just making it – only making it and no more. *Mere* is dismissive. One usually finds it, sad to say, modifying *academic*, as in "merely academic," in which *merely* and *academic* conspire to degrade each other.[34] But well into the eighteenth century *mere* could also be an enhancer, an emphatic term expressing the notion of absoluteness, sheerness, entireness, perfection. In fact, the root and first sense of *mere* listed by the OED is "pure," as in wine unmixed with water. Thus Othello 's herald can speak of *total* loss as the "*mere* perdition of the Turkish fleet"; or Bassanio can tell Portia in that play about scales, severable bodies, and talionic justice:

> I have engag'd myself to a dear friend,
> Engag'd my friend [Antonio] to his mere enemy [Shylock]
> To feed my means.
>
> (3.2.260–262)

And in the same play *mere* also bears its minimalist sense as when Portia says of Shylock, "He shall have merely justice and his bond." Yet observe that "merely justice" still retains its sense of "perfect, full, pure" as in "mere perdition," which is in fact exactly what it portends.

With *mere* too we see a word that can pretty much mean itself and its opposite, and yet both senses of *mere* converge at a point, the point of getting precisely there. In the obsolete sense mereness is about purity, which extends to include notions of absolute, entire, sheer, perfect, downright, the perfect instance of, the thing itself in all its unadulterated and pristine perfection. But our mereness, the mereness of barely making it, is about mere sufficiency and nothing more. There is a notion of exactitude here, too, but with a whole different feel. It is the exactitude of having just made it across that very sharp divide separating inside and outside. Both merenesses meet at the pure thing, but from contrasting points of view: thus Shylock gets "merely justice and his bond." *Mere* thus behaves analogously to *just*, with its contrasting movements of intensifying and downtoning. *Even* too can combine the dismissiveness of our *mere* and the emphasis of the emphatic *just*, as in "Even an academic is not afraid of that," in which the *even* has little to do with the precision of exclusivity. When the standard set is the courage of the usual academic, *even* means that everyone qualifies; we are in a world of complete inclusiveness.

Enough of *just* and *even*. My point is merely to call attention to how central the notion of justness and evenness is to providing exactitude of reference in our everyday language. Even when *just* and *even* mean virtually nothing, it is often with them that we measure our words. There is a theory of justice in our most routine conversation, and it is a theory of justice as getting to even, a theory in which measuring and balancing are the name of the game.[35]

Paying for *Peace*

Getting back to the zero point on the scale is part of the deep structure of other notions central to doing justice, to settling disputes, to remedying wrong, to making and keeping peace. Take the word *pay*: justice worthy of the name, to repeat, is about payment, payments back and payments for. *Pay* comes from Latin *pacare*, which means to appease, pacify, reduce to peace. And as the OED reports of *pay*, "the sense 'pacify' [was] applied specifically to that of to 'pacify or satisfy a creditor'." Remarkable: the English word *peace*, coming via Latin *pax* from *pacare*, derives from the idea of paying.

Peace is about settling accounts, paying back what you owe. Peace that does not involve evening up scores and restoring the balance is not peace among equals. Rather, it is about being subdued, enslaved, or reduced to a client; or being too lazy or too scared or too forgiving to insist that what is owed you be repaid. Peace, in other words, that is bought by the forgiveness of debts (notice that forgiveness is itself a term of creditor–debtor relations) must be carefully inspected to verify that it is not motivated by cowardice. As between equals, peace means settling accounts, paying debts, satisfying and thus pacifying those who have a claim against you.

The same notion is also embedded in German *befriedigen*, in which the notion of satisfaction, gratification, and pacification go hand in hand. In *befriedigen* it is the root meaning of peace – *Friede* – that generates the notion of payment, of the satisfaction and discharge of debts, thereby inverting the direction of Latin *pacare*, in which the root idea of paying off a debt generates the idea of peace. The connection of ideas works in both directions, so profoundly interdependent are they. Peace demands repayment; repayment brings peace.

The idea that peace and payment share a common core runs deep, not just in Indo-European languages but in Semitic ones too. The root of *shalom*, the Hebrew word for peace, the *shin-lamed-mem* (*sh-l-m*) root, has a core meaning of to pay back in kind, to make whole.[36] It too is about payments, but more of the variety of an eye for an eye, in which a more exact equivalence is sought, either by restitution of the very thing taken or a reasonably identical facsimile: as in your life for my life, your tooth for my tooth. Unless accounts are in balance, there is no basis for peace. Unbalanced accounts means you must beware the avenger, for he will be out to pay you back and will be justified when he does so.

They were not naïve about this. Once the balance was struck people might well upset it again, but if they did they would be without right when they did so. The popularity of their cause would suffer, something that mattered considerably more to them than it does among us. One could seldom go it alone in these kinds of societies. Everyone except the stupid, the clumsy, or the sociopathically aggressive would think twice before rocking the boat without just cause. In the idiom of the sagas, getting to zero meant there was peace "for a while," and that was no mean achievement. These saga people were wisely practical. Justice bought time; it was unlikely to be a permanent solution as long as there was scarcity and people were moved to compete for honor and status and other scarce resources.

And it should also be noted that the idea of paying back readily expanded beyond the concerns of corrective justice narrowly conceived. Thus Langland's *Piers Plowman* puts the principle of *redde quod debes* ("pay back what you owe") at the moral center of its redemptive vision. *Redde quod debes* is less about corrective justice, though that too, than distributive justice. It is about the duties of the rich for the poor.[37] The interconnection between distributive and corrective justice runs deep, but "getting even" in its various senses is at the core of both, and thus many a social reformer and social revolutionary has seen fit to conceptualize claims for distributive justice in the diction of corrective justice. Property is declared to be theft. And if it is stolen the victim of the theft has a right to satisfaction, a right to get even, does he not?

TWO

The Talion

IT IS NOT ALWAYS READILY APPARENT to the principal parties when they are even, hence the need for an oddman as noted. The image of the scales suggests it needn't be all that hard to figure out; the instrument will provide an answer. It is merely a mechanical operation. But what are we to weigh against what? What properly enters into the accounting? What does discharging a debt involve, especially in as much as these debts are as likely to be debts of honor, humiliation, and blood as of sheep and cows and shekels? Do you, for instance, pay back with interest?

Getting Even?

Consider our own use of what it means to get even: if you get even by bringing the pan on the left back up to its neutral position, by one account you are back to where you started, back to zero; but by another account you have been undercompensated, for, if the debt is of honor, the wrongdoer enjoyed a certain amount of time indulging in the pleasures of looking down on you and of gloating at your humiliation; he has not been made to disgorge his pleasure. Or if he withheld or took your ox, he got to enjoy its labor while he had it.

Fair compensation requires this: you had me down, and now it is my turn to have you down, to witness and delight in your humiliation as you delighted in mine. That is what is so rightly captured when we say, I'm going to get even with you. The justness of this is easy to see if it is my ox you misappropriated. I should get not only my ox back, but also the rental value of the ox for the time you had it. This is the elementary stuff of one's first month in law school.

When the debt is of honor (and in an honor society few undischarged debts do not engage one's honor) the notion of getting even is understood to embody a hostile intention to make the other feel your pain, to get him down, if not to obliterate him. At a minimum it means you want to make sure you (and others) can *see* he is as humiliated as you were seen to have been. And if we can with some degree of confidence blame the wrongdoer for having started it – that is, if his wrong can in no way be seen as merely having taken his turn in a relationship of hostile turn-taking known as feud – then the wrongdoer deserves an extra kick in the pants for upsetting the initial equilibrium. But there is nothing extra in the humiliation of the initial wrongdoer to compensate adequately for the humiliation suffered by the first victim. It is merely squaring the account, as any justice worthy the name would require.

Pieties as old, even older than Socrates[1] – along the lines of two wrongs do not make a right – beg the question, for the second "wrong" of recompense is not a wrong but merely what justice demands. Or so the counterargument goes, one associated not just with bloodthirsty avengers but with no less a promoter of human dignity than Kant. Kant, however, was only restating an idea that had enjoyed a healthy life in a wide range of cultures spanning millennia. Edgar Allan Poe puts the idea nicely: "What can be more soothing, at once to a man's Pride and to his Conscience, than the conviction that, in taking vengeance on his enemies for *in*justice done him, he has simply to do them *justice* in return?"[2] And as long as that man's internal scale is in balance, so that it measures the wrong done and the value of his payback in accord with community norms, he will indeed simply be doing justice in return.

And if the incident is but one round in a continuing hostile relationship, what then? Must getting even be thought of only as a one-shot deal, or is it merest fantasy to think that evenness can be obtained for anything more than "for a while"? Can't the case be made that *closure* is a cant term to indicate that no one gives a damn anymore? When people still care enough to contend, time itself is one of the things to be set in the pans of the scale. We can thus make time (and turns, as in my turn–your turn) into a kind of money, trading unevennesses back and forth – as in now I am down for a while, now you, now me again – and it all comes out in the wash as part of an ongoing agreement to maintain roughly equal hostile relations. But to get the accounting right requires a lot of practical wisdom and patience, even courage at times.

Where there is a will to continue hostile relations in feud, or friendly relations in, say, gift exchanges and feasts, getting perfectly even risks bringing the relationship to a close or putting it in an awkward condition of how to justify the next move. But one party usually finds an excuse to start it up again, either with another dinner invitation on the positive side, or with another insult or a killing on the negative. He will often allege that things really weren't even when he does so, although in fact they were even enough that should he have had no desire to continue relations he could have done so without feeling himself to be in a position of dishonor, or as having dishonored the other. It seems that enough fuzziness can be generated in all but the simplest of money debts and even in them too. Is it not often the case that in situations of "closure" one side thinks the other got the better of the deal? Don't many terminations of relationships, either hostile ones or amiable ones that just run out of gas, leave one side feeling he got the short end of the stick, suspecting the other party is chortling or engineered the termination to his advantage?

But it is important from the start to recognize that what I call talionic cultures were not single-minded or single-purposed regarding payback. Antitalionic arguments were available and regularly made. One did not have to wait for Christianity to appear on the scene to make them. They came quite naturally, as you might guess, to people about to be whacked by an avenger. These anxious souls pressed upon the avenger of the blood all kinds of reasons why forgiveness and forgetfulness were good ideas. Thucydides records an instance, and the sagas are full of them.[3] They were also readily made by third parties pressing the interests of the wider community in peace. Indeed talionic and antitalionic arguments could be made by the same people, depending on their structural position in a dispute. If situated as a mere third party they talked peace, forbearance, patience; but if they were cast as a victim, then blood was their argument, although that argument could be made by third parties too when they suspected the victim was being forgiving out of cowardice. That said, it was still the case that in talionic cultures the demands of payback were the default position, the initial presumption, and the matter to be addressed.

Getting the measure right so that both parties can sense the rightness of the measure gives rise to remarkably subtle ways of evaluating and compensating for harms. The worry about how hard it is to come up with equivalences is at the core of primitive systems of justice, and it is hardly something we have adequately resolved today. Among us, once outside the schedules of prices listed for body parts in the worker's comp schedules, we must face the issue of how to assign a dollar value to a person's loss. Legal scholars dispute endlessly which measure of damages will best capture the real damage so as to make the victim "whole." Though we do not officially make criminal punition compensatory, we have not rid ourselves of the idea that it too is a payment, a discharge of something owed by the criminal, and in any event we must put a value on a particular punishment so as to commensurate it with other punishments meted out for other crimes. We thus worry about proportionality within a grid of punishments, which mostly comes down to assigning various numbers of years to different offenses depending on their badness, years thus providing the means and measure of payment, rather than eyes, teeth, lives, or money.[4] That time is the measure of value and the means of payment gives a special vividness to the tired proverb "Time is money," but what anthropologists call "special use money" it is.[5]

Consider the law of the talion, the law of retaliation, of tit for tat, whose classic formulation is the biblical eye for an eye, tooth for a tooth. Never mind for now that the rule gets stated in varying ways and different contexts in Exodus, Leviticus, and Deuteronomy, each raising its own substantial interpretive problems. It is more general matters that I wish to focus on. We take the talion as a classic statement of irrational revenge, as an emblem of a society so blind to good sense as to prefer two one-eyed people to one.[6] We are embarrassed by it and sneer at those who advocate it, thinking them barbaric and cruel. The embarrassment of some people drives them to attempt to rescue

God's word from charges of cruelty and vulgarity by arguing that in its historical and cultural setting the talion was a *limitation* on revenge and bloodfeud. You are limited to *only* one eye or one life for an eye or a life, not two or three. They see it as an ameliorative and progressive rule, leading to a kinder and gentler world.[7] Maybe, but that seems only half right, if right at all, for the rule provides more than just a top limit – no more than one eye or one life; it also sets a bottom limit – no less than one eye or one life, either. No letting your cowardice, that is, incline you to be forgiving. Not that the talion does not permit, even in fact require, wiggle room, but that is a complex matter that I will turn to later.

Others have argued that the biblical formulation of the talion was a rejection of the vicarious liability – hitting X for the wrongs that Y did – that accompanied the earliest formulation of the talion in the Mesopotamian laws, where, for instance, if one were to injure the son of man, it was the injurer's son who was the object of expiation. Or if a man raped another's wife, the rapist's wife was to be raped in return.[8] The biblical talion, so it is argued, limits the payback to the body of the wrongdoer alone. Leviticus and Deuteronomy are clear that this is the case, but Exodus is rather less so, for we still have God insisting in the chapter before the Exodus talion that He is "a jealous God, visiting the iniquity of the fathers upon the children unto the third and fourth generation of them that hate me" (Ex. 20.5).

Still others have pointed out that the talion can be read as a strong statement of treating people equally, at least for those not enslaved, for the lost eyes and teeth of slaves are dealt with by giving them their freedom rather than a right to their master's eyes and teeth (Ex. 21.26–27).[9] Philo of Alexandria offers a different reason for freeing the slave: if the master were to lose an eye for his slave's eye he would make the slave's life a living hell "and avenge himself on one whom he regards as a mortal enemy by setting him everyday to tasks of an intolerable kind."[10] Hammurabi's laws explicitly limit the equalizing aspect of the talion by making the stricture applicable only within a juridical rank. Thus if a person of the *awilu* class takes the eye or breaks the bone or knocks out the tooth of another *awilu*, he is to lose his eye or tooth or have his bone broken; but if an *awilu* blinds or breaks the bone of a commoner, he shall weigh and deliver 60 shekels of silver.[11] Body parts were not appropriate media of exchange across juridical status lines. The Israelite society reflected in the Book of the Covenant (Ex. 20.22–23.33), however, lacked the different juridical classes of free men of *Hammurabi*, recognizing, like saga Iceland, only two distinctions: slave and free. But as soon as the boundary between slave and free is crossed, the strict eye for an eye gives way to other measures no differently than in *Hammurabi*.

Those who advocate the equality reading argue that the talionic legislation – an innovation in Hammurabi's code and later adopted by the ancient Israelite codes – was an attempt to have the polity criminalize what before were private matters, and thus to make sure the wealthy could no longer buy themselves out of suffering mutilation for the harms they had inflicted.[12] For reasons I shall demonstrate, the talion did not have this effect. For now suffice it to say that the rule does less to bring the rich within the ambit of the law (they always were within its ambit, for they have assets that make it worthwhile to sue them) than to get the poor into it. For what the talion does is to give the poor assets to satisfy claims. The rule does much to help solve the social problem of the insolvent wrongdoer whose poverty makes him judgment-proof. Not having sheep to pay his debts he now has his body or body parts. The rich, as before, may well still be able to buy off the plaintiff's knife if the plaintiff prefers to sell his right to the rich man's eye for sheep, silver, or slaves.

You must be wondering, but what good does your eye do me? Who wants someone's extracted eye? How can that make me whole? Make me whole with money, as the American tort system professes to do. Without wanting too much to ruin my story by telling the end before the beginning – which is but one of several reasons academic writing gives the reader little incentive to go beyond the introduction – it comes down mainly to this: we can satisfy ourselves today with bland assertions that one of the goals of tort law is to make the victim whole (recall that the root of *shalom* also involves the concept of restoring wholeness), but, as we will see, we do it on the cheap. Talionic cultures were invariably honor cultures, and that led to a more complex interplay between injury and conventional money substances than is the case now.

If I can rightly take your eye, you will be scared of me. That is worth something; it makes the compensatory regime of the talion one that cannot help but keep honor firmly in its sights, for fear is bound up in some nontrivial way with respect and the talionic principle is above all a principle of just compensation. The compensatory aspects of our tort system keep honor out of it and we may be wise to do so, because at the official level in which our law operates, honor is a value that can be admitted only in the very restricted domains of actions for defamation and libel, which are conceived in a much narrower way than was the all-encompassing moral and social notion of honor as it was constituted in cultures of honor and revenge.

Students of honor culture know that honor and revenge were not merely backward-looking, evincing an irrational obsession with sunk costs, though that too; the successful players in the honor game also knew how to look to their future. But that does not make them utilitarians. Looking to the future meant looking to the future quality of your honor, and this meant that you really did have to look backward now and then and show you were capable of what an economist would call irrationality. There is much truth in Hamlet's "rightly to be great / Is not to stir without great argument / But greatly to find quarrel in a straw / When honour's at the stake." And you could not just fake your irrationality in the interests of rationality; the smart ones saw through such faking.

Being feared was not a bad thing, as long as you were not feared too much (because that could get you killed by other forward-looking inhabitants of your culture). Taking an eye when you had a right to, at least every once in a while, might have some forward-looking virtue to it, because in many an honor culture honor was at its core captured by our maxim "Don't tread on me." A good modern might see in that saying how the no-harm principle needs to be formulated when there was no responsible government power worth the name or when one had to look not just to his honor but to his and his family's safety as well. And then too one can never underestimate the basic moral and aesthetic justness of getting perfectly even. Honor has an extraordinary transformative power: it can make currency of no value, a worthless dead eye, into something of great value.

The Compensation Principle

Heirs as we are to an antirevenge discourse that owes much to Seneca and the stoics,[13] we think of revenge as going postal and blasting away, but revenge cultures did not think of it that way. For them, revenge was not just an ethic but an aesthetic, the aesthetic of proportion and balance. People were well aware that there was a poetics and poetry of revenge, which was partly the reason it was the subject of the stories they most often liked to tell.[14] A man who went postal and took excessive revenge was understood to be acting not only without right but also without taste. Not that such immoderate souls could not capture the imagination and become epic heroes on account of their excessiveness. Thus we have Achilles, and to a lesser extent Egil in the sagas and David in the Bible, and also Lamech, the veracity of whose exploits we must trust to his own boast to his wives, who for all we know might have been rolling their eyes. Would, though, that his saga had been preserved:

> Adah and Zillah, hear my voice;
> you wives of Lamech, hearken to what I say:
> I have slain a man for wounding me,
> a young man for striking me.
> If Cain is avenged sevenfold,
> truly Lamech seventy-sevenfold.
>
> (Gen. 4.23–24)

But if the Old Norse evidence is any indication, such immoderate people had the effect of eliciting and uniting opposition against them. The Norse even had a proverb to that effect: "Short is the life of the immoderate."[15] In short, an avenger who exceeded his warrant either made amends for his excesses or was taken out. (The proverb was not about gluttony.) Revenge cultures understand that wrongs must be repaid. The politics of disputing focused on three main issues: one, what the precise medium was to be employed to repay the obligation and in what amount; two, a corollary of the preceding, whom to hit on the other side; and three, when to pay it over. This book deals primarily with *whats* and *how muches*; for the *whens* and *whoms* I direct you to other books if you are so inclined.[16]

What is argued over is not whether compensation is due, but in what specie payment is to be made: whether it shall be in eyes, or teeth, or corpses, or sheep, or cows, or silver, and how much. The core issues are the means of payment – not whether there will be a reckoning and payment – and the amount of payment in whatever specie decided on as appropriate. The same mercantile diction was employed whether the specie was blood or money, captured so nicely in the Hebrew root *go'el*, *gimmel-aleph-lamed*, which is translated variously in the nominative as avenger or redeemer, the person who buys back. Taking blood was no less compensatory than taking money.

The once dominant view of legal historians – a view that arose in the nineteenth century and that is untenable in the face of the evidence, although one still hears it recited as gospel in law schools – is that revenge systems gave way to compensation systems, which then paved the way for state-delivered justice, amidst general rejoicing at the progress. The fact is that revenge in blood invariably coexisted with means of paying off the avenger by transfers of property or money-like substances in lieu of blood.[17] Revenge always coexisted with a compensation option. The conceptual underpinning was exactly the same in either case: both revenge and compensation were articulated solely in idioms of repayment of debts and of settling scores and accounts.[18] Revenge was compensation using blood, not instead of money, but as a kind of money.

Thus it is that when the rabbis interpreted the talionic passages in the Torah not to require actual eyes and teeth to be paid over but rather money compensation, they were not, as David Daube has pointed out, willfully misinterpreting or missing the point of the talion but were "only work[ing] out something of which at least the beginnings were there; they did not impose upon the text a line entirely alien from it."[19] The rabbis recognized that the core idea was one of payment and repayment. The problem for early talionic culture was not the conceptual one of being too primitive to understand notions of exchange, but the practical one of how to measure value and then how to find an appropriate means of payment once value had been determined. In a sense, the problem was one of money, of how to fulfill the standard money functions of providing a means of payment and a measure of value.

Remember that the classic formulation of the talion arose before coinage was general, before there was easy and ready money that was of a given weight and purity and whose value was clear. All kinds of things were called on to play various moneylike roles. And even after coinage came into existence – first appearing in Lydia in the sixth century B.C. – it was often in short supply. The Bible contemplates shekels as a measure of value, as do the older Sumerian, Babylonian, and Assyrian laws. But those shekels were units of weight, not coins of a specific weight of silver, not until after the Exile. Thus it is that when Jeremiah acted as *go'el* and redeemed his cousin's field, he "weighed him the money, even seventeen shekels of silver . . . and took witnesses, and weighed him the money in the balances" (Jer. 32.9–10).

One should not think that because the sources mention units of account to measure value that the substance of those units – say, silver or gold shekels, barley or oxen – was actually paid over. The substance providing the unit of account or measure of value was only occasionally also the means of payment.[20] Medievalists hardly need to be reminded of this, it figuring so prominently in our sources.[21] King Ine of Wessex (c. 700) thus provides in his laws that although wergeld is valued officially in silver shillings, actual payment can include "a man and a mailshirt and a sword, if need be, in each 100 shillings."[22] The measure of value is shillings, the means of payment are a live human body and defensive and offensive weaponry. In his way of thinking such weaponry was an extension of the human body anyway, one step away from being personalized and valorized as legs and arms. And is not the biblical talion functioning much as this law of King Ine?

There is a hedge I must make: we will see more than once in what follows that people did not think of payment in blood as of equal moral and aesthetic value with accepting compensation in sheep or other property to buy off their right to take blood. There was a presumption that blood was the noblest form of specie, or at least the most poetic. As I shall discuss in greater detail, people were suspicious of those who cashed in on the death of their kin, who, as the sneering Viking idiom would have it, "carried their kin in their purse" or, in the Kabyle version, who "eat the blood of [their] brother," for whom "only [their] stomach counts,"[23] just as today we might experience a bit of guilt or fear that we are not quite grieving over the death of a relative who made us the beneficiary of a million-dollar life insurance policy. The problem exacerbates itself: for if you demanded more money because it is less honorable to take money rather than blood, you made yourself look more suspiciously like a person who carried his kin in his purse and thus might be tempted to set up his kin in order to collect for their bodies. Suffice it to say for now that they still believed that a reasonable balance could be struck with money as well as with blood, and were rather good at finessing the issue.[24]

The Euphony of Eyes and Teeth

So why did the ancient Hebrew legislator not prescribe, as the seventh- to eleventh-century Germanic codes would do, an eye for 50 shillings, a tooth for 6, a middle finger for 4, and trust the parties to stipulate what kinds of goods had to be handed over as a means of payment to satisfy the measure of value stated in terms of silver shillings or shekels?[25] Was it that the biblical lawgiver liked the cadence and elegance of such a tough-minded statement of pure equivalence, of an eye for an eye, a tooth for a tooth?[26] Was it above all that the litany of equivalences sounded good, sent chills up the spine? And if it sounded good, why was that? It seems to have grabbed the compilers of the Pentateuch; why else did they repeat various versions of the talion three times? It has been noted by commentators, moreover, that none of the three appearances of the eye-for-an-eye formula of the talion in the Torah is demanded by the context; they look very much like interpolations inserted for emphasis and not altogether appropriately, especially in Leviticus and Deuteronomy.[27] It might be that aesthetics is much of what it is about.

The biblical formulations are not limited to eyes and teeth. It is as if the legislator and compiler got too excited to stop, especially in Exodus: "life for life, eye for eye, tooth for tooth, hand for hand, foot for foot, burn for burn, wound for wound, stripe for stripe." But the subsequent iterations abridge the Exodus formulation. Leviticus adds breach for breach, to eyes and teeth, but drops the others; Deuteronomy keeps the lives, eyes, teeth, hands, and feet of Exodus but drops burns, wounds, and stripes.[28]

The only members common to all three versions are eyes and teeth.[29] There seems to be a mysterious force that moves to distill the rule to its most arresting formulation. And by the time we get to Jesus the abridgement had already arrived at its perfect modern form. For Jesus there is a special salience, an attention-grabbing power in "an eye for an eye and a tooth for a tooth." Forget about lives, hands, burns, feet, wounds, and stripes. Says he in the Sermon on the Mount, "Ye have heard that it hath been said, an eye for an eye and a tooth for a tooth." It was the phrase everyone remembered, for Jesus assumes "ye have heard it said" and indeed ye have. "An eye for an eye, a tooth for a tooth" was already something of a proverb in the year 30 A.D.

Daube has argued that Jesus knew that the talion as stated was not literally applied in his time. No eyes or teeth, he says, were extracted in Jesus' day for the kinds of injuries detailed in the Covenant Code of Exodus, only money and movable property.[30] Two centuries earlier the rabbis had already interpreted the talion to mean that money compensation was what the rule required. In Daube's view, Jesus is thus using the talionic formulation more generally to argue against merely suing for money damages for the insult of having one's face slapped. He is urging that one endure the shame with stoic passivity. Turn the other cheek; do not seek to collect damages in a lawsuit. He was rejecting the root idea of seeking any kind of compensation, whether blood or money, for injuries of humiliation and dishonor in this world.[31]

But if Daube is right, it means that Jesus used the abridged talionic formulation solely because of the terrible beauty with which it states the principle of compensation, of getting even. Jesus was thus drawn to the graphic statement of the talion in the same way we are, because it has a compelling ring to it, because it perfectly states a general principle of just recompense that he is arguing should be rejected even in the softened form to which the rabbis had reduced it.

What is it about eyes and teeth? Why do they make for so much more compelling a combination than ears and noses, feet, and even lives? Eyes and teeth, in all the formulations in the Torah, go hand in hand. The tooth always follows immediately upon the eye. Something draws them together. Perhaps it is this: eyes and teeth are on the face. When Oedipus gouges out his eyes Freud would have us think that he was holding back, as if the tragedy was somehow more about a failure in proper sexual object selection than a failure of vision, in all its senses; as if castration was somehow more unthinkable an act of self-mutilation than blinding oneself, even in a world in which self-castration was not uncommon fare.[32] Eyes represent us at our most vulnerable and most beautiful, at our most individual, and at our most dignified and sentient, representing in the words of Philo of Alexandria "the best and lordliest of senses."[33] And women have them too.

Why losing a tooth, though, such common fare in all but the softest of sports? Surely the taking of a life, the loss of a hand or a foot, the infliction of a burn or a stripe, is more arresting than the loss of a tooth, even discounting for the special seriousness of facial disfigurement should one of the top incisors get knocked out. A person bent on disfiguring his enemy, making him (or especially her) so ugly that he or she becomes monstrous, cuts off the nose.[34]

The power of the tooth as an image depends in great part, it seems, on its being coupled with the eye, and this is why it follows the eye in all talionic formulations. It is not the pain of its extraction, but that a tooth contrasts the vulnerability of the eye with the hardness of our animal weaponry. The image is of inclusiveness, everything from great value to small. Then note too that both an eye and a tooth are discrete and as such neatly and discretely extractable. Other body parts shade into one another because they are made out of the same flesh as the parts right next to them, such as ears, hands, feet, tongues, noses. But an eye can be precisely an eye, a tooth precisely a tooth; their boundaries are clear. This gives them a special salience.[35]

Might part of the horror of the eye and tooth formulation lie in the small hint of cannibalistic fury that one fears might accompany paybacks?[36] Thus Hecuba says of Achilles: "I wish I could sink my hands in that man's very liver and eat it." And Achilles to Hector: "I wish I could eat you myself, that the fury in my heart would drive me to cut you in pieces and eat your flesh raw."[37] Thus Ezekiel (39.18): "Ye shall eat the flesh of the mighty, and drink the blood of the princes of the earth."[38] And though both Hecuba and Achilles, and perhaps Ezekiel, are knowingly speaking hypothetically and with grand and passionate hyperbole, there is more than a suggestion that they might ctly as they say should the body of their enemy present itself ____ their rage subsides.

With these images of an avenger desiring to eat his enemy, contrast the form of gruesome revenge in which the avenger tricks his enemy into eating his own children. Thus Atreus' revenge on Thyestes in the Greek world, Gudrun's on Atli in the Germanic world, Titus Andronicus' on Tamora in the Shakespearean.[39] And Israel in the Hebraic, though not tricked into such repast, shall be reduced to it (Ezek. 5.10):

> Therefore the fathers shall eat the sons in the midst of thee, and the sons shall eat their fathers; and I will execute judgments in thee, and the whole remnant of thee will I scatter into all the winds.[40]

These images of cannibalism are meant to be images of excess, not of balance. Can some of the evocative brilliance of the biblical talion's eye/tooth formulation lie in the suggestion of just how fine the line is between talionic equivalence and balance, on the one hand, and reciprocity gone mad, as when fathers who eat sons are eaten in return by them, on the other?

Put aside these hors d'oeuvres for the moment: I return later to partibility of bodies inviting notions of their comestibility. Let's just say that the eye/tooth statement perfectly captures the rule of equivalence, balance, and precision in a stunning way. It holds before us the possibility of getting the measure of value right. Eyes and teeth, like discrete grains of wheat and barley or peppercorns, once abstracted from their bodies, look fungible and suitable to being plopped in the pans of scales. Perfect balance of fungibles, almost like coinage – in fact very much like coinage.

THREE

The Talionic Mint: Funny Money

MONEY GIVES US EQUIVALENCE in the form of A = B, with two unlikes being equated by a price. But one never trusts that A really equals B; the buyer often fears he got cheated (why did the seller agree to hand it over for that price if he wasn't getting a good deal, a good deal at my expense?), the seller, that he got shorted (I surely could have gotten buyer to agree to more if he agreed so readily to that!). The price of silver might rise the next day, whereas eyes might suffer a glut and lose value.

But if I state my principle as a rule of identity, A = A, rather than of equivalence, A = B, then I can indulge the thought that I struck the balance exactly right. The price is a just price, an eye for an eye.[1] We can smudge this too-pretty picture by worrying whether a blue eye equals a brown, a nearsighted one a 20–20 one, or the eye of a loser the eye of a person of honor. Still the rule as stated makes the poetic claim of identity, a powerful statement of getting the price exactly right.

Body Parts and Money

The classic statement of the talion mints some coin. It makes eyes into a form of money, or a money-like substance. First, eyes become the legal measure of the value of eyes, thus serving a crucial money function. That purports to solve the inadequate or inaccurate pricing of eyes in terms of other commodities. But were eyes ever to be a means of payment, a second crucial money function? Were you actually supposed to pay over an eye? If not, we are back to the problems of finding an equivalent specie to measure the value of eyes – shekels, oxen, grain, goats, or whatever.

Trading an eye for an eye is not quite barter; eyes are doing money-like work in a way a pure bartered item is not.[2] These people understood that money-like jobs could be done by various kinds of specie. And one of the most common forms of specie was human beings, both as a measure of value and as a means of payment. As late as the nineteenth century, Russians (and also slave-owning Americans) measured the value of estates in units of souls, that is, serfs or slaves. One had a 300-soul estate or a 2,000-soul estate.[3] The early Irish laws measured value in units of slave girls, and there is reason to believe slave girls at times also served as a means of payment.[4] Even when the payment is meant to be made in gold, the measure of value may not be quite separated from the human body, as when Achilles says he will not accept even Hector's weight in gold as a ransom.[5] In that case is the prime measure of value gold, or Hector's body mass?

The Hittite laws figure humans as a means of payment and as a measure of value: "If anyone kills a man or a woman in a quarrel, he shall bring him for burial and shall give four persons, male or female respectively. He shall look to his house for it." (If the killing were accidental the number of persons to be paid over was reduced by half.)[6] So too in saga Iceland: a killer might pay himself over to the master or kin of his victim, substituting himself for the victim, occupying the latter's vacated place. In one case a man accepts the killer of three of his servants into his household because the killer was understood by everyone to be a man of ability, worth three average men.[7]

The Hittite solution of paying for people killed with people seemed to Charles Buckley, a San Francisco electrician, the only way to make proper amends to the parents of a four-year-old girl he ran over while drunk in 1922. He offered his own five-year-old Isabel as compensation, and Mrs. Buckley joined in the offer. Dollars, to his mind, was not the right money for the occasion.[8] Under a German-brokered deal in early 2004, Israel released and paid 436 prisoners to buy back one live Israeli businessman held captive and the remains of three soldiers killed in Lebanon.

There are a multitude of provisions in the early Mesopotamian codes, the Germanic codes, the Bible, and others that figure humans as means of payment for debt.[9] The institution of debt slavery from saga

Iceland to biblical Israel to ancient Sumer bears witness to humans as gages for security of payment, and to the fact that they were actually paid over. Thus Exodus 21.21 refers explicitly to a slave as his owner's *money*: "And if a man smite his servant, or his maid, with a rod, and he die under his hand; he shall be surely punished. Notwithstanding, if he continue a day or two, he shall not be punished: for he is his money."[10] More is meant here than the slave is his owner's property; by calling him "money" there is a hint that the slave is already a pledge for a debt owed to the owner. It is even the case that Indo-European words for "to be worth" and "value" have at their root the notion of the exchange value of a man put up for sale, or redeemed from slavery or capture.[11]

But parts of humans? Their eyes, feet, teeth? You can make a whole human work off his debt or replace your lost son or brother, or serve as a hostage to secure an agreement, but what can you do with a subdivided body – before, that is, the day of kidney, cornea, and heart transplants? There is an answer, and let me work toward it by degrees.

In the Sermon on the Mount, before Jesus counseled turning the cheek instead of following the principle of an eye for an eye, he had already referred to eyes a few verses earlier, eyes that had committed the sin of looking lustfully on a woman. If seeing was the first attribute one normally associates with eyes, the next thing about them in Jesus' mind was their extractability:

> And if thy right eye offend thee, pluck it out, and cast it from thee: for it is profitable for thee that one of thy members should perish, and not that thy whole body should be cast into hell. And if thy right hand offend thee, cut it off, and cast it from thee: for it is profitable for thee that one of thy members should perish, and not that thy whole body should be cast into hell.
>
> (Matt. 5.29–30)

First eyes, then hands; both, it seems, are punished for their transgressions. But in fact something deeper is going on with their excision. They are also serving as a means of payment. Had Jesus stopped with the "pluck it out and cast it," or the "cut it off and cast it," the severing would be punitive. But he justifies the severance, not by alleging the

33

just desert of the offensive hand or eye, but by talking the language of investment and risk management. The offending eye and hand are buying insurance. Better to pay over your eye and hand now than suffer your whole body tossed into hell later.

Mere metaphor, the rhetoric of overstatement, you say? But Jesus is careful to make his metaphors still adhere to the realm of reason. When you look on a woman to lust after her and have thus committed adultery in your heart, you do not pluck out both eyes even though both were doing the desiring – only one of them. Jesus knows he is not quite offering the sinner a bargain too good to believe by asking for only one eye, but he is not asking the impossible, for two eyes, a price that no one would pay.

There were some who took him at his word, though not for eyes: thus the early father of the church, the brilliant Origen, castrated himself to make sure he was not tempted to sin, or so that others would not suspect him of sneaking a little pleasure here and there.[12] Castration, recall, was not an altogether uncommon operation for Stoics and early Christians to undertake, to say nothing of the eunuchs needed to serve various cultic functions in pagan temples, which should give us pause as to what extent Jesus was merely engaging in a bit of poetic license. In fact Origen's solution to sexual temptation was common enough that the Council of Nicea (325 A.D.) ruled that priests who voluntarily castrated themselves should be suspended.[13] The Norse god Odin, too, thought it well worth it to pluck out his own eye as the price for obtaining a drink of Mímir's well and with it the heavenly art of runes and verse.[14]

The paying of a body part as compensation is made explicit in the laws of King Alfred, which provided that if anyone was convicted of public slander "he shall compensate[15] for it on no easier terms than that his tongue be sliced off (*þonne him mon aceorfe þa tungon of*); and he cannot redeem it cheaper than at a price estimated in accordance with his own wergeld."[16] Given that another provision in Alfred's laws rates the tongue equal in value to an eye, which in turn is set at one-third the price of the whole person, you must pay, assuming you to be an ordinary free man, 66.67 shillings to keep it.[17] And if anyone raped the slave of a *ceorl* ("churl, a free man")[18] he had to pay the *ceorl* five shillings, but if a slave raped a slave he had to "pay with his genitals."[19] While it is hard not to discern a punitive and disciplinary element to the kind of money demanded of the slave, the diction of the provision speaks of payment and compensation, not punishment.[20]

The body and its parts figure at the deepest core of ideas of payment, value, exchange, tribute, tax, measurement, insurance, and money.[21] Even tumors, emerods (a quainter form of hemorrhoids), were symbolically excised as an excise,[22] a means of compensation, when the Philistines returned the ark they had captured with a reparation payment of "five golden emerods and five golden mice" (1 Sam. 6.4). The Philistines were desperate to rid themselves of the plague by the magical means of sending away representations of it. But the Israelites did not understand the golden tumors and mice as anything other than a compensation payment for having disrespected the ark. They showed no concern that by accepting effigies of tumors they would catch the disease.

And almost too obvious even to note: corpses and body parts, if not quite given over as hostages, are nonetheless held as hostages. The *Iliad* provides grand example, but there are a myriad from elsewhere in the Attic world. And some also in our own time: in 2004 Palestinian militants held the head of an Israeli soldier and other pieces of Israeli flesh hostage, as Israeli soldiers combed the sand for other stray pieces of their fellows to prevent them from falling into enemy hands. *The New York Times* reported that the Palestinians "hoped to trade the soldiers' body parts for prisoners held by Israel."[23]

It gets hard to discern at what point ideas of punition come to replace (but never completely) ever-weakening notions of body parts as a means of payment and measure of value when they are chopped off as part of a legal judgment. It is a complex topic, but I offer three quick instances from the second code of King Canute c. 1015 A.D. §30 deals with the recidivist troublemaker who has already failed one ordeal, §53 with an adulterous wife:

§30.4: and should he be shown guilty a second time there shall be no other compensation acceptable except that his hands or feet or both be cut off...

35

§30.5: and if he still does greater mischief then he loses his eyes; his nose and ears and upper lip and his scalp are to be cut off, whichever of these those whose decision it is to make decide; thus one shall rebuke while protecting the soul.

§53: if a woman, whose husband is alive, fornicates with another man, and it becomes known, it shall be a total disgrace to her, and her husband shall have all her property, and she shall suffer the loss of her nose and ears.

There is a progression here. In §30.4 the idea, though somewhat tongue in cheek, is that hands and feet are a special kind of money suitable for the occasion. The butcher shop of §30.5 evinces frustration more than anything else; the lawmaker is lashing out punitively. But even here we see a small hint of Jesus' insurance idea. Jesus, of course, kept the premium comparatively low, and he gave one the option of taking his words figuratively, rather than as a real inducement to dismemberment. Not Canute. The knives are out. How else are you going to save the soul of such a reprobate recidivist unless you make his body pay protection money for the soul it houses?

It taxes the sympathetic imagination of people now to try to see that the concern to protect the offender's soul expressed in §30.5 is anything but the worst kind of bad faith. And it must have knowingly been so for some of them, too, who could not deny their pleasure in the cruelty of saving souls, but those who could deny their pleasure, or in fact took none, might sincerely believe in the kindness being shown the culprit's soul, if not his body. When we get to §53, though, the adulterous woman loses not only her property but also her nose and ears; the idea of compensation has lost out completely to ideas of punition, even as regards the loss of her property. The point is to render her so physically repulsive that she will have sexual virtue foisted upon her and leave her so poor that no one will be inclined to overlook the disfigurement for the benefits of her property.

Paying Gods in Bodies and Blood

One uncanny, imaginative, and not quite dismissible theory by Bernhard Laum (1924), working mostly with early Greek and Indian evidence, claims to find the origins of money and value measurement in the partibility of animal bodies.[24] That so many words for money are also the word for cow or cattle would seem to make the observation trite at least to the extent that a live animal is meant: thus Old Norse *fé* (cattle, sheep, money), and Old English *féoh* (cattle, cows, property), from which we get Modern English *fee*, are cognate via the effects of Grimm's law with Latin *pecus* (cattle), yielding our *pecuniary*.[25] To be noted too is that *cattle* and *chattel* are different dialect forms of the same French word, with *chattel* developing a more general and money-like meaning of movable property.[26] Cows and sheep are among the earliest measures of value, and their ties to the idea of money persist at the most basic levels of our money talk.

But what Laum is after is to show that the idea of the moneyness of animals comes not from their use in normal trade – the unit of a cow or an ox is too large in value, to say nothing of their large mass, to be a regular means of payment – but from their use as sacrificial victims. The place to look for the origins of money, he argues, both as a measure of value and a medium of exchange,[27] is at the temples, in offerings and gifts to the deity. Laum finds that the whole idea of generalized measures of value, the idea of standardization itself, comes from separating out ritually pure animals for sacrifice. Animals of the same species were compared with each other, and from the comparison a normalized type was created, a qualitative norm. Rules of cultic sacrifice generate rules of quality and measurement: we thus arrive at a unit of the standard sacrificial ox, bull, ram, or lamb.[28]

These sacrifices meant roasting the animal and carving it up, handing out portions to the celebrants – with certain portions such as backbones and thighs, as in the *Iliad*, or breast and right thigh, as in Leviticus (7.31–32), taking on more value than other portions.[29] The parting of the animal, with some parts having special value, suggests Laum, is the first small prefiguring of the symbolic representation of value that would eventually yield coinage. Laum did not use Aztec evidence. But the Aztecs, not having domestic native animals of much size to bother sacrificing, made do with humans, and as Inge Clendinnen deadpans, the body of a warrior's victim was "nicely apportioned in accordance with a strict system of priority, with the torso and right thigh awarded to the major captor; left thigh to the second; right upper arm to the third; left upper arm to the fourth; right forearm to the fifth; left forearm to the sixth."[30]

The animals used were animals sacred to the deity, usually bulls or oxen in ancient Greece and India; in some respects the animal was seen as an avatar of the deity, so that what was being rendered to the god as a gift offering was the god's own to begin with, or even the god himself. We can see shades here of achieving appropriateness and equivalence via identity: pay a god to the god, pay an eye for an eye. Not only in ancient sacrificial cults but in Christianity too: in what came to be the dominant theory of the Incarnation, miserable judgment-proof fallen mankind could not make proper amends to God, so God had to become a perfect man (and hence suitable for sacrifice), one of sufficient worth to square the account, by paying himself to Himself.[31] The sacrifice of Christ is merely another manifestation of the talion: God for God, who is also a partible sacrificial lamb who is then also the object of worship.[32]

I offer here a word of caution. A narrative whose basic structure is more than two millennia old takes the form that in some earlier and more brutal state of the society – mostly lost and obscured in primal mists – it was humans that were sacrificed to the gods. Humans were the first and obvious choice to buy off the gods' anger or to prevent it if they were currently in a good mood. Thus we have stories of Iphigenia and Isaac, stories that we accept on their own terms as being about cultures finally coming to their senses and realizing that human sacrifice was nasty and quite costly too. Better to offer cheaper substitutes instead.

But why assume that human sacrifice necessarily must give way to animal? Are we altogether sure that it was animals that were substituted for humans and not the other way around? Poor Isaac is under the impression that sacrifices involve sheep, and in his advanced day it does not occur to him to think that a human would be offered up, let alone himself: "And he said, Behold the fire and the wood: but where is the lamb for a burnt offering?" (Gen. 22.7). And what must Jephthah's daughter have thought about the regressive tendencies of her dad? Backsliding there appears to have been.[33]

If God is willing to accept a ram for Isaac in the Old Testament after demanding Isaac for a lamb, He is not willing to let matters go that cheaply in the New, where no mere lamb, but only a God/man will do. In the Old a ram represents a boy/man, in the New a man/God represents a Lamb, *agnus Dei*. We stand the metaphor on its head: the ram as symbolic man is morphed into the man as symbolic lamb, metaphors of animal sacrifice come to provide the justification and symbolism of later human sacrifice, thereby turning what the Roman authorities meant to be a ritual of punition into a ritual of compensation, and thus of redemption.

Laum's argument follows the traditional account detailing ever cheaper sacrificial substitutions. He must be largely right, but the movement is not without disruptions and regressions. Laum locates the very idea of substitution and the consequent symbolization of value in the domain of the sacred and the sacrificial, in which arena he claims the idea of making one thing expiate for another first arises: a bull stands for the god, a part of a bull for the whole, eventually even the spit (the *obelos*, which still lives as the name for this symbol: †) on which the piece of meat is roasted comes to stand for the meat, and finally the spit becomes a kind of proto-money and provides the name for the basic Greek coin: the obel. Next time you eat shish kebab be respectful of its impressive ancestry.

Rather than kill a valuable animal, why not substitute a cheaper animal, then further substitute cakes baked into the shape of the expensive animal, or offer pieces of metal with animal pictures stamped on them, and lo, we are at something looking very much like a coin, which the temple authorities, according to Laum, minted, loaned, and banked. Where else would you find or need money changers but in the temple?[34] Or at least right next door. Drive them out and there must be an end to the daily sacrifices. Even our coins cannot shake an intimate association with body parts; we give them heads and tails. The coin is thus turned into an animal, and coins invariably sport the human heads (often severed heads at that, as on the nickel, dime, and quarter) of our gods – Lincoln, Jefferson, Roosevelt, Washington – but bear symbolic tails.

More recent scholarship might mistrust this account, but in the end newer theory provides more grist for our mill. The essence of religious sacrifice lies in substitution.[35] Sacrifice simply must come to terms with some idea of substitution, whatever mystifications it feels necessary to construct around it. You can really sacrifice the god only once, and the sacrificer, in expiation, can really sacrifice himself only once. Deicide and suicide end the matter right there for all time, unless a system of ritual substitutions is devised not just for the god but for the sacrificer too. In the ancient Vedic system of sacrificial substitutions there is much manipulation of the idea of "equal," of equivalence, as ever lower and cheaper victims are substituted, in which it is both admitted and denied that equivalence is maintained. Write Wendy Doniger and Brian Smith, "Extolling the substitute as the 'equal' of the original is, one might say, a stratagem for constituting it as a proper substitute."[36]

But surely this is much of the very story of the history of money, as people and sheep give way to ornamental metals, which give way to paper, in which for a greasy dollar a clerk hands me a glorious blueberry-swirl ice cream cone. The extraordinary amount of energy the church put into elevating the value of the communion host in the thirteenth century can be nicely seen in this light.[37] The same kind of self-deceptions and manipulations of the idea of equivalence are at the basis of our tort system, in which one is made "whole" with money for the loss of a limb, and at the basis of a monetary system in which the money does not also have a use independent of its money function. A paper dollar is only money; it is not also a sheep, a peppercorn, a human, or an ell of cloth. If a wheaten wafer can be God, then surely a greasy dollar can be an ice cream cone. Commensuration and substitution go hand in hand, to the great advantage of religious ritual and hurly-burly market transacting. With so much play in the joints of what can stand in the place of what, of what can equal what, a wealth of opportunity arises, and so, too, the possibility of getting ripped off.

Laum, as others have done, connects the idea of wergeld, the price of a man, with the notion of sacrifice. The origins of the Germanic word *geld* lay in the idea of sacrifice to the gods, and hence it came to bear the sense that produced its meaning of a tax (*Danegeld*), tribute, and, in modern German, money.[38] The idea of wergeld is not, he claims, understood to be compensation for a material loss. Nor is it about restoring honor, but rather about fear of the dead not resting quietly.[39] My own suspicion is that Laum is mistaking cause for effect. Ideas of unquiet dead demanding that their killings be atoned cannot be separated from ideas of settling accounts, ideas of compensation; the unavenged dead person's accounts are imbalanced, and he has an interest in setting them to rights. The religious ideas of the unquiet dead do not precede the ethics of revenge and payback; it is demands of paying back and getting even that come first and generate second-order beliefs of unsettled dead, or of angry gods who need to be appeased. That the dead are consumed with the compulsion to even their accounts is hardly surprising when the same idea is the predominant principle of justice among the living.[40]

Others, too, keep the sacral out of wergeld; they would attribute to wergeld itself the origins of money as a standard of value rather than, as Laum does, attributing money's origins to sacrificial dismemberments. Thus Simmel in his discussion of wergeld: "To reduce the value of man to a monetary expression is so powerful ... [that] this tendency not only makes money the measure of man, but it also makes man the measure of the value of money ... The value of the human being is considered here to be the principle of classification for the monetary system and as the determinate basis for the value of money."[41] Numismatist Philip Grierson adopts Simmel's argument, adding the observation that it is highly likely that the proper etymology of the word *worth* derives from *wer*, that is, from man.[42] Man is the measure of value.[43] The idea of determining the value to be paid over for dead bodies and for damaged parts of live ones comes first and then gets extended, both Simmel and Grierson argue, to domains of trade and the market via the stepping-stones of brideprice – the purchase of wives by payment to her family – and slavery.

To be noted, too, is that splitting up an animal, if not a human, may be a purely secular matter of determining legal damages. There is not a whiff of the sacral in Exodus 21.35: "When one man's ox hurts another's, so that it dies, then they shall sell the live ox and divide the price of it; and the dead beast also they shall divide." The live animal is worth more alive than split up dead; it is therefore to be sold so as to transmute it into more readily partible substances, like silver or barley, which can be easily and accurately divided. But the provision does not require the carcass of the wronged ox to be sold and the proceeds of it split, for the carcass is now readily divisible in kind without any further loss in its value. The provision, in effect, splits up two animals – the live one by splitting up the proceeds of its sale, the dead one by carving it up with cleavers and saws. Each of the contending humans gets just as much life and just as much death as the other.

Cutting Up Bread, Cutting Up the Body

Laum stops before taking his evocative thesis as far as it could go.[44] For instance, what exactly is Jesus doing at the Last Supper by making the bread stand for his body and then ripping it into pieces and having his followers ingest them? Or what of the doctrine of the Real Presence of Christ in the communion host, to say nothing of the common practice of stamping images of Christ or the Lamb onto it?[45] Here we again have striking symbolic reminders of the partibility (and digestibility) of bodies. And even here there is a hint of money: do we not have the idea of the part representing the value of the whole, indeed the part bearing the congealed value of the whole, where the symbol, like a coin or a bill, becomes the object of value because it is accessible, transferable, and uniform? What of eating sacrificial lambs, as well as eating *with them* as in the Last Supper, if it be not that both eating them and eating *with* them are about creating and fulfilling obligation?

Eating together joins people in knots of reciprocal obligation, and eating them literally binds them to you as the god becomes your sustenance and your fleshly substance, either when you eat the kabob on the *obelos* or the bread that Jesus hands you. You are what you eat. And the faithful are to eat their gods/God. There are more than a few medieval miracle stories in which doubters bear witness to the truth of the Real Presence by seeing the communion wafer turn into a child at the moment the priest elevates it, who is then adored, torn into pieces by the priest, handed out, and chewed up.[46] There is no separating feasts and feuds, bodies and money, eating, obligation, and exchange.

The same set of ideas, embodying the centrality of eating, tearing apart and distributing, obligation and debt creation, is embodied in our word *lord*, which is a contraction wrought by time on early Old

English *hlafweard*, literally "loaf guard, loaf owner." And by slow decay *hlafweard* becomes *hlaford*, then *hlaverd*, then *laverd*, then *lord*. And the name for servant or household member? *Hlafæta*, loaf-eater.[47] And like the disciples of Jesus, the loaf-eaters owed their lord obedience and loyalty, and some of the burden of avenging him if slain. The lord's bread *is* the lord, his very substance, and hence it "becomes" you in every sense of the word. And those you eat bread with also become companions, that is, people who eat *panis* (bread) with (*com*) each other. The idea of paying homage to those you eat – whether it be Jesus or sacrificial beasts, or your prey, or your host's wherewithal – runs deep, and it is almost an anthropological commonplace that we compensate those we eat by making them into lords, masters, and gods of a sort.[48] The fish, Dagon, is the god of fishing people; the bull and ox of the ancient Greeks, the lamb of the Christians who trace their descent to shepherds. One even can see in the totemism of cartoon animals – the Looney Tunes gang, Gary Larson's cows – an attenuated form of this kind of worship.

Thus, too, consider the medieval obsession with worshiping parts of saints' bodies, pulling them apart, putting them in silver and gold encasements and transferring them, stealing them, holding them for ransom.[49] The trade in relics was a trade in body parts every bit as active, and often as like a gray or black market as the trade in cadavers is for body parts and medical research now.[50] And the relics of saints were no less medicinal; infused into water and drunk, they had the power to cure. Thus ingesting the saint also created an obligation to further venerate him and perhaps compensate those who administered his shrine.

And circumcision? Jewish males have for more than three millennia bound themselves in a covenantal relationship with the deity by paying over a piece of flesh, and one of the services God undertakes in return is to play the *go'el*, the avenger, the redeemer on our behalf. It was about sealing a deal for the purchase of protection. And sometimes it could be about buying a bride, as when Saul put a price on the hand of his daughter Michal of a hundred Philistine foreskins.[51] David paid that and added a hundred-foreskin tip (sorry) to boot (1 Sam. 18.27). In the Christian exegetical tradition Jesus' circumcision prefigures the

43

Crucifixion and the sacrifice of his entire body (as was the case with those two hundred Philistines who first fell to David's sword before they would sit still enough for their nether parts to be excised by his knife). Thus Milton's meditation upon Jesus' circumcision:

> He who with all Heaven's heraldry whilere
> Entered the world, now bleeds to give us ease.
> Alas! how soon our sin
> Sore doth begin
> His infancy to seize!
> . . .
>
> For we, by rightful doom remediless,
> Were lost in death, till He, that dwelt above
> High-throned in secret bliss, for us frail dust
> Emptied his glory, even to nakedness;
> And that great Covenant which we still transgress
> Intirely satisfied,
> And the full wrath beside
> Of vengeful Justice bore for our excess,
> And seals obedience first with wounding smart
> This day; but oh! ere long,
> Huge pangs and strong
> Will pierce more near his heart.[52]

God and His son surely understood that blood and body parts work as money and as obligation-creating and obligation-confirming substances. In the ancient Mediterranean world – in Greece, Rome, and Israel – covenants, alliances, and contracts, reports Burkert, "[could not] be made without sacrifice" or cutting off some bits of flesh. Thus the Hebrew verb "to cut" (*karat*) is also used to mean "to make a covenant," or as we might say "to *cut* a deal."[53]

The Hebrew metaphor of cutting a covenant could be revivified to brutal comic purpose if its original vividness had become a dead metaphor. When in the Book of Samuel Nahash the Ammonite encamped outside Jabesh-Gilead, the desperate men surrounded by Nahash sued for peace: "Make (cut) a covenant with us, and we will serve thee." Nahash countered with a condition that took "cut" literally, just as God had meant it in Genesis: "On this condition will

I 'cut' it with you, that I may thrust out all your right eyes."[54] The suggestiveness of cutting does not stop there. The men of Jabesh sent to Saul for help; the messengers found him herding oxen. Saul took a yoke of these oxen and "cut them in pieces, and sent them throughout all the borders of Israel" not only to give those who thought not to heed his call an object lesson of what would happen to their oxen if they did not come, but also to oblige them formally to respond to the summons.

And if Nahash can make grim jokes about cutting convenants so can an angry God, furious because the people who had released their Hebrew slaves persuant to a decree of King Zedekiah immediately set about reenslaving them. Says God:

> You have not obeyed me by proclaiming liberty, every one to his brother and to his neighbor; behold, I proclaim to you liberty to the sword, to pestilence, and to famine.... And the men who transgressed my covenant and did not keep the terms of the covenant which they made before me, I will make like the calf which they cut in two and passed between its parts.
>
> (Jer. 34.17–18)

God is making reference to the same ceremony that Saul used to summon the people to attack Nahash. The cutting up of the calf is what "cuts" the covenant and suggests also the sanction to be levied against those who breach it. God too delights in playing with talionic equivalence by playing with words so that the failure to liberate a slave earns one the "liberation" to the sword.[55] What a wondrously allusive world this world of blood, flesh, body parts, money, pledges, and talionic paybacks is!

FOUR

The Proper Price of Property in an Eye

WE HAVE TWO COMPETING VISIONS of days gone by. They are either times of torture, mutilation, human sacrifice, humans living short, nasty, brutish lives, or they are the good old days of decent simplicity, duty, dedication, and true love. The Aztecs, the Romans, and the various horse peoples who occupied the vast steppes of Asia, and occasionally decided to visit their sweetness and light on peoples to the west and south of them, provide us with plenty of ammunition to justify the first; and period-piece movies featuring the English gentry or our own self-deceptions about our grandparents and our childhoods we claim as proof of the latter.

Probably no reader of this book has a hard time believing that people actually carved up bodies in the bad old days, so why, you might ask, am I taking so much time to prove that an eye for an eye meant an eye for an eye? Of course it did, you will say. And I am certainly not about to deny that people mutilated humans in war, as they still do today, or as part of religious festivals,[1] or to train doctors and make medicines, but my claim is more than that: it is that bodies and body parts were understood by them to be measures of value (clearly), as obligation-creating (clearly), and also as a means of payment – that is, as obligation-discharging (clearly in the case of whole bodies, as in matters of debt slavery or chattel slavery, marriage, fostering, and hostage taking, but also, a little less clearly to be sure, with body parts).[2]

Can we better firm up our case about body parts being money-like? The Bible does not show us eyes and teeth actually paid over.[3] What we get instead is the statement of a rule, and one is never sure whether the rule was a dead letter to begin with, whether honored in the breach

46

by being aspired to but never actually adhered to, or simply bargained out of as a routine matter.

Let us repair for a moment to the Twelve Tables of Rome (usually dated to the fifth century B.C.). The first law to be noted for our purposes, from Table III, though much debated as to its exact meaning, speaks to the body offered as security for a debt. Several provisions allow for the creditor to fetter the debtor and load him with weights, but when a debtor is bound to several creditors and has been unable to satisfy his obligation on three consecutive market days, his body is to be divided among the creditors, apparently by carving it up, for the law stipulates that if one of the creditors cuts more or less than his share it is not to be held against him.[4] With that provision from Table III consider the famous statement of the talion assigned to Table VIII: *si membrum rupit, ni cum eo pacit, talio esto*: "If he destroys a limb, unless he compensates him or makes peace, let there be retaliation."

The first provision from Table III deals with an insolvent debtor whose body is to be cut in pieces to satisfy his multiple creditors. This is not a matter of the talion. There is no doing unto the debtor what he has done unto his creditor. In matters of money debts, after all, the talion would simply require repayment of the money with interest. The talion proper is in Table VIII, and it deals with extracting compensation from a tortfeasor. What the Twelve Tables do, as we shall see, is put both contract and tort creditors on very similar levels of bargaining power.[5] Pay back your loan, or we carve you up; and pay for my leg you destroyed, or I destroy yours.

If the Twelve Tables give the contract creditor bargaining power like that of the tort creditor, the Torah does no such thing. Just because the talion might be the rule for standard kinds of bodily harm in the Exodus Book of the Covenant does not mean that the corresponding debt collection rules need follow the harshness of Roman practice. The rabbinic tradition is remarkably indulgent to the plight of the debtor, and the rabbis took their warrant from ample provisions in the biblical text. There is, for instance, a positive command to lend to the poor (Deut. 15.8–9); rabbinic tradition forbids appearing before one's debtor, even to pass before him, lest he take fright or feel ashamed; the debtor's tools and phylacteries are exempt from levy; one must not take a pledge from a widow, even a rich one (Deut. 24.17); the creditor cannot use self-help to distrain property but must go through court process, nor can he search his debtor's house to see whether he is withholding assets (Deut. 24.10–11); even the court's representative cannot enter the debtor's house. Most remarkably, the debtor still gets to use any pledge he gives over to his creditor who must return it to him during the hours he needs to use it (Ex. 22.26; Deut. 24.12–13).[6] This leads Maimonides to wonder what the value of the pledge might be to the creditor. He finds it in this: "that the debt will not be canceled by the advent of the Sabbatical year."[7]

Property Rules and Liability Rules

It is a different world when a biblical tort creditor faces his injuror under the law of the talion. Observe two people bargaining over an eye one knocked out of the other in a talionic society. Let us call our two actors V for victim and W for wrongdoer.[8] V says to W, "I want you to pay me for my eye you gouged out at the party last night." W answers, pulling out his worker's compensation schedule, "OK, here's 25,000 shekels." V: "No way. I would never have agreed to give up my eye, to sell it to you, a perfectly good and useful eye, for a measly 25,000 had you tried to buy it from me *before* you just up and took it. You are trying to get away with paying me what it is worth after it has been blinded, with a little sop for my pain and suffering and my loss of value as a possible slave or soldier. To hell with that. I do not deem my eye priceless; but no way you would have coaxed me out of it for less than a few million shekels." W: "Nope, 25,000 is what the insurance company says it is worth." V: "But the law in this jurisdiction, I have just been informed, stipulates that I can take your eye as recompense, and this is what I am going to do." W: "Oops, well how about 5,000,000 then? I really was only joking when I offered 25,000."

Put aside the problem that W is unlikely to have the wealth to pay five million. In the interests of the hypothetical let us assume him good for it. In the law school world the analysis of this bargaining situation is as likely to be taught in Property as in Torts; it is standard first-year fare.

Its relevance in Torts is obvious, but it also belongs in Property because lurking in it is a theory of property put forward more than thirty years ago by Guido Calabresi and A. Douglas Melamed.[9] Briefly presented it goes like this. First a culture decides to create and then assign to a person an entitlement in a thing. In this case V, not surprisingly, holds the entitlement to his own eye; he owns it. Next, the polity decides how to protect the entitlement it has conferred on V. In this model, it has a choice between two types of protection. The entitlement can be backed by what the authors call a property rule or by a liability rule. Property-rule protection means the entitlement is transferable only at a price the entitlement-holder (in this case V) is willing to accept. No one can take it unless he agrees to V's terms. V has the sole power to determine whether and for how much he will give up his entitlement.[10] Liability-rule protection, however, will, under certain circumstances, compel V to transfer his entitlement for a price – not a price he gets to set, but one that will be determined by a third party, such as a court or an arbitrator or an official compensation schedule.[11]

As a general matter property-rule protection means voluntary transfer by sale or gift; its domain is the market or under the Christmas tree. Liability-rule protection, on the other hand, involves involuntary transfer by accident or by force such as robbery, or eminent domain; its domain is the courts. Thus suppose I lose my eye in a car accident for which you were at fault. In our legal order you must pay me for the loss of my eye. But you get it at a bargain. I can get only what the court, or the worker's comp schedules, or the insurance company says is the going rate for an involuntarily transferred eye as long as it still leaves me with one good one. You do not have to pay me what I would have demanded had you bargained with me ahead of time for the right to take it (assuming for the sake of the hypothetical that I could legally agree to have my eye gouged out). But that is the problem with accidents. One does not usually set about to do them on purpose, and so all the bargaining must be done after the transfer has been effected and the damage is done. My eye in such a regime is cheap for the taking.

Compare, though, how much improved my bargaining position is in a talionic regime, and thus how much pricier my eye will be. The talion structures the bargaining situation to simulate the hypothetical bargain that would have been struck had I been able to set the price of my eye *before* you took it. It does this by a neat trick of substitution. Instead of receiving a price for the taking of my eye, I get to demand the price you will be willing to pay to *keep* yours.[12] It is not so much that I think your eye substitutable for mine. It is that you do. You will in fact play the role of me valuing my eye before it was taken out, and the talion assumes that you will value yours as I would have valued mine. The talion works some quick magic: as soon as you take my eye, in that instant your eye becomes mine; I now possess the entitlement to it. And that entitlement is protected by a property rule. I get to set the price, and you will have to accede to my terms to keep me from extracting it.

The bargaining game I envisaged here is a powerful allegory of perfect sympathetic identification, perfect because unsentimentalized. Sentimentalized emotions, it has been noted, come cheap, for the mere price of turning on the TV, renting a DVD, attending various academic lectures on social injustice, or, closer to home, writing with enthusiasm about the talionic world as if it were a world I, a nervous insomniacal academic, would thrive in. The talion, though, gives you a powerful impulse to imagine and value my loss as if it were your own, because it is about, in fact, to be your own. For you to save your eye, you are going to have to pay an arm and a leg.

An arm and a leg? Is it not remarkable that body parts still continue to function as measures of value in everyday speech? There is, of course, a threat in measuring value in arms and legs, a threat that they or something like them will also be excised as the means of payment. In the Aztec world, people employed a similar figure of speech: "You will pay with your entrails." In their world there was a genuine risk that the speaker was not speaking figuratively.[13] Even our milder idea that you cannot get blood from a turnip equates blood and money just as many revenge cultures did regularly.[14] Our obsession with the body's partibility has nothing to do with the fear that Dad may be mad at me for loving Mom: it runs so much deeper than that tired story, so deep into our primordial past that I suspect it is a reflex of being torn apart not by Dad, but by Bacchantes or animals, or an angry Hecuba or Achilles, and supped upon.[15]

Lest you think I am making up this bargaining situation in the manner philosophers are wont to do with their implausible hypotheticals, let me present a case from medieval Iceland that offers some pointed proof that the bargaining played out pretty much as I imagined. An Icelander named Skæring gets into a dispute with some Norwegian merchants who have put into port in Iceland. They chop off his hand (merchants in those days were tough guys and were often themselves indistinguishable from Vikings). Skæring runs to his kinsman Gudmund, who is the local big man, and asks for help. Gudmund, with a group of men, rides to the Norwegian ship and demands that they compensate Skæring at a price he, Gudmund, shall name. The Norwegians agree, and Gudmund hits them with a very stiff price, almost as much as they would have been expected to pay had they taken Skæring's life. They balk at paying the price named, despite having agreed beforehand to pay whatever Gudmund adjudged to be appropriate; they argue that the hand of an undistinguished guy like Skæring should not carry such a high value and that Gudmund is simply gouging them, not adhering to certain norms of reasonableness. Gudmund says, OK, forget it. I will myself pay Skæring the exact amount I adjudged you to pay, "but I shall choose one man from amongst you who seems to me of equivalent standing with Skæring and chop off his hand. You can then compensate that man's hand as miserably as you wish."[16] The Norwegians pay up.

Thus the lesson of sympathy is learned. The Norwegians now can feel just how much Skæring valued his hand before he lost it. Indeed they so feel Skæring's pain that if there were, say, twenty-five Norwegians in the group Gudmund threatened, not an unlikely number, and each thus had only a one in twenty-five chance of being selected to lose his hand, they were not about to take the gamble. That means that property-rule protection for Skæring's hand is worth at least twenty-five times more than liability-rule protection.

Would Gudmund really have taken the hand? What would be the point of that? What, ask prudent and practical and even kindly souls of utilitarian bent, could he do with it? Yet the Norwegians surely believed he would take it. Such threats were credible because presumably they were carried out every now and then. Cases like this show that body parts and bodies filled more money functions than merely setting a measure of value; they also could function as means of payment. And that is precisely what constitutes the threat value that gives Skæring something close to a property-rule price for his hand even after it has been involuntarily transferred.

Sometimes, though, I may simply want to take your eye, taking my compensation in your pain and humiliation, not caring in the least that I may also be enhancing the credibility of any future threats I may have to make. I may have no thoughts of the future at all, only of my present desires fueled by thoughts of the past wrongs done me. I want the pleasures of my Schadenfreude now. Adding anger and hatred to the victim's motivations may mean only blood or hands or eyes will work to assuage my dishonor, not conventional forms of money. Thus Proverbs 6.32–35 regarding the anger of the cuckold: "He will accept no compensation, nor be appeased though you multiply gifts."

Humiliation of the wrongdoer could also be obtained more rationally by taking W into debt slavery to work off what he owes because it is highly unlikely W is going to be good for the price. Taking him into your household may give you the pleasure of ordering him around, whipping him, or having him simply not matter, that is, treating him to the usual indignities of slavery. But would you be able to sleep at night with W resident in your abode? Why not transfer him to someone else to whom you owe a sum? Not *sell* him to your creditor, but *pay* him to your creditor. W becomes currency, by shuffling, if not exactly running, through the slave market, from place to place.

Humiliation aside, sometimes it is purely rational, as noted earlier, to pluck out that eye and chop off the hand, or take the pound of flesh from right around the heart. It means that the next time, and for quite a few times thereafter, you will not have to. People will, I bet, be very careful around such as the likes of you and will make sure they fulfill their undertakings where you are concerned. And remember: they did not have insurance as we do now, so it was all the more important that you take care to have your threats be believable. That was a form of insurance against future harms that might otherwise be directed your way. In my writings on the Icelandic sagas I have sought to hammer home the point that the wise bloodfeuder did not need to respond aggressively to every wrong done him; in fact, he was stupid and had a very short life if he did so. He just needed to make sure people thought him perfectly capable of avenging in blood the *next* offense done him.

One other practical matter. There were ways of forcing people who overvalued the harms done to them to accept a compromise. The good opinion of third parties could quickly shift from the victim to the initial wrongdoer if the victim was unwilling to settle and insisted on the point of honor. They might even cease to be third parties and join forces with the second party. It is likely that there were strong pressures for V not to gouge W; he was not to set a price that looked unseemly, all things considered. Josephus, writing in the first century A.D., comments on the talion thus: "He that maimeth a man shall undergo the like, being deprived of that limb whereof he deprived the other, unless indeed the maimed man be willing to accept money; for the law empowers the victim himself to assess the damage that has befallen him and makes this concession, *unless he would show himself too severe.*"[17]

It is the "unless he show himself too severe" that merits a few words. The holder of the property right to the eye of the person who harmed him was bound, it seems, by certain rules of reason, by certain customs, not to insist on the full enforcement of his rights. There must have been a fairly generally agreed-upon sense of what it was fair to demand, or at least of certain upward limits beyond which you could not go without losing your right or your honor. That is the message that underlies the story of Skæring. The Norwegians felt Gudmund had violated certain customary limits on what he could ask for a hand of a guy like Skæring, even though they had granted Gudmund the right to ask whatever he wanted. That Gudmund overreached is a risk that the Norwegians bore because Gudmund had the power to make them bear it. Gudmund rubs their faces in it with ostentatious irony by offering to pay the same outrageously high sum himself to Skæring if he can take a Norwegian hand for it. Nasty wit abounds in the world of the sagas.

Josephus indicates, however, that there were enforceable limits, presumably by having the price V set be subject to review by an oddman. We have just such an Icelandic case.[18] And might this not be the way to explain the notoriously difficult phrase in Exodus 21.22 that immediately precedes the statement of the Exodus talion: "If men strive, and hurt a woman with child, so that her fruit depart from her, and yet no mischief follow: he shall be surely punished, according as the woman's husband will lay upon him; *and he shall pay as the judges determine"*? Daube believed that the italicized clause was a later interpolation.[19] His view was that the husband had unfettered property-rule protection for accidental harms; he alone had the right to name the price. It seems much more likely to me, contra Daube, that there was to be an oddman present, or soon reachable, when the husband declared the amount due him, to set aside overreaching awards.[20]

Life Is Cheap?

We do not have the evidence to prove whether talionic societies had more mutilated people around than did more liability-rule-oriented compensatory systems. My guess is that the accidental and intentional taker of an eye had a good chance of ending up a debt slave. Perhaps some kind of proof for this hunch can be found in the institution of debt slavery itself and the numerous strictures governing it in the ancient Mesopotamian, biblical, and also medieval Icelandic codes. Further support can be inferred in the Bible from the stern admonishment *not* to accept compensation in cases of manslaughter or homicide: "Ye shall take no satisfaction for the life of a murderer, which is guilty of death: but he shall be surely put to death. And ye shall take no satisfaction for him that is fled to the city of his refuge, that he should come again to dwell in the land, until the death of the priest" (Num. 35.31–32). Such a prohibition against taking compensation assumes that it was a strong temptation in killing cases, maybe even a standard practice, and if for killing then surely for lesser harms. And the most valuable piece of property most accidental harmers would own would be their own bodies, intact, as laboring machines.

In any event, it is far from clear that a talionic society produces more one-eyed people than a nontalionic society. I suspect they may have produced fewer. People would be singularly careful about other people's eyes under the rule of the talion. Although there might be a few saliently brutal compensatory extractions of eyes and severances of hands, it just might be that there were considerably fewer accidents,

54

because the cost of an accident was so very high. There is a stunning law in the medieval Icelandic code that makes the point: "There shall be no such thing as accidents." I have discussed this provision in detail elsewhere, but suffice it to say that it puts the burden on the accidental harmer to pay up or else be treated as an intentional harmer and killed.[21] In such a regime I know I would be really careful.

We are wont to sneer at talionic societies and say that life is cheap, nasty, and brutish among such violent souls. But cheap is exactly what life is not among talionic peoples. The reason such societies may often be so poor is not because life is cheap, but because life is so expensive that it is hard for them to free up capital to build roads and factories. Imagine if the costs of replacing horses with automobiles meant that every road fatality gave the victim's kin a right to kill or to extract a ransom measured at the value the person at fault placed on keeping his life! It is that life is cheap among us, despite all our piety about dignity and the pricelessness of human life. We put prices on it all the time, and not very high ones either. I buy life insurance at pretty good rates. I judge that my family thinks me only slightly undervalued at the $2,500 per year that I pay out in premiums to buy them the right to about $1,000,000 when I die. Don't be too harsh in blaming me for attributing to them such a low estimation of my own worth: I want to make sure they miss me too.

How closely related in deep motive are our ideas of insurance and insurable interests, and theirs of revenge? We need to be paid for the losses of loved ones and body parts much as they did, or something is out of joint with the world. Is not life insurance a way of demanding compensation from God, the Wrongdoer? And add to that the point made a few pages ago that the capacity to make creditable threats was its own kind of insurance.

One of the reasons we gave up, officially at least, on the talion with the power it confers on victims to get fairly compensated is that it is so much cheaper to do it our way. Besides, over the course of a lifetime we are as likely to play the role of W as often as we are forced into the role of V. What it comes down to is that we let our own wrongdoing balance out and cancel the harms we endure. Today you smash my fender, tomorrow I smash someone else's, who in turn hits another who then eventually nails your fender. We believe it all comes out in the wash. I pay you a lowball figure on the understanding that that is what I will accept from you when it is my turn to be V. Keep the cost of accidents down. As a society we are a whole lot richer for our decision to operate the way we do, if not nobler. Richer, that is, as long as the price we pay is not so cheap as to make us not care at all whether we cause harms. But then we leave it to the insurance companies to police the truly careless person; they may not quite get a pound of flesh, but they will make sure he will suffer something for the harms he inflicts.

My point about life being dearer in talionic culture than in ours is a cheap point in some ways, a debater's point. We should not confuse our own tolerance for statistical deaths on the highways with callousness. Honor cultures valued people who were players in the honor game quite highly, but they could be extraordinarily callous to the suffering of those whom they deemed to be without the capacity for honor.

One question to ask, though ultimately not answerable given the evidence, is whether victims on average actually got more compensation then than now. My suspicion is that in high-stakes feudlike situations, the ancients were committed to steep compensation because that was the only way peace had a chance (and the parties were likely to be rich enough to buy peace); but for injuries that cross status lines liberal democracies do a better job of leveling some of the disparity in treatment between the weak and the powerful. If in the Psalms and Prophets God had to be the Redeemer – that is, the avenger of the blood – for the poor, for widows and orphans, that is because they were not getting much help from human avengers. The state now takes up that burden; and though some still feel they have a better chance asking God for help, on average it seems that God's justice was even slower and more erratic than that delivered by the state on behalf of the poor.

To be the protector of the poor and weak was a moral demand recognized by the earliest statelike authority, and a king considered it to reflect well on himself that he could offer justice to the weak. This from the prologue to the laws of Ur-Namma, Sumer, c. 2100 B.C.: "I did not deliver the orphan to the rich. I did not deliver the widow to the mighty. I did not deliver the man with but one shekel to the man with one mina. I did not deliver the man with but one sheep to the man with one ox . . . I eliminated enmity, violence, and cries for justice. I established justice in the land."[22] Powerful stuff, by anyone's criteria.

A colleague comments that although we may in fact give cheap liability-rule protection to our body parts and lives in the realm of accidents, consider, he says, the amounts we spend on health care to keep our bodies living long and painlessly. We are willing to pay through the nose for life, he says; it is not cheap in the least.[23] To which I, assuming the role of defender of honor culture, reply: those obscene amounts we pay to grant ourselves extra unproductive years bespeak less of our virtue than of our vice, less of our commitment to human dignity than to our lack thereof. We are so afraid of death and pain that we will bankrupt our grandchildren's generation to add on more useless years at the butt-end of our days than we know what to do with. Cowardice, lust, luxury, slothful ease. There is no honor in them at all. We price ourselves more highly as pleasure machines than as working beings. Indeed, pain has become such a scarce commodity that we actually pay for the opportunity of experiencing it in extreme sports or in ever more recherché forms of sex, of which indulgences we are all supposed to be tolerant because, you know, human beings all bear their equal portion of dignity. O tempora, o mores. O tongue only half in cheek.

To speak more precisely: it is not life itself that is expensive in talionic honor cultures, but honorable life that is expensive. And honorable life need not mean a short life either. It was not always death before dishonor. It was also live to fight another day so that you could get even with the person who dishonored you. But you had to fight on another day. Honor did not allow for refusing to redeem lost honor.

FIVE

Teaching a Lesson: Pain and Poetic Justice

THE FORMULATION OF THE TALION in Exodus adds stripe for stripe to the litany of lives, eyes, teeth, hands, burnings, and wounds that are to be compensated for in kind. Stripes are less about mutilations and disfigurement than about pain.[1] Stripes are given to inflict pain, but they are an inadequate proxy for the pain actually felt. Although I can guess that you will value your hand as I value mine, I cannot in the least be sure you will feel the pains of a lashing to the same extent I do.[2]

Pain thresholds, people have always known or suspected, vary greatly. Implicit in various forms of racism and classism is the view that the lower orders, whoever they may be, are impervious to pain, either from being accustomed to it or from being too insensible and stupid to feel it. And then, too, some people are better at taking it than others whatever their class, sex, or race. It was always a riddle I could never solve when the guys I played with and against when young could take hits that I could not imagine taking myself and thus shied away from, to the tune of their taunts. Was it that they had no nerve endings and hence were manifesting no virtue at all but simply felt no pain, or was it that they felt it but did not fear it or were not averse to it the way I was? Could it be they actually liked getting hit? Pain and pleasure have such an unseemly relationship, each never quite knowing how to keep neatly to itself.

Instruction on Feeling Another's Pain

Nothing presents the intersubjectivity problem, of getting at another's consciousness, more starkly than trying to understand another's pain, as to both intensity and quality. This makes pain less useful as a measure of value than bodies, lives, eyes, or teeth. Yet the talionic principle is desperate to find a way to use pain as a means of payment. And lashes are what we must settle for. We can count their number; we can measure the damage they do to the skin and flesh, but we cannot measure the pain suffered, even if we employed a measure such as decibel level of screams or quality of groans, for these can be faked or be elicited by very different pain levels.

But there are some clever ways to finesse the problem. And where else but in an Icelandic saga do we see precisely this issue addressed with great sophistication and wit? Do not let the names confuse you. A man named Hrafnkel (Raven-kettle)[3] killed a young shepherd of his, Einar, for riding a horse he, Hrafnkel, had dedicated to the god Frey. The shepherd's father, old Thorbjorn, with the help of his nephew Sam, commence a lawsuit against Hrafnkel. But they find it hard to get support for their claim; people are afraid to go against Hrafnkel, whom the saga introduces as an "unevenman," an unjust man. Just when Sam and old Thorbjorn sink into despair an adventurer comes forward named Thorkel, who offers to help them by interceding on their behalf with his powerful brother, a chieftain named Thorgeir. Thorkel, the adventurer, advises Sam that in order to convince Thorgeir to join with their cause they had best stage a little charade.

It so happens that Thorgeir the chieftain is laid up in his booth at the Allthing, the annual assembly where the courts meet. An infected boil on his foot has been depriving him of sleep and the boil has just burst the night before. He is now finally getting some sleep with his sore foot extended on a board. Thorkel tells Sam and old Thorbjorn that the old man should go into the booth:

> "It seems that his vision is badly failing on account of old age. When you, old man," said Thorkel, "come to [Thorgeir's] hammock, rush hastily toward it and smash into the footboard and take the bandaged toe, and yank it toward you, and we will see just how he reacts."
>
> Sam said, "I know you mean to give us useful advice, but this does not strike me as advisable."
>
> "You have two choices: either you do as I tell you, or don't ask me for help."

One can understand Sam's dismay. Here he is in the practical and unpreachy world of an Icelandic saga, and some weirdo insists on staging a scene out of a different literary genre. And that is just what Thorkel means to do: he is about to preach to his brother, to deliver a homily on pain and sympathy and he wants to act out the exemplum.

Old Thorbjorn plays his part; he slams into Thorgeir and jerks his sore toe. Thorgeir awakens with a jolt and starts yelling at the old man. Thorkel then steps into the booth and begins:

> "Don't fly off the handle at this, brother. There is no harm done. People often do worse than they mean to; they do not always pay as much attention as they should when they have a lot on their mind. Your excuse, brother, is that you have a sore foot that's been hurting you. Only you really know how much. It just might be that an old man is not any less in pain over the death of his son for whom he has received no compensation and has no likelihood of getting it. Only he really knows how much that hurts. A man with that much on his mind can't be expected to pay careful attention to what he does."
>
> Thorgeir said: "But I don't think he should blame me. I didn't kill his son; he shouldn't be seeking revenge on me."
>
> "He does not wish to avenge himself on you," said Thorkel, "but he approached you harder than he meant to and that is mostly because of his bad eyesight. But he wants your help..."

Why this stagey moral tale? Because Thorkel knows we do not feel another's pain. He is no less sophisticated on this score than Adam Smith, and both are a whole lot more sophisticated than anyone today who is inclined to use the phrase "I feel your pain." Or if we actually manage to generate some sympathetic pain by an act of imagination or kinesthesia we surely do not feel it as intensely or as long.[4] Pain, to be understood, must be brought home as one's own. And because one cannot transfer one's own pain in the same way one can transfer blood, sheep, or coin, one must employ a rough proxy, as Thorkel does here. The physical pain of having a sore toe yanked is meant to provide a rough idea of the pain of having an unavenged son. The lesson in sympathy that is being taught is clearly of an ilk with the lesson the talion teaches. You will begin to feel the pain of the loss of my eye to me when I am holding my knife to yours. Sympathy is carved in the flesh. Fellow-feeling in this world does not mean sentimental indulgences in pity and self-congratulation for being a person of such refined sentiments; it means helping the weak wreak revenge, which is just how God positions himself in the Prophets and Psalms, an avenger of those who need help taking it.[5]

To bring the point home Thorkel gives his brother a real pain, and the pain is all the more frustrating to Thorgeir because he cannot avenge it. Just as the young shepherd Einar was not an appropriate target of revenge for Hrafnkel on grounds of his age, rank, and triviality of the horse-riding offense, neither is old Thorbjorn on account of his age, rank, and triviality of the offense someone Thorgeir can strike back at.[6] Moreover, says Thorkel, this was an accident. And the accident is excusable not only because it was an accident but also because old Thorbjorn's inattentiveness is so easily explained, so justifiable; his grief is that distracting. Can't you feel his pain, brother?

The *unavengeability* of the pain the old man visited on Thorgeir is crucial, and it is by virtue of that unavengeability that Thorkel cleverly manages the impossible; he is able to commensurate the pain of grieving for a dead son with the pain of a sore toe, psychic sorrow with physical pain – not by measuring them on a pain index, but, brilliantly, by placing them on a frustration index, the frustration of not being able to take revenge for the pains. That frustration unites all humanity in railing against misfortunes and injustices; it is a pain everyone trusts everyone else to feel in the same way and with levels of intensity that are predictably and pretty confidently observable. Frustration is like disgust and anger in that regard; it largely solves the intersubjectivity problem. Thorgeir cannot avenge being bumped into because he can't justifiably lash out at an old man for an "accident," and old Thorbjorn can't avenge his son because he is old and powerless. Both are laid up after a fashion. But now each can understand the other's pain, for they are made to feel the same kind of pain: vengeance stymied.[7]

Thorkel is careful to make the case clearly. It is not that the old man has a dead son that prompts his distraction. It is the frustrating disequilibrium brought about by a dead son *"for whom he has received no compensation and has no likelihood of getting it."* The misery of

61

mind is of having no prospect of getting back to even. A dead son adequately valued by a quid pro quo in blood or some other specie restores the mind, exchanges grief and confusion for satisfaction and order.

But what is poor Thorgeir to do? Must his toe go unavenged? Embedded in Thorkel's homily is the idea that not all pain is avengeable and not all lashing back is justifiable. Some pains must be endured without amends, for there is no one who can justifiably be lashed out at for the harm. Thorgeir thus claims that old Thorbjorn shouldn't take out his misery on him by bumping into his sore foot, while Thorkel reminds his brother that he should not be taking out the pain of his foot on an old man for having bumped into him. Old Thorbjorn is in effect saved by a plea of accident. Such pleas are available in vengeance cultures but mostly only to the old, to children, or to those who do not matter. The obvious irony is that this was no accident. It was a fake accident. No wonder, as I have written elsewhere, that these people were suspicious of claims of accident.[8]

Thorkel's point, though, is nicely made: guys, there is someone we can take all these pains out on and it will gain us nothing but honor. But, says Thorgeir, all one gets from going up against Hrafnkel is dishonor, because he always wins. Thorkel's response: then we are no worse off than everyone else, because they have already lost to him. We are treated to another aspect of this grim social and moral economy of pain and humiliation and honor: you are made better off by everyone else's pain and discomfiture.

There is among them, notice, no less than among us, a deep desire to have recompense not only for wrongs, such as a murdered son, a gouged-out eye, a chopped-off hand, but also for misfortunes, such as having an infected toe, or being ugly, or having it rain on your picnic. It is hard for the person bearing the pain to draw a distinction between pains that are merely unfortunate and pains that justify blame and revenge. We still today want to hit back at anyone or anything that harms us. Do you not curse the toy left on the stairs you trip over? Do you maybe kick it, even sentence it to the death of the trash can or the thrift shop? Do you not think that something or someone is owed for your pain? Sometimes you owe it to your own self. We curse ourselves, or cuff our own forehead with the heel of our palm, when we do something stupid or when our own inabilities seem inexcusable to us. Who is hitting whom when that happens, who is cursing whom? What accounts are being settled? But accounts are being settled, are they not?

Deuteronomy's Artful Talionic Lesson

Let me at this point revisit the notion of the "beauty" of the talion that I touched on earlier. The classic formulation of the talion embodies a narrative in as succinct a form as it is possible to condense a story. It has a beginning, a middle, and an end. Beginning: you took my eye; middle: threat and bargain; end: I restore my honor and dignity by taking yours from you and now we are even. The notion of getting even is inseparable from the aesthetics of justice.

And hovering over the story is a mystic image of a balance-beam scale. The scales provide suspense, in the double sense of suspense: one, the pans are suspended from the balance beam, and two, the suspense of watching them swing up and down after the weights are dropped in to see whether they will hit the even point. Have you not experienced that small rush of anticipation, or simply the extra intensity of focused attention, when in some rare circumstance, perhaps in a market in what gets called the third world, you watch the scale swing as the weights are dropped into one pan to get it to even? Will the shopkeeper have to add more or take some away? Or will he give you the benefit of his own coming up short on guessing the weight? Even the steelyard-type scale in the gym provides a similarly gripping suspense story as you slide the weight into ever more depressing spaces rightward before the end of the arm detaches itself from the top of the swing limiter and begins its slow descent into restricted space. It is all a bit like roulette.

All this is the stuff of good stories. There is an urge to poetize justice, to make sure it is the stuff of good stories; the moral point, we believe, is enhanced when it elicits a triumphant smile, a small frisson at its perfection, as it surprises both its victim and the audience alike in its aptness, at how perfectly it settles all outstanding accounts, banishing the hobgoblins of incommensurability. It is the brilliance, by the way, of the "Road Runner" cartoons to invert our sympathies utterly, by making us loathe the poetic justice that sadistically hoists that fecund genius Wile E. Coyote with his own petard. Too much poetic justice begins to look unjust. Not all hostile plots recoiling on the head of their authors are images of justice; some are also images of the sadistic malevolence of the gods. That poor coyote is the emblem of all that is comically tragic about human designs or, in his case, of his simple quest to get a meal but to get it in style. In a talionic culture one expected justice to have poetry and feel right; it was from the poetry that much of the sense of satisfaction of justice done was derived, with *satisfaction* bearing both its sense of a particular feeling state and its legal sense of the condition of having all debts quit. The satisfaction was borne of the sense of its rightness.

Take the case codified in Deuteronomy 19.16–21:

> If a false witness rise up against any man to testify against him that which is wrong; then both the men, between whom the controversy is, shall stand before the Lord, before the priests and the judges, which shall be in those days; and the judges shall make diligent inquisition: and, behold, if the witness be a false witness, and hath testified falsely against his brother; then shall ye do unto him, as he had thought to have done unto his brother: so shalt thou put the evil away from among you. And those which remain shall hear, and fear, and shall henceforth commit no more any such evil among you. And thine eye shall not pity; but life shall go for life, eye for eye, tooth for tooth, hand for hand, foot for foot.

The deuteronomist considers the punishment meted out to the bearer of false witness to be talionic punishment; thus his restatement of the classic formulation of the talion to wind up the section.[9] But the talion is doing different work here from what it does in the classic situations that require finding equivalences to compensate harms involving mutilations, injuries, and death. Here the wrongdoer is not a bungler or even a violent brawler but a perjurer, a particular kind of intentional harmer, and the punishment is meted out even when his evil intentions were thwarted and no harm was done. Unlike the standard talionic situation, perjury does not provide much of a starting point for a private bargaining session.

The action takes place in court, and without too much forcing we can see the court as avenging a wrong done to itself. But mostly the passage looks to be an example of "teaching a lesson" rather than of compensation. The talion is not doing its usual compensatory work, as it was in Exodus, Leviticus, the Twelve Tables, or the tale of Skæring. Yet neither we nor the deuteronomist feels the eye-for-an-eye imagery to be inappropriate in this setting. It can do work justifying instructional punition, no less than state a principle of compensation. Why? Partly because at a deeper level the talion is understood to state an aesthetic principle of poetic justice, in which the core idea is the exactitude of the fit, the perfection of the matching.[10] Let the punishment fit the crime, and what better principle of fit than the golden rule of the talion: "Then shall ye do unto him, as he had thought to have done unto his brother"?

Perfection of fit is also coupled with another principle of poetic justice: its irony, so that the wrongdoer can be understood to be the author of his own punishment.[11] And sometimes the irony is pushed to its limits by making what we find to be particularly chilling uses of vicarious liability – of making someone other than the actual wrongdoer pay the price – which biblical law, though not God, pretty much rejects. An example alluded to earlier will make my meaning clear. Thus *Hammurabi*:

> If a builder constructs a house for a man but does not make his work sound, and the house that he constructs collapses and causes the death ... of a son of the householder, they shall kill a son of that builder.
>
> (§230)

Whoever thought that law could dispense utterly with dark humor? And if the law cannot, can we blame the Jacobean playwrights for indulging in their over-the-top fantastic revenges, in which the avenger is first and foremost a decadent artiste of making the punishment fit the crime: "Is thy union here?" Or the matchless inventive perversity of *The Revenger's Tragedy*: "Have I not fitted the old surfeiter / With a quaint piece of beauty?" says the avenger, remarking on his painting his dead love's skull with poisonous cosmetics to attract the amorous attentions of the old duke, who poisoned her for resisting his lustful advances.[12]

It is a nice puzzle to determine how seriously committed to certain forms of vicarious liability so-called ancient or primitive cultures were. Something in the *Hammurabi* provision smacks of an intellectual exercise, a game played in the scribal schools rather than a practical regime of liability. That does not mean, though, that people didn't exact revenges along such lines. Such revenges are common fare in folktale and legend, where they are meant to be darkly humorous and brutally clever. It is justice with a knowing smirk. Thus the provision from the Middle Assyrian Laws (1076 B.C.):

> If a man lays a hand upon a woman, attacking her like a rutting bull, and they prove the charges against him and find him guilty, they shall cut off one of his fingers. If he should kiss her, they shall draw his lower lip across the blade of an axe and cut it off.
>
> (§9)

There are of course other interpretations, particularly of the series of laws at *Hammurabi* §§229–231, which deal successively with the liability of a builder for various deaths caused by his faulty building. Raymond Westbrook argues – in a way as chilling as my view that these provisions are the stuff of a cruel, elegant joke – that the central principle in vicarious liability is one of mitigation. If your bad workmanship kills the householder, you go; if it kills the householder's son, your son goes; if it kills the householder's slave, you supply him with a new slave. In other words, says Westbrook, the builder's liability is ever less as he kills someone of ever lower status.[13] Still, it does not seem to me plausible to rid a scheme like this of the purposeful artistry of its overdone fearful symmetry, the symmetry and dark irony being surely as dominant a principle as mitigation.

It is not only ancient lawmakers who let their imaginations take flight in order to effect talionic punishment; punishment theorists who wish to combine a commitment to talionic retribution with opposition to capital punishment can find some strange ways to satisfy the demands of the talion. Thus the talion is claimed to be fulfilled not by killing a murderer but by inflicting upon him some redescription of what murder "really" is. If murder is defined as "the deprivation of ability to complete life's projects," then, lo, it is satisfied by imprisonment. Creative imagination can make the notion of "same" and "like" and "equivalent" do all kinds of funny things. Jeremy Waldron, in his mild defense of the talion, proposes the following "talionic" response in the case of perjury:

> Perjury may or may not do harm to an assignable person, but it certainly impedes the ability of the courts to function. That is one of its wrong-making features. The offender has experienced that characteristic as agent, but what would it be like for him to experience it in some other role? Maybe a person guilty of perjury could be denied access to the courts for some specified period in the future. Or some property of his could be confiscated and returned to him (or not), depending on the toss of a coin.[14]

I have noted that there is a lot of play in the joints of notions like balance and equivalence, but at least it still had to look like equivalence. If bloodfeuders were nervous about exchanging blood for money because payment in silver for blood did not look talionic enough, why should we think Waldron's punishment for perjury would do anything but elicit guffaws?

In the Deuteronomy talion, we moderns, and even some ancients, might still see a compensatory principle lurking behind its punitiveness, that it is still a story about settling accounts: the perjurer is paying for his crime. But that is not the deuteronomist's take. He is not talking about repayment of debts incurred. To be sure, he is concerned with fitness, if not quite balance, the aptness of making the punishment fit the crime, of having what the offender thought to do to his brother redound upon his own head. He wants to drive evil from the land and he must find a way to teach a lesson, to focus everyone's attention. And the wit and beauty of ironical deserts has a way of doing that. For in this setting the punishment is meant to be utilitarian as a first-order matter, not just as a pleasant by-product of vengeful urges.

The deuteronomist expressly means to deter others who might be inclined to cook up sham cases and bear false witness: "And those which remain shall hear, and fear, and shall henceforth commit no more any such evil among you." And because the terse tough beauty of the classic formulation of the talion terrorizes, the deuteronomist hopes it will provide a stunning and impressive object lesson. In short, it will "teach you a lesson": you are to hear (with your ears) and fear (in your heart), and your eye? Your eye is not to do what it may tempt you to do when you witness rough justice; it is not to pity: "and thine eye shall not pity." The deuteronomic talion adds the notion of "teaching a lesson" to the notion of "getting even" that characterizes the formulations in Exodus and Leviticus, just as in our own speech we will often find both idioms – getting even and teaching a lesson – to be equally appropriate to explain the ministering of justice.

Coda: Mixing Metaphors: Paying Back and Paying For

I have noted that revenge is conceptualized in vengeance culture in the idiom of debt and credit. But there is a clash of two competing paradigms, each of considerable antiquity. Who is understood to play the role of creditor, and who the debtor, in these remedial interactions? There is a pay *back* model and a pay *for* model. In the former it is the avenger – that is, the victim or his representative – who owes a debt of blood; he pays back the wrongdoer or someone on the wrongdoer's side, the wrongdoers being understood as creditors, those who are owed repayment. When it is blood we are talking about, the avenger owes and is duty-bound to repay. But nowadays, and back then too, the wrongdoer could be styled as the debtor; he owed amends, and surely when it was compensation in sheep or silver rather than blood that was to be paid over, it was clear that he was the debtor, the ower, whereas the wronged party, his victim, was the creditor, the owed. And then when the state or a king intervenes to demand a cut or to exact punishment, the wrongdoer must pay *for* his wrong to some entity like the state or someone like the king in place of or in addition to the person he directly harmed.

To this day we mix our creditor/debtor metaphors when revenge and punishment are the subject. We say "payback time," casting the wronged party as the debtor, while at the very instant he strikes and thus pays him back, he also thinks of having made the wrongdoer pay up, pay *for* his wrong, each party being cast both as creditor and debtor as we switch seamlessly from one set of metaphorical assumptions to another.[15]

In the payback model it is easy to see how we can cast the avenger as debtor, as someone who owes, but how do we understand the wrong-doer to be a creditor, except by definition as a formal matter to keep the metaphor of payback consistent? The sagas give us an answer. The Icelanders did in fact understand that the wrongdoer had given something to the victim when he wronged him. With cold wit, saga characters refer to insults and injuries as "gifts," ones of negative value to be sure, but gifts nonetheless: says one Icelandic mother to her husband and sons after they have been made the objects of scurrilous insults, "Gifts have been given to you, father and sons alike; and you would scarcely be men if you did not repay them."[16] Insults and harms are conceptualized as so many gifts, and gifts create an obligation to pay them back, to make a return gift of like for like. Receiving gifts makes you a debtor. Odin himself lays down the law in this matter, specifically referring to gifts of negative value: "Give back gift for gift."[17]

When you do me a good turn I would scarcely be worthy if I did not make a return, for one good turn deserves another. And when you do me a bad turn I would again be something less than worthy if I did not return the favor, for one "good" turn deserves another. The core principle is that everything, good or bad, that was given over raised an obligation to repay. Not only among the Vikings but also among the Greeks and Persians (and though we resist the notion, among us too): thus the prayer of Cyrus reported by Xenophon asking "that he might live long enough to be able to repay with interest both those who had helped him and those who had injured him."[18] The principle of paying back debts demands we "avenge" gifts, no less than harms, by paying them back in kind. One can see the golden rule as only a slight modification of this basic moral rule of mandatory reciprocity.

To add one more layer: paying back is also congruent with buying back, with redeeming. For payback time is also buy back time. One repays the negative gift to the wrongdoer and thereby redeems one's honor.

SIX

A Pound of Flesh

WITH THE EXCEPTION OF A CAMEO appearance or two I have kept Shylock in the wings, but it is time to give him a full scene. I need barely mention *The Merchant of Venice,* and the reader can fill in the blanks as to how well suited the play is to this book's themes. There are body parts and human flesh acting as a money substance; we have scales, knives, justice, revenge; measuring and meting. At the core of the play's thematic structure is the question of what counts as money and how it should behave; what symbolizes and stores value best. Even the folkloric casket story, which embarrasses us now and mostly seems to reveal the stupidity of the princes of Morocco and Aragon – of course it is the lead casket, you idiots, don't you folk in folktales know the first thing about a folktale? – and which seems so crudely jerry-rigged to the main drama, reproduces the core themes of evaluating human flesh, in whole or parts, by reference to various metal repositories of value. What is moving against what? Is it gold, silver, and lead that are money substances, but Portia is pure soul, pure spirit? Or the other way around? Gold, silver, and lead are pure airy symbol, but Portia is so much meat on the hoof. Pardon the vulgarity: it is not her flesh, that kind of meat, that interests her suitors: it is her dough. She *is* the ducats with which she was "richly left" (1.1.161).

The Merchant of Venice is a troubling play, and not just to Jewish readers like me. Does Shakespeare mean to warrant my cheering on Shylock and my loathing for the heiress-hunting prodigal Bassanio, for the ruthless and hypocritical Portia, who discharges her husband's debts by hijacking the law, for the officious and sanctimonious Jew-baiter Antonio, and for the odious self-hating Jessica, ashamed of her father, who appallingly steals and trades for a monkey the ring her mother gave to her father when he was a bachelor? Or am I like the Oneida Indian kids at the Saturday morning matinee when I was a kid before television came to Green Bay, who cheered in all the wrong places in the cowboy movies, the wrong places being what they understood to be the right places?

Why, though I know better, do I still experience a twinge of bitterness that *The Merchant of Venice* is properly classified a comedy when the feelings I have reading it more accord with the feelings I experience during *Lear* and *Othello*? Can I ever read the play dispassionately, divorced from wanting to see Shylock claim his security interest in Antonio's body? Historicize, Miller, historicize; don't blame a prior age, nor the present one, for its hatred of Jews. Accept the play on its own terms. But what in heaven's name are those terms?

I take some solace that I can enlist William Hazlitt to my cause. After seeing Edmund Kean in 1816 break with convention to play Shylock as more substantial than the usual one-dimensional stock Jew-villain, Hazlitt wrote, "Certainly our sympathies are much oftener with him than with his enemies. He is honest in his vices; they are hypocrites in their virtues."[1] And it is not as if Elizabethans themselves were of one mind about Venetians, about merchants like Antonio, spendthrift aristocrats, and the competing demands of law and equity. Does not the play, I try to reassure myself, supply the means to critique the various positions taken in it? Shylock's speeches on revenge and Christian hypocrisy are unnervingly forceful and nearly untraversable even for those inclined to favor the mercy party, who, it is to be noted, never do outargue or outreason Shylock but must resort to arguments ad hominem and force majeure to defeat him.

Even in the smallest of details we find the hypocrisies of the Christians exposed. Thus Antonio smugly[2] informs Shylock as he approaches him for a loan:

> Shylock, albeit I neither lend nor borrow
> By taking nor by giving of excess,
> Yet to supply the ripe wants of my friend,
> I'll break custom...

> (1.3.56–58)

71

We do know that Antonio lends at zero percent interest; no hypocrisy there. But we surely do not see him *borrowing* at the same low rate. That he must seek out Shylock indicates the market for zero-percent loans could hardly exist as anything more than a pipe dream. No Christians, it seems, are willing to lend to Antonio at the rate Antonio lends to Bassanio. Even Antonio, the only person we actually see lending gratis, appears to be motivated in his lending practices more by hate, by the pleasure he takes in harassing Shylock on the Rialto, than by charity (3.1.49), with the one exception of the loan he makes for love to Bassanio. (Not that Antonio does not figure to bind Bassanio to him by means of his generosity. Bassanio clearly feels himself obliged to Antonio. The love Antonio bears Bassanio has occasioned more than its share of comment.)[3]

One wonders how a merchant can be so economically naïve, unless he is guilty of the most willful self-deception.[4] And the self-deception must be powerful indeed, for it must turn blind eyes everywhere it looks. There are those among the play's Christians who are not self-deceivers when it comes to thinking economically. There is Portia, Lady Justice herself. No figurative blindfold prevents her from making out like a bandit, saving her own assets by having her husband's debts paid off with money expropriated from Shylock. But the most sophisticated Christian economic thinker in the play is the clown, Launcelot Gobbo, who has no trouble understanding the effect of demand on prices, perhaps having acquired this way of seeing the world from his service in Shylock's house:[5]

> *Jessica:* I shall be sav'd by my husband, – he hath made me a Christian!
> *Launcelot Gobbo:* Truly the more to blame he, we were Christians enow before, e'en as many as could well live one by another: this making of Christians will raise the price of hogs, – if we grow all to be pork-eaters, we shall not shortly have a rasher on the coals for money.
>
> (3.5.17–23)

The transmutation of Jews into Christians will increase consumption of pigs and drive down the price of money in relation to pigs. There is no way to separate bodies, flesh, and money. They travel in the same circle.

Few plays have inspired so much critical controversy as to their plain meaning.[6] I know it is unsophisticated even to ask, but so much of the dispute about the play's plain meaning focuses on the question of who the good guys are. The Christians? How good are we supposed to think they are? That is up in the air for anyone but the most rabid Jew-hater. And even he might wonder why Antonio should lend gratis, or why Bassanio shouldn't mind his accounts better, or why Christians, with the exception of Antonio, should spend so wildly on their present pleasure, trusting to borrow without apparently a thought to repayment, unless a convenient Jew appears to be plucked.[7] What happens when there are no Jews left to plunder? How is the seemingly endless luxury of Belmont funded? The knowledge that it is the plundering of Jews that saves their way of life when it is about to bankrupt itself is a knowledge that even relatively minor characters seem to possess. Thus Lorenzo, in a dig at Shylock's expense, is moved to speak a word of Hebrew to indicate the miracle of continued wasteful pleasure the Hebrew Shylock's expropriated wealth and substance offers them: "Fair ladies, you drop *manna* in the way/ Of starved people" (5.1.294–295).

Shearing Fleece and Eating (Human) Flesh

But back to my chief themes. How much is money like sheep; how much are sheep like humans? Let us begin with the fact that both can be fleeced and then proceed with the fact that both are meat and can be consumed. The play's Christian men in quest of well-endowed ladies openly see themselves as Jasons questing for golden fleeces. Says Graziano about the success he and Bassanio have had at wooing, "We are the Jasons, we have won the fleece" (3.2.240); a fleet of fleecing Jasons at that: Bassanio, Graziano, and Lorenzo. Earlier we are told that Portia herself is something of a ewe: "Her sunny locks hang on her temples like a golden fleece." But the "many Jasons" that "come in quest of her" (1.1.169–172) do so to fleece Portia because she is "richly left" and thus ripe for fleecing.

It is part of the benignity of the world of Belmont that the fleecers never have to scruple about fleecing ugly ewes, but were Portia ever so ill favored as to beauty, there would still be Jasons aplenty to shear her. One loves where there is money; and so even Jewesses are prizes for impecunious Christians as long as the Jewesses have rich fathers who can be stripped bare. Does not Jessica enfleece herself with gold? "I will make fast the doors and gild myself / With some moe ducats, and be with you straight" (2.6.49–50).

The incarnation[8] of money in sheep and in human flesh invites ideas of comestibility as well as of fleecing. Sheep and other money forms are food for the mouth and maw. Hints of (human) flesh eating lurk about the play. Shylock hints at it by denying it: "A pound of man's flesh taken from a man, / Is not so estimable, profitable neither / As flesh of muttons, beefs, or goats..." (1.3.161–163). Yet his very first words to Antonio – "Rest you fair good signior, / Your worship was the last man *in our mouths*" (1.3.55) – suggest something more unnerving. Yes, I know, he means Antonio is in their mouths as the subject of the conversation he and Bassanio were just having. But Shylock extends the common form of the expression to make it more disgustingly graphic, more distasteful. Usually it is not a person that is in one's mouth in this sense, but his reputation or some deed of his, some news, some praise or blame, some *abstraction*, as when Othello says to Cassio, "Your name is great / In mouths of wisest censure..." Shylock's way of putting it does not put words or names in his and Bassanio's mouths so as to make the mouth an organ of speech; he instead metamorphoses Antonio into dessert – "the *last* man in our mouths" – thereby making the mouth an organ of alimentation and predation; in Shylock's usage the metaphor has become disgustingly nonabstract and violently nutritional.

What are the limits to the kinds of flesh humans can consume? Jews cannot eat pigs, but can Christians eat Jews (the Eucharist and Lorenzo's manna)? Can Jews feed on Christians (the blood libel)? And if you think I am going too far, what suggestions of cannibalism are to be excluded in a play that features playing butcher to a human body to carve a rib steak from near the heart, specifically denominated as a meal-size portion, a pound of meat? Only a few critics, at least among those I have read, pay heed to the suggestions of cannibalism. But images of it abound, and had Shakespeare known Hebrew he might have made something of the Torah's word for usury – *neshekh* – which means "bite."[9] Graziano views Shylock as a ravenous man-eating wolf. An invitation to dine among Christians is seen in terms of hostile consumption of human flesh: "I'll go in hate to feed upon the prodigal Christian" (2.5.14–15), although earlier he said he would not eat "with" them; the irony is, though, that it is Shylock who will be served up as manna to feed the endless sinkhole for wealth that is Belmont. Even Bassanio sees his own insatiable demands for money as having engaged his friend to his mere enemy "to *feed* my means." Ravenous maws abound. Friends not only eat friends out of house and home, but cause their very bodies to be served up for the sacrificial feasts of their enemies.

And if Shylock does not mean really to eat Antonio, he means to make Christians nervous that *they* might well end up eating him, unknowingly ingesting molecules of Antonio like so many Thyestes, Jasons, and Tamoras:

> *Salerio:* Why I am sure if he forfeit, thou wilt not take his flesh, – what's that good for?
> *Shylock:* To bait fish withal, – if it will feed nothing else, it will feed my revenge.
>
> (3.1.45–48)

The barely suppressed idea is one Hamlet delights in: Antonio will progress through the guts of his Christian friends, who feast on the pork that fed on the fish that fed on Antonio.

And hints of the easy exchangeability of edible and money-like sheep and goats with money-like (and edible) humans arise subtly and casually, as when Shylock alludes to the story of Jacob acquiring his birthright. Jacob's hands and neck are draped by his "wise mother" in the skin of two freshly slaughtered kids to trick his blind father into believing Jacob is his much hairier brother, Esau. The tale is one of a human dressed in the skin of the very kids that he serves up to his father, to mimic not the food that is being eaten but his brother, who is being fleeced.[10] The next time you speak of your children as kids – that is, transform them into goats the better to love them (and gobble them up) – keep this in mind.

One body comes within a hair's breadth of being carved, with the prime cut tossed in the scale. Others are portioned virtually, as a way of indicating passionate commitment. Bassanio thus tells Antonio he would give the Jew his "flesh, blood, bones and all,/ Ere thou shalt lose for me one drop of blood" (4.1.112–113); later he makes Shylock an offer of ten times the principal sum of the loan, on pain of losing his hands, head, and heart if he does not repay it (207–208). Even Portia, likewise expressing love but in a context of no threat, sees herself as a sum, a sum of parts, that she wishes were greater so that she could bestow even more of herself and her goods on Bassanio, whom we maybe should not trust not to sunder them and sell them off piecemeal (3.2.157).

We carve up the body all the time rhetorically, but in a play that takes these metaphors seriously, Bassanio's offers must be attended to more closely than usual, as we would if we heard them uttered in the Tlatelocan marketplace in the Aztec world, when one heard the casual but chilling insult of a hawker's wares: "What merchandise have you brought to sell? Do you want to sell your intestines or hearts?"[11] Bassanio cares deeply to rescue his friend, and he talks the language of corporal severance to show how deeply he feels. Let us grant him the sincerity of his passion. But that does not mean we must grant him the same level of sincerity as to his offer to lose "flesh, blood, bones and all," as he declares. Bassanio is exaggerating. That offer is not meant to be taken literally, although it may be rather dangerous to exaggerate in a play that achieves its comic triumph by a deliberate refusal to accept the clear meaning of a forfeiture clause in a bond.[12]

His follow-up offer of ten times the principal on pain of losing hands, head, and heart has a more serious look to it because he suspects Portia is good for 30,000 ducats, and now that he has won her golden fleece, her wealth is his to dispose of. He is thus certain he will not forfeit and so can make the offer to dismember himself if he fails to pay the promised sum. Portia herself earlier offered "double six thousand, and then treble that" when at Belmont they got the news of Antonio's difficulties (3.2.298–299). She too sounds as if she is exaggerating for effect, but the effectiveness of the exaggeration seems to depend on her being good for 36,000 ducats. Bassanio has pretty good information as to her net worth, it being what caught his attention in the first place, and thus to offer up his body in default of 30,000 ducats offers no serious risk to his body at all.

Have Mercy

As discussed earlier, Shylock's property right in a pound of Antonio's flesh is a powerful bargaining tool. He does not have to part with the right except on his terms. And he is offered now double, triple, and possibly ten times (depending on how seriously we are meant to take Bassanio's offer) the amount of the principal sum to waive his right to flesh. Still not high enough. His "lodg'd hate" for Antonio drives up the price of Antonio's flesh so that it can no longer be measured in ducats, or at least in the astronomical amount of ducats that would have to be raised to buy off his hate. Shylock says it is a whim, a "humour" of his, to order his values so, but it is his right to do so and he makes the argument about what are now known as property rules exceedingly well in the process (4.1.40ff.). Antonio's flesh is the only specie that can satisfy the debt, a debt Antonio owes in Shylock's mind, not for the 3,000 ducats he advanced to fund Bassanio's heiress-hunt but for the debt Antonio raised by treating Shylock like a dog.

Shylock is not speaking figuratively when he enumerates Antonio's ways of treating him. Antonio berates him in public spaces while Shylock is doing business; he calls him a "misbeliever, cut-throat dog," spits on his "Jewish gabardine," and kicks him (1.3.101–124). Shylock is not exaggerating. Antonio proudly confirms the litany of abuse and promises more of it, even as he asks for a loan:

> I am as like to call thee so again,
> To spet on thee again, to spurn [kick] thee too.

You cannot expect a Jew to like it, even if Shylock confesses to have "borne it with a patient shrug, (For suff'rance is the badge of all our tribe)." Shylock has been a good Christian all along, turning the other cheek in the face of kicks and slaps just as Jesus counseled, and still the spitting and kicking continues.

It seems we are again locked in a bizarre exchange system. If revenge breeds revenge in return, like breeding like, what does sufferance breed? Not mildness on the other side, but more berating and beating. This is utterly consistent with a motif that runs through the play of like not producing like. Money is not allowed to produce its like; that is what usury is.[13] And it seems that more than a few humans in this play behave as good Christian money should, by not producing like. Thus parents and offspring cannot recognize each other, for like cannot produce like. Old dim-sighted Gobbo, Launcelot's father, does not recognize him; just as Isaac in Shylock's account cannot recognize which of his sons he is blessing. Jessica refuses to recognize Shylock as her father by abandoning family and faith.[14] And although Shylock's mother is "unhallowed," Christians suspect that her son was in some magical way not her legitimate offspring.[15] So why should mildness produce mildness? That would be usury, like so much money producing money. There is no trusting offspring nor the offspring of one's actions, unless the action is revenge.

Antonio promises to repay Shylock's loan upon Shylock's body with spit, phlegm, and kicks even before Shylock has agreed to lend and well before Shylock has decided to waive interest in lieu of a fleshly forfeiture. It is as if Antonio, by not-so-oblique suggestion, put the idea in Shylock's head to offer the terms he offers. If Antonio will not borrow or lend at usance, and if by Antonio's view barren money should not generate money, well then Shylock will use one of the standard accepted ploys to evade the usury prohibitions, one that Antonio seems willing to countenance. Antonio is not, I think, being ironic, when he sees "much kindness in the Jew" (1.3.149) for stipulating "no doit of usance" and substituting instead the forfeiture clause of "an equal pound" of Antonio's fair flesh.[16]

Shylock decides to transact in precisely the specie suggested by Antonio: the natural body and its substances. How poetically just to make the security for the loan a pound of Antonio's meat, when it was with the excreta and secreta of that body that Antonio promised to repay Shylock anyway. To the Jewish idea of talionic justice of paying for eyes and teeth with eyes and teeth, add the Christian idea of Incarnation, of transforming spirit and abstraction into flesh so that it can be sacrificed and paid over to satisfy an angry Creditor. The combination produces a world in which bodies, as we saw in previous chapters, are money, the medium of paying back, of paying over, and thus the medium of justice and revenge. I am not imposing my hobbyhorse on the play: the idea of equivalences among people, sheep, and money runs deep in the play's diction and melodies. Thus the repeated pun of "Iuwes," Shakespeare's spelling for Jews, "ewes," and "use" (the word for interest).[17]

Shylock wants his pound of flesh because he hates Antonio, but his hate seems to rise to the fore less because hatred consumes his character than because, except for the news of Antonio's ships being lost, nothing has gone right for Shylock of late. He is caught in a fury of frustration. His daughter, whom he loves, has run off, stealing a good portion of his money, which he also loves, and taking the ring his wife gave him and trading it for a monkey, a ring he would not have parted with "for a wilderness of monkeys" (3.1.122). One senses he loved his wife, Leah, more than anything, a kinder Jacob than Jacob, surely a better husband than Bassanio or Graziano is likely to be, and no less a protective father of his daughter than Portia's was of her, though less given to whimsy.

Piously, we are to believe that the play reveals the triumph of mercy over justice, though justice hardly gets a fair shake in the play, and mercy, well, spare me such mercy. Shylock is made to be a parody of Lady Justice: he stands in court, scales in hand, with his knife ready, subbing for the sword. He is even figuratively blind to the requests that he relinquish his claim for mercy's sake.[18] The knife-wielding Jew, though, is more than a parody of Lady Justice; he is the Christian nightmare image of the circumciser; he is The Flesh Exciser incarnate, so to speak. Christians never were quite sure what Jews actually did to their eight-day-old boys. They fantasized the whole kit and caboodle got snipped: not just the prepuce but the "sealed bag," their "jewels, two stones, two rich and precious stones" (2.8.18, 20).[19] Antonio, resigned to death in the trial scene, calls himself a "tainted wether," a wether being a gelded sheep; he comes very close to making himself a ewe of sorts, or indeed a Iuwe/Jew and what we know him to be too: a moneylender.[20] Antonio sees himself as a deformed sacrificial lamb. Circumcision, prefiguring Christ's sacrifice, is on his mind.

It has been pointed out, quite correctly, that Shylock is being nastily witty in choosing to take the flesh from "nearest his heart," for the heart is where St. Paul says a Christian is to be circumcised. Under the old law circumcision meant cutting real flesh (flesh is an early-modern English euphemism for penis, as "meat" is still today),[21] but Paul figuralized circumcision, spiritualized it, made it, under the new law, circumcision of the heart (Rom. 2.29). Shylock is about to circumcise Antonio precisely where Antonio's faith says a Christian should be circumcised. Shylock's literalism is cleverer than the ham-fisted literalism Portia will use to deprive him of his rights, even if Shylock is embarked on a cruel joke. Not to be ignored either is that the Jew with a knife is the image of covenant, of a bond, of the very idea of contractual undertaking, of the fact that in sacred times the first contract required the severance of body parts as confirming and securing the obligations incurred between God and his covenantees. Remember the Hebrew for making a covenant: "cut a covenant."[22]

Shylock simply asks for the rights in his bond, which, as the givens of the play demand, is deemed by all to be enforceable. He is not engaging in any lawyerly tricks; he does not overinterpret or require counterintuitive readings of his bond. Everyone knows exactly what it means; the whole drama of the play requires that its meaning be punch-in-the-face clear. It is rather Portia who will make the law out to be an ass, confirming every layman's view that lawyers can generate any outcome they want by nitpicking and making counterintuitive interpretive moves; law as putty. Christianity connives with a nearly timeless antilawyerly sentiment to make the Law an object of ridicule, as well as of fear and loathing. The Law, in parts of Paul and in one important strand of the Christian exegetical tradition, becomes a tainted word, a somewhat politer way of referring to the Jewish dispensation, the benighted world before Jesus came to fulfill, perfect, and transcend it.[23]

I want to take up certain matters we discussed in the first pages: of evenness, exactitude, and the symbolism of the balance-beam scale. Scales are of varying accuracy. Those good for measuring trucks at interstate weigh stations are not very good at weighing medicines or gold dust. At some point even the most refined of scales bumps up against the effective limits of its precision. Exactitude is exactitude for a purpose, within limits of tolerance; it is about getting close enough given the purpose at hand. Perfect exactitude is something of a fantasy. And in matters of justice it is a good thing that there be play in the joints of the system, just as we want some in bridge spans and skyscrapers lest they snap in the breeze.

All systems of justice have to do with "satisficing,"[24] with making do, at some point, in the presentation and collection of evidence, in the length and relevance of matters in pleading, and finally in the decision-making and remedial processes themselves – that is, in finally deciding how to measure the damages and what constitutes, even in strictly enforced rules, a violation. Is the speed limit broken by going ten miles over, five miles over, one mile over, one inch per hour over; and if the last, are we sure we have a radar gun accurate enough to hold someone to blame when a speedometer is likely to vary in accuracy by 2 percent, depending on how hot the tires are and how much they are over- or underinflated? Even a bright-line rule needs some give. Yes, the sales tax is exact. But do we round up or down when it comes to less than a cent, and is a swap a sale, and is sugarless gum strictly a food so that the exemption on food covers it?

Some things have to be too small for the law to care about if it is not going to get bogged down with trivial harms. A rough rule, captured by the maxim *de minimis non curat lex* (the law does not regard little things), is necessary to provide the needed wiggle room in the normal administration of the law so that the law does not become an object of contempt. Too much should not, as a routine matter, turn on so little. Now enter Portia, who determines the outcome of Shylock's case by abrogating the *de minimis* rule as a practical matter by setting its boundary at such a ridiculously small amount – one grain, or one hair's breadth.

Yet, as we have seen, the bold biblical statement of the talion makes a powerful claim for evenness and equivalence and states it in a way that makes equivalence masquerade as identity. But we all know, and that includes the authors of the Covenant Code in Exodus, that my eye is not your eye. They are equivalent to each other for purposes of the talion, even though yours is brown and mine blue or yours is 20/20 and mine 20/60. No, you cannot pass me your blind one for my sighted one; there are, as Robert Frost perfectly said, "roughly zones." Make the law require exactitude to the significance of the weight of a grain or the deflection of a hair in normal day-to-day transactions in a butcher shop or a grocery store, and the law must be ignored or business will cease. The law must defer to practicalities as a general matter (there is room for some symbolic exceptions), or there is an end to law except as a philosopher's game.

Consider in this light the ironies in Portia insisting on exactitude as a way of undoing the practical possibility of justice. She will have no play in the joints, or so little as not to allow the necessary flexibility for the system to work effectively. With no small sadistic delight, she demands of Shylock that he cut no more and no less than the pound weight in the other pan. Exactitude and evenness are all:

> nor cut thou less nor more
> But just a pound of flesh: if thou tak'st more
> Or less than a just pound, be it but so much
> As makes it light or heavy in the substance,
> Or the division of the twentieth part
> Of one poor scruple, nay, if the scale do turn
> But in the estimation of a hair,
> Thou diest, and all thy goods are confiscate.
> (4.1.321–328)

Portia plays with the word *just*, so that "just a pound," which should mean no more than a pound, is interpreted to mean no more and no less than, so that "just a pound" becomes "a just pound," meaning an exact pound. Portia is using justice's requirement of evenness but is demanding an exactitude that effectively denies Shylock his remedy. The twentieth part of a scruple comes to one grain of barley. And even if Shylock is unsure that his scale is sensitive enough to pick up the weight of a grain, he also knows she has set the standard of precision at a point that is meant to be unachievable. Recall how the Twelve Tables of Rome specifically decreed it a matter of indifference whether the creditors cut off a little more or a little less of the debtor than stipulated: *si plus minusve secuerunt, ne fraude esto,* "If they cut more or less it shall not be deemed a wrong."[25] Shylock knows the jig is up, especially when Portia insists on *no less* as well as no more than a pound. He is thus denied the power to grant the small mercy of not taking as much as he is entitled to, of leaving something for the gleaners of the field.

Nowhere does Portia ever reject the idea of talionic equivalence. She insists on it to a T. Her brand of mercy to Antonio is funded by a perfect requiting and plundering of Shylock; her mercy is but revenge in sheep's clothing, and she cannot disguise her delight in exacting from Shylock everything she could exact: property, faith, dignity, and manhood. Maybe she or the Elizabethan audience is possessed by that culpable complacency that lets them believe that to force a Jew's conversion and then make him pay half or more of his wealth for the privilege is in fact to do him a favor, that becoming a Christian is worth it. Some critics have sought to excuse the happy denizens of Belmont in this way.[26] The conscious experience of the Belmontians' own Schadenfreude in Shylock's utter defeat must give the lie to any self-serving belief that they have conferred a kindness on Shylock. Surely the ever-opportunistic Portia cannot be so easily seduced by her self-interested mobilization of the discourse of mercy, law, and love. Ask Shylock how content he truly is with such mercy. He is offered the classic bargain he cannot refuse and then must register gratitude for the offer.

We now, with the scales fallen from our eyes, can see what is wrong with mercy: it plays favorites. Mercy here comes at Shylock's expense. And even were it to function in good faith, if mercy has to play more than a rare role it is not a good sign for the state of the law or of the polity.

The Humanizing Force of Vengefulness

In this play the Law must be mocked and manipulated by giving the Jew more law than he can bear, and thus to undo the Old Law with law to the greater glory of mercy. Law is made to look worse than it is, so that mercy can look better than it is. Shylock represents the Old Law, and the Old Law is made synonymous with merciless revenge on the one hand, and with an obsessive concern with ritual rather than spirit, form for form's sake, on the other: an eye for an eye rather than mercy, and circumcision of the foreskin rather than of the heart. It was all revenge and body parts. In the Christian view, the Old Law is opposed to mercy and as such it offered no hope for sinful man's redemption, whose offenses to God were so great that he could never make adequate recompense unless God was willing to be merciful. Only via mercy could man receive the gift of salvation; the Law could give him no legal claim to such a gift. Says Portia:

> therefore Jew,
> Though justice be thy plea, consider this,
> That in the course of justice, none of us
> Should see salvation: we do pray for mercy...
> (4.1.193–195)

Mercy, though, did not come for free in the Christian tradition. It was funded by Christ's sacrifice. The Old Law still set the rules of the game, and by its demands for repayment the treasury of mercy was funded. One can see in Shylock's funding of the mercifully good times at Belmont a blasphemous parody of how the Jewish flesh of Jesus, the humiliation of the Jew Jesus, funds the entire Christian mercy system, good times for the elect. In theology as well as in the hurly-burly of getting and spending there is no such thing as a free lunch.

But before the arguments on behalf of mercy are made by the Duke and Portia, Shylock has already stated a very strong case for good old revenge. The speech is famous, and it has been understood since the early nineteenth century to be a powerful argument for humanizing Shylock, who until then had been taken to be a one-dimensional Vice, a caricature, something distinctly less than human:

Salerio: Why I am sure if he forfeit, thou wilt not take his flesh, – what's that good for?
Shylock: To bait fish withal, – if it will feed nothing else, it will feed my revenge; he hath disgrac'd me, and hind'red me half a million,

laugh'd at my losses, mock'ed my gains, scorned my nation, thwarted my bargains, cooled my friends, heated mine enemies, – and what's his reason? I am a Jew. Hath not a Jew eyes? hath not a Jew hands, organs, dimensions, senses, affections, passions? fed with the same food, hurt with the same weapons, subject to the same diseases, healed by the same means, warmed and cooled by the same winter and summer as a Christian is? – if you prick us do we not bleed? if you tickle us do we not laugh? if you poison us do we not die? and if you wrong us shall we not revenge? – if we are like you in the rest, we will resemble you in that. If a Jew wrong a Christian, what is his humility? revenge! If a Christian wrong a Jew, what should his sufferance be by Christian example? – why revenge! The villainy you teach me I will execute, and it shall go hard but I will better the instruction.

(3.1.45–66)

Poor Salerio can make no answer, nor does it seem to me that Portia is able to make much of one either. Says Hazlitt of Shylock; "In all his answers and retorts upon his adversaries, he has the best not only of the argument but of the question, reasoning on their own principles and practice"; and of Portia Hazlitt says, "The speech about Mercy is very well; but there are a thousand finer ones in Shakespeare."[27] Nervous academics, unhistorically historicizing, imposing their nonviolent wishes on a nonpacifist Christianity, seek desperately to claim that Shakespeare's Christian audience would not hear Shylock's speech as a brief for welcome-one-and-all humanism. They, so the view goes, would see his argument as showing how deeply benighted and damned his vision was. He cannot conceive of soul and spirit as the basis of community; in his view only the body and its vulnerability and a visceral urge for justice bind us together as fellow humans.[28]

But who except a Divine or two, the late sixteenth-century version of the pious literary critic, would thus respond to the substance of Shylock's claim? The average Elizabethan groundling, as well as the aristocrat in a better seat, was hardly a pacifist, or nonvengeful. He just loathed Jews. That audience would have a perfect answer to the power of Shylock's speech, and it would not go to its substance. As Odysseus answered Thersites' insightful observations about the costs and benefits of the war against Troy with mockery and a beating, so too it is enough to know that a Jew made any argument, no matter how compelling, to discount it. Thersites and the Jew lose because their words don't count. It is the old riposte ad hominem, a very effective way of disposing of good but vexing ideas that may be employed usefully by people you refuse to countenance. Answer the embarrassing observation by beating the living daylights out of the guy who made it if you cannot quite ignore his point.

Shylock's is a virtuoso performance. He shows that Antonio is more than a garden-variety Jew-hater; Jew-hating pretty much fills up his workweek. Antonio harasses Shylock endlessly, goes out of his way to do it, and with seamless self-satisfaction feels himself virtuous when he does so. Never mind that Shylock is a business competitor of sorts. Once he drives Shylock out of business, one wonders whether it will be as tempting for Antonio to lend gratis. Against Antonio's harassment, his constant mocking, his spit, kicks, and phlegm, his sneers and jeers, the pound of flesh seems a rather modest payback. And as Shylock notes, Christians will understand his motives full well, for he has been their student in these matters. Now it is his turn to play the teacher: "The villainy you teach me I will execute, and it shall go hard but I will better the instruction."

Metaphors of pedagogy come to add a nuance to the diction of debt and obligation. As we saw in chapter 5 using the talion to "teach a lesson" veneers with the diction of revenge a deeper pedagogical motive, as in the deuteronomic account of the talion, where deterrence, not revenge, is the chief goal. Not here, though: teaching a lesson means getting even in style, for how can you blame my vengefulness when I learned it as the object of your revenges? Shylock has no trouble combining metaphors of paying back with interest and teaching a lesson: "I will *better* the instruction."

Teaching lessons necessarily involves impressing upon the one who has wronged you – or on someone who has laughed at you because someone has wronged you – fellow-feeling for pain and humiliation. We are back to our prior discussion of the link between the talion and the generation of sympathetic imagination. Metaphors of teaching a lesson work quite well in payback settings in which the rules of engagement require one to pay back the actual wrongdoer. The metaphor loses some, but not all, of its force when the rules of feud allow you, say, to hit a nephew for the sins of his uncle. In such a setting you can still be understood to be instructing the other *side* on the inadvisability of harming such as the likes of you, but the idiom of "teaching a lesson" is not quite as telling as when the person who is the object of revenge has never directly harmed you. Perhaps the actual harmer may get the point of the lesson when he sees his nephew dead for simply having been his nephew. But it also may be that the uncle's grief for his nephew is not quite so great as his relief at having escaped the avenger, and you, the avenger, might suspect he is more relieved than grieved, whether he is or is not.[29]

There is no denying the moral and rhetorical power of the claim for the brute physical identity of Christian and Jew. One wonders how such an obviously true statement can have the force of surprise, even for a Jew. One does not get chills or feel triumphant if an orator tells you the grass is green or the sky is blue. I can see how a Christian might experience a sense of reprimand at how he has managed to both know that the statement of the physical identity of Christians and Jews is true and yet repress that knowledge so as to act as if it were false. (After all, no Christian man in the play has any trouble seeing beautiful Jewesses as fully human females.) But why does a Jew feel the force of the speech no differently than I am imagining a hypothetical Christian does? Self-hatred? Or is the Jew simply rallying to an exhortatory aspect of the message to remember a truth he has had beaten out of him? Maybe it is nothing more than the delight of seeing the discomfiture the argument is causing Shylock's Christian interlocutor? If that's the case the Jew's joy is a brief one. It is a losing argument, for the same reasons Thersites' was.

Sad, but it does sometimes come as news to Jew and Christian alike that a Jew has hands, organs, senses, a partible body, just like a Christian; that he is nourished in the same way, vulnerable to pain, disease, and death in the same way, and that he too laughs when tickled. Shylock cannot disguise the bitterness in the realization. Look at his example for laughter. It is not the laughter of joy or mirth or even Hobbes's laughter of sudden glory at the expense of another; it is the purely reflexive involuntary laughter in response to the overstimulating torment of tickling. Laughter as mere physical reflex is shared by Christian and Jew; he avoids claiming they share the same sense of humor.

To break the litany of bodily needs[30] and vulnerabilities with the sudden "and if you wrong us shall we not revenge?" is a rhetorical triumph. We must assent, even against our better desires, should we have such desires, or against our conscience, should our conscience instruct us to forgo revenge. The Jew assents because he cheers Shylock on; the Christian assents because he has assent forced upon him by the facts. Christians are expert avengers, especially when it is a Jew who wrongs them. Says Montaigne, "Christians excel at hating enemies. Our zeal works wonders when it strengthens our tendency towards hatred, enmity, ambition, avarice, evil-speaking."[31] But a Christian, unlike the vengeful Jew, is either a hypocrite when he takes revenge or a hypocrite when he insists that Shylock has to justify his desire to take it. It is because of the Christian brief against revenge that Shylock even is put to a justification beyond claiming his warrant in the Christian view of the Jewish Old Law. It is not the Jew who is to turn the other cheek; a Jew is true to his nature – as Christians define his nature, that is – when he is vengeful.[32] That is why one must force Shylock's conversion; now that he is a Christian his nature will be "content" with the mercy visited upon him.

The Merchant of Venice puts obligation-creation, debt-repayment, and satisfaction – and the ways the body figures in securing and satisfying obligations – at the center of the plot. Taking on an obligation, promising, is risky business for creditor and debtor, ower and owed. The creditor's concern is that the debtor remember his undertaking. A forgetful debtor is not a good thing, and debtors are inclined to be forgetful. Getting the debtor's body involved, putting it at risk, is one way of creating a good memory. There are other ways, but it is the relation of memory, obligation-fulfillment, and revenge that takes us next to the world of *Hamlet* and beyond.

88

SEVEN

Remember Me: Mnemonics, Debts (of Blood), and the Making of the Person

IT WAS LIVING BODIES that were at risk in chapter 6. Antonio offered a pound of his flesh as security lest he forget or lest he be unable to repay the debt in coin on time. People are forgetful. We hardly care that we may be forgetful of things that do not matter, though we may fear the onset of senility when we cannot recall the host of little things that used to plague us when we could not forget them. We do care, however, that some people are forgetful of things in which the forgetting works in their interest, as when my kids refuse to remember, no matter how many times I have yelled and screamed, to clean up their rooms, or whatever paltry chores it is their responsibility to discharge. Debtors are inclined to forget. And should they be lucky enough to have a creditor whose memory is not as self-interestedly selective as theirs, well, then they are home free.

Burning in the Memory

How do we develop the capacity to remember in spite of our interest in forgetting, in spite of desires to live in a very shallow present such as the one lived in Belmont? Creditors, it seems, if not debtors, have an interest in their debtors' capacity for memory. They may even develop ways of creating memory in their debtors, arriving at all kinds of ingenious mnemonics, such as making them put something at risk they cannot forget: such as their hands, their testicles, their son or daughter, their pain receptors.

As is often the case, Nietzsche got to the heart of the matter, a bit overstated, as is his wont. "How," he asks,

can one create a memory for the human animal? How can one impress something upon this partly obtuse, partly flighty mind, attuned only to the passing moment, in such a way that it will stay there?

One can well believe that the answers and methods for solving this primeval problem were not precisely gentle; perhaps indeed there was nothing more fearful and uncanny in the whole prehistory of man than his *mnemotechnics*. "If something is to stay in the memory it must be burned in: only that which never ceases to *hurt* stays in the memory" – this is a main clause of the oldest (unhappily also the most enduring) psychology on earth... Man could never do without blood, torture, and sacrifices when he felt the need to create a memory for himself; the most dreadful sacrifices and pledges (sacrifices of the first-born among them), the most repulsive mutilations (castration, for example), the cruelest rites of all the religious cults (and all religions are at the deepest level systems of cruelties) – all this has its origin in the instinct that realized that pain is the most powerful aid to mnemonics.[1]

Debt, obligation, memory creation, and body parts seem to keep coming together. The idea runs deep in the Jewish confession of faith in Deuteronomy in which memory is kept alive specifically by alleging as the grounds of original group memory the experience of slavery, the bound body: "When your son asks you in time to come, 'What is the meaning of the testimonies and the statutes and the ordinances which the Lord our God has commanded you?' then you shall say to your son, 'We were Pharaoh's slaves in Egypt...'" (Deut. 6.20–21).

But Nietzsche also knows that it is in the debtor's interest to cultivate memory too if he wishes to be trusted and lent to again. He must be able to show to others that he is "calculable," predictable. He must be able to make promises and commitments. And so at the end of the very painful process of beating a memory into mankind at the cost of pounds and pounds of flesh, whippings, and debt slavery is created "the *sovereign individual*."

The proud awareness of the extraordinary privilege of *responsibility*, the consciousness of this rare freedom, this power over oneself and over fate, has in his case penetrated to the profoundest depths and become instinct, the dominating instinct. What will he call this dominating instinct, supposing he feels the need to give it a name? The answer is beyond doubt: the sovereign man calls it his *conscience*.[2]

Nietzsche sees conscience as the internalization of the creditor's interest, not the Freudian father's, and the creditor's interest is what gives psychological depth to the individual by giving the flighty Bassanio-like debtor, forever consumed by present pleasure, a way of recalling the past so as to make himself predictable and responsible in the future. We thus acquire a social, legal, and moral future by having a legal past beaten into us. Conscience compels us to pay back what we owe, thereby putting paying back, and thus revenge itself, at the core of the fullest sense of personhood. You will say that this is so much phony exaggerated intellectual drama, the stuff that keeps academics rightly dismissed as fools by the multitudes. But the tale runs deep and it has a truth that I mean to get at, for it is intimately tied up with the themes of this book.

This chapter's crooked tale will tread a strange path. But the notion of debt – specifically debts of blood, obligation, and hence memory creation, and thus too revenge and the partible body – is crucial to our sense of personhood. We will begin with the (after)life of a corpse who met his end by foul play, and unfold the tale of old Hamlet's ghost and his quest to be made whole again in death.

Bloody Tokens and the Relics of the Unavenged Dead

The first thing I ever wrote on the Icelandic sagas more than twenty years ago discussed in excruciating detail a bizarre ritual in which a corpse or parts of a corpse, its head, its blood, sometimes its bloody clothing, were employed to charge a person to avenge it.[3] In one case a wife digs up her recently murdered husband, cuts off his head, hides it under her cloak, and goes to ask her uncle whether he will avenge the dead man. Her uncle declines, reminding her that there are people more obliged than he is to take revenge. She then whips out the head from beneath her cloak and says that the person whose head it was would have avenged him if their positions were reversed. Her uncle, a bit nonplussed to say the least, accedes to her desires.[4]

In another case a woman, again trying to get her reluctant uncle to avenge her murdered husband, dumps the victim's clotted blood all over him as he sits at dinner.[5] She too gets what she wants from her uncle. Variations of the ritual are easy to find in many cultures in which bloody tokens or parts of the corpse are used to mobilize and formally oblige revenge; we are treated to them more often than we wish in news footage from the Middle East. An especially gruesome one from the Bible has a Levite cut up the corpse of his concubine into twelve parts after the men of Benjamin have raped her to death. He sends the parts to all Israel to summon the other tribes to ravage the Benjamites (Judg. 19–20).[6]

Such practices thrived in the medieval setting and were intimately tied up with the worship of relics. Potent remains of saints' bodies and blood kept the saints alive in this world – though dead in the usual sense – doing miracles and also, as those who have suffered the reading of hundreds of saints' lives know, taking revenge (taking revenge and healing are what saints mostly do).[7] The theme of the bloody token or avenging relic is also a staple of Elizabethan and Jacobean tragedy. Heironimo, the avenger in Kyd's *Spanish Tragedy* (2.5.51ff), smears his handkerchief with his son's blood not only to serve as a constant reminder but also to bind him to revenge in a continual reenactment of the bloody-token ritual. Given that such practices are attested widely and are not just the stuff of literary imagination, the grisly horror that characterizes so much Jacobean revenge tragedy looks a little less contrived.[8]

These rituals require that the living mobilize the corpse in its own cause. It is a wife or a mother who preserves the head, props up the body, gathers up the blood and bloody clothing. What happens, though, if the surviving kin of the corpse do not know that the corpse died unnaturally or are otherwise disabled from taking revenge for the corpse, such as, say, when the brother and proper avenger of the corpse is the murderer? That is in fact the situation in the first, by the Bible's reckoning, recorded case of the bloody-token ritual: "And the Lord said unto Cain, Where is Abel thy brother? And he said, I know not: Am I my brother's keeper? And he said, What hast thou done? The *voice of thy brother's blood crieth* unto me from the ground" (Gen. 4.9–10).

Abel's blood must take matters into its own hands (we are surely justified in providing Abel's blood with hands when the Bible provides it with a voice); the blood must call out and oblige another avenger on Abel's behalf because Abel left no surviving spouse, and neither are Adam and Eve in a very good position to act as his avenger, for they are equally obligated to the murderer. One problem among several for Adam is that if he avenges Abel on Cain he leaves himself heirless, which is what happens anyway when God sends Cain away. And thus it is all the more urgent that God provide a substitute for Abel. That is what Seth explicitly is; his name means substitute, replacement, or "appoint instead." "And Adam knew his wife again; and she bare a son, and called his name Seth: For God, said she, hath appointed me another seed instead of Abel, whom Cain slew" (Gen. 4.25). This is pure talion – a Seth, explicitly denominated a replacement Abel, for an Abel, a life for a life.[9] And we see humans already playing the role of money in the first family, and that the talion can be satisfied by substitution no less than by taking a life. And the nice thing about Seth is that he cost no one to pay him over. He owes his very existence to the moral demand to make Adam and Eve whole again.

And another case of fratricide, equally famous, puts the dead victim in the same setting of having to ensure his own revenge. Thus old Hamlet, assumed to have died naturally in his sleep, must perform the vengeance-charging ritual on his own behalf from the grave. He must undertake the burden of informing the living that there is work to be done and then oblige the living to undertake that work. The .ghost is nonmatter; he can leave no material reminder of his charge, no severed head, no clotted blood, no bloody clothing, but there is no doubt that he is performing as ancient a legal ritual as there is, more ancient in the Bible's chronology than covenantal circumcision, for Abel precedes Abraham. Old Hamlet presents an image of himself and leaves a message in words that, once heard, bind Hamlet to obey:

> *Hamlet*: Speak, I am bound to hear.
> *Ghost*: So art thou to revenge when thou shalt hear.

The ghost minces no words. If his first charge to his son is to avenge him; his second and parting words are to *remember* him, to which Hamlet responds with unfeigned hysteria:

> *Ghost*: Adieu, adieu, adieu. Remember me. *[Exit.]*
> *Hamlet*: O all you host of heaven! O earth! What else?
>   And shall I couple hell? O fie! Hold, hold, my heart,
>   And you, my sinews, grow not instant old,
>   But bear me stiffly up. Remember thee?
>   Ay, thou poor ghost, whiles memory holds a seat
>   In this distracted globe. Remember thee?
>   Yea, from the table of my memory
>   I'll wipe away all trivial fond records,
>   All saws of books, all forms, all pressures past
>   That youth and observation copied there,
>   And thy commandment all alone shall live
>   Within the book and volume of my brain,
>   Unmix'd with baser matter. Yes, by heaven! . . .
>   [Writes.]
>   . . . Now to my word:
>   It is 'Adieu, adieu, remember me.'
>   I have sworn't.
>   (1.5.91–104, 110–112)

Hamlet's panicky response focuses not directly on the explicit charge to revenge but rather on the final charge to remember, for the latter subsumes the former. Thus his "I have sworn't" applies most immediately to remembering, and that is why, somewhat obsessively, he commits the words "Adieu, adieu, remember me" to writing. Hamlet is bound to revenge by hearing the grounds that justify it. But the ghost knows that the obligation is not self-enforcing. One can be obliged to do something and forget to do it, can welsh on the debt. Hamlet must remember the obligation, and this remembering, as we shall see, comes to take on a special meaning and does special work.

94

Remembering is thus a form of plighting, a plighting of one's troth. One critic, Howard Eiland, has noted how intimately the notion of plighting is bound up with idea of "to play" and plays are things in *Hamlet*, as we all know, that are meant to catch consciences, just as a plighting is. Says Eiland: "When Hamlet determines 'frankly [to] play' (5.2.232) he is simultaneously *pledging* and *plighting* himself. 'Play' comes from a West Germanic verb, *plegan*, meaning not only to exercise, but to plead for, stake, risk. It is the source also of the verbs 'pledge' and 'plight,' the latter developing from Old English *pliht*, danger, peril... Play, as Hamlet understands it, is not to be opposed to work or seriousness: that it is in fact a form of dangerous committal and that the player is essentially, not passive, but *at stake*." [10]

Take note how deeply the idea of putting things in danger, placing them in a plight, is tied up with keeping one's word, with remembering. We make hostages of whole humans and, as I noted earlier, even of corpses and parts of corpses; Antonio makes a hostage of a part of himself, and most all of us of our troth, along with our homes, to give our creditors and spouses some power to make our memory prompt us to perform as promised. [11]

Remembering the Dead and Not Forgetting Oneself

Consider how deeply remembering informs our understanding of obligation and how deeply obligation informs our understanding of remembering by looking at their contraries: forgiving and forgetting. Although they are analytically distinct, we tend to lump forgiveness and forgetfulness together – forgive and forget. And for good reason. Remembering works against the grain of forgiveness. The Old Testament God does not forget when he forgives; he remembers at least for three or four generations (Ex. 34.6–7; Num. 14.18). Memory provokes; it makes demands to discharge obligations not merely that it preserves but in some serious sense that it actually creates, for memory is assimilable in function, and maybe in form, to conscience itself.

One of the main points that lies near the surface of the sagas and glaringly at the core of *Hamlet*, and even, I bet, in your own experience, is that many of those bound to avenge would prefer to avoid the obligation. Vengeance is scary business for more than the target of it: those targets are armed and prepared to resist, and it is often the case that they have already proven *their* ability to kill, something a first-time avenger has yet to prove. A person obliged to take revenge must resist all kinds of temptations to forgive and forget. His cowardice, his reason mobilize arguments of the sort that forgiveness is a virtue, or that revenge is best left to God or the gods, or that it is an irrational obsession with sunk costs. Excuses. Excuses. As I have argued elsewhere, conventional wisdom conceives of vengeance cultures as barely cultured at all, as all id and no superego: big dumb hot-tempered brutes looking for excuses to kill. But we are no less naturally *homo pullus* than *homo lupus*, as much man the chicken as man the wolf. Prudence may be more natural than foolhardiness, or no less natural. There is good reason to believe that it takes much more socialization labor to produce bloodfeuders than accountants.[12]

But let us not mock accountants. They are after all professional rememberers. What are account books, but mnemonic devices? One hardly needs to be reminded how deeply interrelated are the ideas of remembering and accounting. When Hamlet commits his "Adieu, adieu, remember me" to writing he is playing the accountant, making an entry in an account book, noting debts owing. Then too accounts are stories, primal stories, of what it takes to get even; accounts are also justifying stories, of giving an account of the justness of one's action, of, that is, accounting for our deeds when we claim we are just getting even. What heroic stock our accountants come from.[13]

But I digress. The core belief at the heart of most revenge cultures is that man is more naturally a chicken than a wolf. Thus revenge cultures are invariably shame cultures and have to devote enormous cultural machinery to getting people to remember past wrongs. They develop elaborate means of goading, shaming, and humiliating to recall people to their dangerous duty they would as soon forget. If you are reluctant to avenge, others will treat you much as Hamlet treats himself in his "Oh what a rogue and peasant slave am I" soliloquy. People, especially the women in these cultures, would not let you forget, though sometimes they might let you forgive when prudence not only was sensible policy but could be made to look like an honorable one too. One wonders whenever it was, contra Nietzsche's account, that people were allowed to live hedonically in the present, with uncultivated memories. Nietzsche's description of early man before memory was pounded into him is more apt as a description of twenty-first-century man on whom little makes much of a memorable impression, he being bombarded with too many faux images marketed in bulk as "unforgettable."

Yet remembering, even still, is a richly obligational notion, which is perhaps why we opt for forgetfulness; remembering is intimately involved with paying, paying back, with reward and punishment. We thus remember people in our wills, or remember someone with a tip, though tellingly "remember" in such settings now sounds a little old-fashioned if not quite obsolete. But for Hamlet there was no doubt that to remember meant to be mindful of duty, to be mindful of one's proper role; remembering involved reminding oneself or recalling oneself to one's proper place.

Then too, as we touched on briefly earlier, Jesus combines themes of remembrance with ideas of the body's partibility in a ceremony of obligation-creation. Behind the words of Luke's account one can almost hear the ghost of old Hamlet. Like the ghost and like Abel, Jesus presents his own body to his "avengers" in a performance of the bloody-token ritual: "And he took bread, and gave thanks, and brake it, and gave unto them, saying, this is my body which is given for you: this do in remembrance of me" (Luke 22.19).[14] The body and blood bind its recipients, oblige them to remember, and what are they to remember? Jesus has just announced that one of them will betray him and that he is about to be killed. Maybe "avengers" can do without its scare quotes. (And in case the disciples miss the message, he comes back and displays his wounds after he is dead.) Evidence that the faithful were to be God's avengers is not hard to find. A law of King Æthelred (the Unready) dating from 1014 thus makes it an affirmative duty of a Christian to "*avenge* offenses against God most zealously."[15]

To remember, in the sense of to be recalled to one's proper role, means above all not to forget oneself: "Comfort, my liege; remember

97

who you are. *K. Richard*. I had forgot myself: am I not king?" (3.2.82–
83). To fail to remember oneself, to forget oneself, is to fail in one's duty
or one's dignity. It is a signature trope of characters in the Jacobean
drama to remind themselves of who they are amidst the general collapse
of their worlds by invoking their own names to shore up the fragments
of their being, claiming still to be the very person they feel is being
annihilated by hostile forces: "I am the Duchess of Malfi still," "I
am Anthony yet," and thus the chilling force of the failed attempt at
the same trope: "Who is it that can tell me who I am? *Fool*: Lear's
shadow."[16]

Take these relatively innocuous lines:

Horatio: Hail to your lordship.
Hamlet: I am glad to see you well.
Horatio, or I do forget myself.
(1.2.160–161)

There are more than a few ways to play these lines, but I suspect
Hamlet is a bit distracted, having just completed his first soliloquy,
when Horatio, Marcellus, and Bernardo enter. And he fails to recognize
his friend fully, not in the sense of failing to know who he is but in failing
to give him his proper due. Thus the form of Hamlet's self-reprimand
is to claim that his failure to remember Horatio properly is really a
failure to remember himself – "or I do forget myself." It is an incident
of no special significance, though in Shakespeare such unimportant
moments have a certain uncanniness to them, for very soon Hamlet is
going to be charged to remember not just an obligation to greet a friend
with proper focus and attention, but an obligation to say farewell with
proper focus to a father who has been slighted in death:

So, uncle, there you are. Now to my word:
It is 'Adieu, adieu, remember me.'
I have sworn't.

The ghost's charge to remember does not mean merely to keep in
mind. It means to *carry out* an obligation that must be kept in mind.[17]
To remember his father is to restore his father's being, to put him back
together in honor and spirit, to restore equilibrium by paying back one

very large debt that was incurred in his death. To remember means to revenge.[18] Thus it is that when the ghost reappears in the bedroom scene his first words to Hamlet are, "Do not forget." He comes to whet, to sharpen, he says, Hamlet's blunt purpose, purpose being figured as a sword, an avenging weapon, that has lost its edge. And although we may think that Hamlet has been doing nothing but remembering to the point of neurotic obsession, that is not the sense, evidently, the ghost takes "remember" to have. The only sign of having remembered is a completed revenge, just as remembering you owe a debt that you still fail to repay can properly be understood to be a failure of your memory.

The Happy Dead

Why does the ghost care? Why does Abel's blood care? Why do the dead call for revenge? It is less a matter, I believe, of the guilty and anxious consciences of the living projecting their fears on to the dead, than deeper anxieties about the integrity of personhood and the self. The anxiety is only partly about bloodguilt. It is more about the wholeness of the self, a desperate concern to make whole again that which has been broken or fractured by the dishonor of not having been remembered properly. This self is not quite the same person as the one Nietzsche declares to be the sovereign individual, that creature who is the end product of generations of creditors beating calculability and conscience into the minds and bodies of their debtors, though it shares some of his features.

We can get a feel for the force of this self that the dead care to repair, or the living undertake to fix for them, if we recall the concern those Renaissance characters had not to forget themselves as their world crumbled around them, of their struggle to remember themselves in a way that meant more than maintaining sanity but also evinced their concern to behave in a manner that dignified and conformed to a standard they held and that others held them to too: I am Anthony yet; the Duchess of Malfi still; am I not king; Lear, Lear, Lear.

When can one call a life happy? Must we wait until we die before we can judge whether ours was a happy life? That is what Herodotus has

Solon say: "Until he is dead, keep the word 'happy' in reserve. Till then, he is not happy, but only lucky."[19] "That is why," says Montaigne, "Agesilaus replied to someone who called the King of Persia happy because he had come so young to so great an estate, 'Yes: but Priam was not wretched when he was that age.'"[20] Will we even know whether we can call a life happy at death? For what if your reputation suffers after your death or you leave weak and contemptible offspring and you become known more as being the father or mother of a race of cowards and fools than for any of your virtues when you were living? You end up pitied.

In honor cultures, it matters not only how you die but also that you are avenged if you die in a way that demands revenge be taken. A dead man's honor, and thus his well-being, is not just restored by revenge, it can even be enhanced by it. One Icelandic saga, in its concluding paragraph, offers a certain legal expert's reasons as to why Grettir was the greatest of Iceland's outlaws. Two of the reasons need not concern us, but the third and most important had nothing to do with Grettir's accomplishments when alive: "The third reason was that his death was avenged way out in Byzantium, the only Icelander of whom that could be said."[21] Those who witnessed that killing in Byzantium years earlier had this to say at the time: "This [Grettir] must have been something special given that Thorstein traveled so far from home to avenge him."[22]

When even outlaws are ranked according to their excellence at being outlaws, it should not be surprising that revenges are ranked according to various criteria. Revenge for Grettir was doubly special: (1) because he was the only Icelander ever avenged in Byzantium and (2) because his avenger traveled so far to take it. (In a later chapter I will discuss how deep the compulsion to evaluate, rank, and order is.) Most important, for our immediate purposes, is the social and moral fact that although some of the honor of a successful vengeance taking belongs to the avenger, a good portion of it accrues to the corpse, Grettir. The avenger, Thorstein, does not have his own saga, and he is only a minor character in Grettir's, almost an afterthought.

Now we can see clearly what's in it for the ghost: honor, well-being, evenness, an integrated self, and thus, though the word is poisoned by its touchy-feely associations, closure, but still better captured by the idea at the core of Hebrew *sh-l-m*: to be made whole, to pay back in kind, to be at peace. The wronged corpse cannot do it alone. Without Thorstein, his avenger, Grettir might have finished second to Gisli for best outlaw; but that is the least of it. To be unavenged is to be mis-remembered, not quite forgotten, though in a sense that too. Without Hamlet to settle matters the ghost will remain a debtor, imbalanced and sneered at by his brother the homicide, who beds his wife and wears his crown. The ghost desperately needs Hamlet to remember him properly. He can assist Hamlet by reminding him of his duty, though unlike others in his predicament he cannot provide the grisly power of a bloody token; he must resort to apparition. Once old Hamlet is prop-erly remembered, young Hamlet benefits too. He has done his duty, restored the family honor, and saved himself continued self-reproach or, should his conscience treat him too gently, then the shame of being taunted as a coward by future visits of his father's ghost.

Hamlet defines much of his own self in its relation to remembrance and revenge. It is almost too trite to say that revenge figures centrally in creating personhood, identity, and selfhood for the living in an honor culture. In honor-based societies it is impossible to talk about concepts like the self, the person, even about character, without talking about honor, for ultimately your inner life, your private self, was very much a reflex of your public life and self. Honor was what provided the basis for your counting for something, for your being listened to, for having people have second thoughts before taking your land or raping you or your daughter. It even governed how you spoke, how loudly, how often, and to whom and when, and whether you were attended to when you did; it governed how you held your shoulders, how tall you stood – literally, not figuratively – and how long you could look at someone or even dare to look at him at all. And what was the state of one's honor who found suspect reasons to avoid avenging one's father, one's sister, or direct wrongs to one's self?

Nor need a focus on revenge produce a flatness of character, turning the avenger into a mere Vice in a morality play.[23] Is not Hamlet proof that complexity of character and an ethic of revenge can do rather nicely together? But what we often overlook is that the whole basis for

Hamlet forging his identity and depth of character in this way is an act of homage to the ghost's desperate attempt to have his (the ghost's) own fragile personhood set right in the moral order. This remembering of the ghost manifestly is not about constructing a glorious reputation for old Hamlet, about being remembered in a good light as a figure of consequence. A good and glorious reputation old Hamlet already had and still retained; the ghost evinced no concern on that score.

Grief, Guilt, and Tormenting Ghosts

When we first meet Hamlet he is remembering other things:

> Must I remember? Why, she should hang on him
> As if increase of appetite had grown
> By what it fed on; and yet, within a month –
> Let me not think on't – Frailty, thy name is woman –
> $(1.2.143-146)$

Hamlet's memory is focused on what his mother should be remembering but is not. It is her behavior with his father he remembers, and as memory is wont to do it seems to give him present cause to blame his mother for her failure to mourn properly. Yet if Gertrude mourns not enough, Hamlet's mourning is mistrusted as being excessive. His grief is all "seems," a pose, overblown, stagy, unmanly, in bad taste. Claudius suggests that Hamlet is forgetting himself, in the sense of lacking decorum, of having bad manners. But Claudius has a greater concern beyond Hamlet's bad manners; though a lecher, a drunk, and a fratricide, Claudius is not stupid. He has no wish to recall Hamlet to true grief, for no different from madness, grief in great ones must not go unwatched.

Claudius has reason to worry about Hamlet's grief. There is an intimate connection between grief and memory creation, and thus revenge. It is not infrequent in vengeance cultures to let the women grieve, even hire them for the purpose, but men, men are supposed to repress their grief so that it can metamorphose into anger or into vengeful purpose. An old man in a saga, Kveld-Ulf, who took to bed stricken with grief at the death of one son, was chided by his surviving son "that there were more fitting things to do than to waste time lying in bed, 'it is my advice, that we go take revenge instead.'"[24] Head-hunting cultures or cultures imbued with powerful witchcraft beliefs may transmogrify grief into a desire to kill, to seek a death for a death.[25] Does the cagey Claudius fear that even aimless and stagy grief will provide the basis for more worrisome motives down the road? Grief is like a ghost, charging the male mourner to satisfy his grief by having it move his soul to bloodier sentiments.

Hamlet, we all know, greatly feels the burden of the ghost's charge. Instead of being remembered with a handsome legacy of an office or a summer home in his father's will, he is misremembered, burdened, charged with the obligation to discharge the debt his father cannot repay. In this world turned upside-down by incompleted obligations, by foul murther, it is the living son who must remember in his will – that is, in his capacity for intentional action – his dead father. Living and dead combine in this ceremony of mutual remembrance to impose and undertake obligations of the greatest moral moment.

Could it be that the primal fear that generates the belief that the murdered dead will return to haunt the living is not that he will haunt his killer, but that he will haunt his reluctant avenger? The guilt of the murderer takes a backseat to the guilt and shame of the tardy and fearful avenger. The ghost of old Hamlet does not appear to Claudius. The conscience the ghost seeks to burden is not that of his murderer. The unavenged dead focus their attention on their avengers. Why bother bothering your enemy, even if he used to be your brother? You would have an interest in haunting your enemy only if you have no surviving kin or no kin of sufficient character to avenge you.

In this agonistic world, even in ours, it is not your known enemies who are the greatest danger to your well-being. You expect no good from them; and unless you are very stupid, an enemy cannot betray you. That is what family and friends are in a position to do, for who tend to be your enemies but former friends and family who have betrayed you? It is those you trust, by definition, those who can betray trust, who are in a position to let you down, as Claudius did to his brother, and as the ghost fears his surviving son may do to him by not properly remembering him. There is maybe less risk to your honor in dying violently at the hands of your known enemy than in dying secretly at the hands of your brother; but if you are unlucky enough to have died in either of these ways the greatest risk to your honor is to be survived by weak, lazy, or contemptible kin who will not see that you are properly valued. So hound them from the grave you must.

The Mnemonics of Wergeld and the Fragility of Well-Being

The ghost wants blood. Wergeld is not an option in *Hamlet*. Yet the cultures we have been concerned with provide alternatives to blood. What about being remembered in the form of a transfer of sheep, cows, and the various forms of blood money?

As we have discussed, paying in blood always coexisted with options to pay in other kinds of money. Blood made for better stories and generally, as we have noted, more honor. (The connection between honor and good stories is not accidental but partly constitutive of honor.) Taking more regular forms of money and waiving your right to payment in blood was not dishonorable by any means, unless people felt you were motivated by cowardice or greed rather than by a concern to accede to the wider demands of neighbors and friends to take the more peaceful course. Exacting a large settlement from the killing clan could be read as a public testimony to the fear you, as an avenger, inspired, as well as public estimation of the value of your dead kinsman. There was, in other words, the possibility for genuine honor in a peaceful resolution that traded sheep or silver for blood.

Consider England of the seventh through ninth centuries, when the laws named status rankings by wergeld amounts, so that in some Anglo-Saxon kingdoms there were 200-shilling men, 600-shilling men, and 1200-shilling men.[26] Such cultures had no qualms about measuring human value in money units. The dishonor was not in being priced, as some among us believe, but in being low-priced. But I imagine there were a slew of anxieties that might plague a 1200-shilling man of middling sensibility. Here are just some of the problems. It is one thing to legislate that a man is worth 1200 shillings; it is another to collect that much if your 1200-shilling brother meets his end by having his skull split by a person he quarreled with. Wergeld is likely to be forthcoming only if the kin of the corpse constitute a genuine threat to take revenge.[27] This is yet another reason it is misguided to think that compensation signals a softening of the hard principle of talionic justice. Compensation is a possibility only if revenge is a very likely probability. Who is going to pay you enough to assuage your honor if he does not fear your ability to reclaim your honor by killing him if he does not pay up?

Suppose you are a 1200-shilling man. What if your kin can get only 200 for you? Imagine the opportunities for mockery and irony if your kin cannot get the 1200 shillings the law says you are worth. In a mercantile economy there would be jokes about going cheap, about being marked down, discounted, but even in this premercantile order one can imagine the wit that would be funded by your kin selling your life for less than full value. And if your kin could get only 200 shillings for you what were you then? A failed 1200-shilling person, or a "newborn" 200-shilling person? And are your kin reconstituted at a lower order juridically or just in the rough standings as gauged by the calculus of honor and shame? "Hey," one might fear hearing, "here comes our friend the 99-shilling man."

What uncertainty of identity in such a simple society whose social and moral order we conventionally understand to have raised none of the anxieties surrounding identity that we moderns like to think are of more recent vintage. The usual flat account is that identity was secure back then. You were what you were born to be and that was it. But honor societies never let your identity be a lock. It was always being challenged. The mere designation of a dead kinsmen as a 1200-shilling man means his and your identity must be proven in the field of honor. Pay over 1200 or else, or else, dammit, we no longer are entitled to our social position.

We have no certain evidence from the Anglo-Saxon world that such rerankings and reorderings in fact occurred at death in those instances when the kin were not, for whatever reason, able to collect what they were entitled to collect. We do have evidence though of wergelds being revised upward during life. One text, well known to students of Anglo-Saxon, preserves strictures assuming the upward mobility of a churl, a trader, or even a scholar who might so "thrive" as to become a thegn and thus receive a new higher wergeld. To qualify, a churl needed to acquire a certain amount of property, a trader needed to "travel three times over the wide sea on his own," and a scholar had to do what comes naturally to scholars: stay chaste. Priests are given very secular inducements to live up to their vows. Thus King Æthelred rules that a priest who remains celibate will get his wergeld raised to that of a thegn.[28]

We have suggestions in the Icelandic saga literature that posthumous redefinitions of identity also took place. One's status could be redefined upward if the corpse was compensated for at a rate higher than the person was entitled to in life. One man, for instance, who was thought to be a juridical slave ceased to be one in death, not because death liberated him from servility but because his master was able to exact a free man's compensation for him, rather than the standard slave payment, when he was killed: "Did you really pay a hundred ounces of silver for Atli's killing, enough to make him out a free man?"[29]

There is a paradox at the core of accepting blood money in lieu of blood. The money is supposed to buy peace and it sometimes does, but it contains within it incentives to violate the peace it was meant to secure. The problem is that the means of payment can act as a bloody token, for in a way, it is a token of blood. The money memorializes the dead man it replaces. Here is how it works: You kill my uncle. You offer to pay me 200 shillings as compensation to buy off my right of revenge. You hand over a purse. The purse with its silver now stands in place of my uncle. The reason we can strike the bargain is that I feel my uncle is worth that amount and my honor and his are reasonably restored and preserved by accepting it.

So what do I do with the purse of silver? Buy a replacement uncle? What does silver buy in my culture other than peace and corpses? It seems, rather, I might be moved to hang the purse on a hook right above the seat my uncle used to occupy when he visited. The purse thus reminds me of my uncle, reminds me that I took money for blood, and serves to symbolize both a peaceful resolution by virtue of my having received this equivalence for him in settlement and something else more unsettling.

Although many preferred the peace in the countryside that a negotiated settlement like this would yield, people did not always trust
those who, as the nasty Norse saying mentioned earlier would have it,
"carried their kin in their purse," that is, exchanged blood for money.
They whispered among themselves: "That less than heroic Edmund forgoes revenge, claims himself a good Christian for doing so, and ends
up rich by selling the corpses of his kin at top shilling. I wouldn't be
surprised if he provokes his kin into doing things that will get them
killed so that he can trade his right of revenge for the money." And
Edmund suspects they are saying things like this even if they aren't,
even though he knows that the last thing sensible people want is for
him to recruit forces and turn the valley into an armed camp.[30]

But it is not just the neighbors he fears are saying that. It is the purse
that says it to him every time he sits down to eat and sees it hanging
on its peg. In fact, that is why he put it there. The purse of silver is his
uncle's ghost, come to remind him that he did second best by him. A
law from early Norway worries about people who might make a living
settling for the deaths of their kin: "No one, either man or woman, has
a right to claim atonement three times, unless he has taken revenge in
the meantime."[31] The suspicion is not unlike the one the police have
when a person dies of foul play and he had, a short time ago, made
you the beneficiary of a $5 million life insurance policy.

It ends like this. Edmund breaks the settlement and kills the brother
of his uncle's killer. And now a meeting is arranged by people interested
in keeping the peace, and it is determined that Edmund must pay the
kin of the victim 200 shillings for his deed. The grim paradox? Edmund
simply hands back the same purse he was handed for his dead uncle a
few years earlier. Thus *Njál's saga*: "Njal took the purse and handed it
to Gunnar, who recognized it as being the money that he himself had
given Njal [for Svart's death]."[32] The money was not earning interest,
except that the money was not sitting still either; it was working on
behalf of Edmund's dead uncle, working to make sure he got remembered right.

What role does compensation play, compensation that legal historians and biblical commentators have been telling us reveals a progressive

evolution from a world of revenge to a world in which people learn to suppress vile revenge and settle their differences more rationally? The compensation, the purse in my example, goaded the avenger, egged him on; and worse, it actually financed his breach of the same settlement by which he acquired it. And the irony is not lost on Edmund's uncle's killer when Edmund hands him back *his* purse and silver. The same purse buys two corpses. The compensation paid for Edmund's uncle finances the next round of hostilities, finances the very revenge it was meant to supersede.

These people understood only too deeply the grim ironies of how compensation could provide the means of undoing the peace it secured. *Njál's saga* shows how subtle their understanding and planning were on this score.[33] So why then does anyone pay it? It is a long story that I have told before, for which the short answer is that compensation bought peace *for a while* and buying time gives a chance for passions to cool and the peace to become reasonably permanent. These were practical souls. Peace for a while was not to be sneezed at.[34]

This vignette is not a far-fetched hypothetical but is supported by examples from feuding cultures from the Mediterranean to the northlands: memory, money, and revenge, all holding hands in an intimate way.[35] When we think of the time value of money we think of interest, perhaps usury laws; and those who lived in honor cultures did too, but they also understood that the time value of certain kinds of special-use moneys, such as purses of silver paid over for an uncle, had a different relation to time. It was all about memory and memorializing a claim in the past that obliged you to remember, to even things up in the future: "remember me." Indeed.

EIGHT

Dismemberment and Price Lists

WE CANNOT LEAVE wergeld just yet. First read this law from England,
c. 1015 A.D.:

> The oath of a twelve-hundred man is worth the oaths of 6 *ceorls*
> (churls); therefore, if a person needs to avenge a twelve-hundred
> man he will be fully avenged by killing six *ceorls* and his wergeld
> is the wergeld of six *ceorls*.[1]

Funny that the text does not just say that the wergeld of a churl is 200
shillings or that the wergeld of a 1200 man is 1200 shillings. Instead
it chooses to value the 1200 man in terms of churls and vice versa,
while the shillings remain unexpressed. When we say that something
will cost you a cool million, we know that "million" means a million
dollars. And I suspect they knew that the bare number 1200 meant 1200
shillings, but then what do we make of this text contemporaneous with
the one just quoted? "The wergeld of a twelve-hundred man is twelve-
hundred shillings. The wer of a two hundred man is two hundred
shillings."[2]

Why must the obvious be hammered home so, unless it is no longer
obvious? Had the number-based status terms become something of
a dead metaphor so that they needed to be enlivened by reminding
what the numbers stood for? Maybe people were settling for what
they could get – settling for, say, 70 percent on the shilling – and this
was deemed a sign of a general decay of order and values, and the
provision was meant to assert the nonnegotiability of the price. Could
this be why in the first provision the unit of value is stated not in
shillings but in men, to emphasize the seriousness of the valuation of

ranked men? A 1200 man is valued at the price of six *ceorls*. Or is the compiler simply defining his terms before proceeding, giving the most basic statements of the official exchange rates of nobles for commoners, of men in general for shillings?

Whatever the answers to these questions, one gets the sense that these provisions are not loose ways of talking. If anything the provisions are meant to tighten up looseness and talk tough: six churl corpses pay for one thegn corpse. The way they talked about value had ramifying effects that ran rather deeply into domains where we now feel it should not run. As in death so in life: a thegn's oath, in a lawsuit, is worth six times the oath of a churl. The higher your wergeld the easier it was to make your proof in court. In Wessex, for instance, oaths of exculpation were given values: you might have to swear an oath of the value of the item in dispute,[3] or of the value of a certain number of hides of land,[4] and not infrequently an oath of a value measured in multiples or fractions of wergelds. You might thus have to swear an oath of the value of the king's wergeld if you were accused of plotting against him, or of a lord's if plotting against him.[5]

Having a high wergeld did not, however, always work to your benefit. It was not only the amount your kin could claim at your death, it could also be the price *you* had to pay to redeem *yourself* from punishment, as when King Edgar prescribes cutting out the tongue of a false accuser unless he redeem himself by paying his own wergeld.[6] Other laws measure fines in the amount of the wrongdoer's wergeld, even in multiples of it.[7] It thus could be the case that your wergeld ended up costing you more in mulcts assessed to you during your lifetime than it gained your kin at your death, unless having an easier time meeting the value assigned to your oath made up for the liabilities.

Sometimes, it seems, there were advantages in having a low value. A concern for symmetry, consistency, and conceptual elegance leads to perversely progressive results. A perfect example comes from Hammurabi's laws, which provided that a commoner had to pay less for being cured by a physician than a high-status *awilu* had to pay, so as to reflect the different social value of curing one rather than the other.[8]

Even the sweet-souled Aztecs punished nobles more severely than com-moners for the same offense.[9] One effect of all this was to give wergeld itself, in Anglo-Saxon England at least, a money function; although its value was measured in shillings, the standard unit of account, wergeld became a unit of assessment in restricted legal settings in its own right – pay two times your wergeld, pay half your wergeld.

Slave Values

Monetizing human worth makes us nervous, especially when it is as up-front and unembarrassed as this. Though we are only a little embar-rassed about monetizing social status, and not embarrassed at all when we rank athletes (or even academics) by the contracts they can extort from the foolish and desperate, there are certain domains, those that touch on our beliefs about fundamental human dignity and value, in which we demand considerable amounts of persiflage. I suggested in chapter 7 that openly monetizing human worth might also make the denizens of wergeld systems a little nervous: the fear of dying at a dis-count might not be adequately balanced by the hopes of being marked up or dying at a premium. We think talking this way smacks of slav-ery, and in America at least we must avoid talking in ways that so much as hint at retaining the ideational accoutrements that accompa-nied the moral low point in the nation's history. Talking about humans as money or property is not, we feel, consistent with certain pieties we have regarding the proper way to talk about the immeasurable special-ness of human value.

Talionic cultures, feuding cultures, wergeld cultures, were anxious about slavery too, not as an institution, not morally, but because it was a real hazard to the free. A free man in Alfred's kingdom risked being captured in war and sold across the sea. That is what Vikings pretty much did for a living. But the risk was a peacetime risk too. Selling humans was a lucrative business and it was not beyond some to sell their neighbors or their kids across the sea.[10] And debt slavery awaited you should you not pay your debts. Behind simple buying and selling lay the risk of enslavement.

Slaves had a price too, but it was not given the dignity of being denominated wergeld.[11] Wergeld was a price with a higher "value"; it was the price of free people. Slaves had purchase prices like cows. Yet sometimes it was hard to keep the categories straight, because both wergeld and the price of a slave were measured in shillings or ounces of silver, and then lo, one shades rather by degrees into the other. The conceptual border between slave and free, in not a few slave societies, often had trouble preventing breaks in the figurative barbed wire separating them. An Icelandic law shows free people's value measured in terms of slave value – slaves, not free, providing the standard. Thus, a betrothal was not legal unless the woman was actually worth the brideprice the groom paid: "It is a sound match if she would not fetch a lower price were she a slave woman and had such ill health, or would not fetch a lower price because of other failings or defects."[12] The groom can get his money back and back out of the deal if he overpaid for his free wife; or presumably he could pay her true value, as measured on a slave scale, and marry her anyway.[13]

But for our purposes the point is that in some settings it might be necessary to think of the free as virtual slaves, so as better to get at their true worth.[14] Might it not be that one of the hidden moral costs of slavery for free people was to know that the exchangeability of people in slavery, and the consequent use of slaves as measures of value, offered the constant risk that you or your child was not even worth a defective slave?

Nothing, however, in the idea of justice as getting even need generate or support slavery; indeed in some respects the talion is an idea that is risky for hierarchical societies to generalize too widely. And such societies were careful, as I have noted, to limit the application of strict talionic rules when harms occurred across boundaries separating social rank. The talion operated in its full vigor only within a social ranking; it was an eye for an eye in *Hammurabi* among *awilus*, but not between an *awilu* and a commoner or between a commoner and a slave, just as in the Bible the strict talion did not operate between slave and free. The same was true on the positive side in gift exchange. Gifts between rough equals followed a different system of accounting than gifts up and gifts down.[15]

The Sum of the Parts

King Æthelberht 's laws have a claim to being among the earliest matter written in English. Æthelberht ruled in Kent from roughly 590 to 616 A.D.; his laws are preserved in a manuscript penned some five hundred years later, from exemplars since lost. There is no reason to doubt their genuineness, for reasons I will not go into here in any detail beyond noting that the twelfth-century scribe was careful to preserve archaic linguistic forms that were no longer current in his day, and the style itself is "primitive" in content and grammatical form when compared with the Anglo-Saxon codes as they developed over the next four hundred years from 650 to 1050.[16] Æthelberht's laws have a bare-bones in-your-face quality, which you will experience for yourself in the following portion I have translated. I present what is conventionally numbered as §§33–72, the personal-injury section, in its entirety. I italicize the provisions that I devote special attention to, but it is important to get a feel for the context, the organization, and litany-like quality of it.

Imagine that you are going to write down the first laws for your society. Would you devote roughly half of the ninety you pen to what follows?[17] I render the Old English pretty much word for word to the extent, at least, that maintaining intelligibility will allow. For some of the provisions the precise sense will be a bit obscure, but most are gruesomely clear.

33. If grabbing of hair occurs, 50 sceattas[18] for compensation (*to bote*).
34. If baring of a bone occurs, compensate with 3 shillings.
35. If notching [or cutting] of a bone occurs, compensate with 4 shillings.
36. If the outer covering of the skull is broken, compensate with 10 shillings.[19]
37. If both[20] are [broken], compensate with 20 shillings.
38. If a shoulder is lamed, compensate with 30 shillings.

39. If either ear cannot hear, compensate with 25 shillings.
40. If the ear is struck off, compensate with 12 shillings.
41. If an ear is pierced, compensate with 3 shillings.
42. If an ear is gashed, compensate with 6 shillings.
43. If an eye is out, compensate with 50 shillings.
44. If the mouth or the eye is disfigured, compensate with 12 shillings.
45. If the nose is pierced, compensate with 9 shillings.
46. If it [the piercing] is on one cheek, compensate with 3 shillings.
47. If both are pierced, compensate with 6 shillings.
48. If a nose is otherwise gashed, compensate each [cut] with 6 shillings.
49. If [it?]²¹ is pierced, compensate with 6 shillings.
50. He who shatters a chinbone shall pay 20 shillings.
51. For the four front teeth, 6 shillings each; the tooth that stands next to them 4 shillings; that which is next to it 3 shillings; and those after, a shilling each.
52. If speech is damaged, 12 shillings.
    1. If the collarbone is broken, compensate with 6 shillings.
53. He who stabs through an arm shall compensate with 6 shillings.
    1. If an arm is broken, compensate with 6 shillings.
54. *If [one] strikes off a thumb, 20 shillings.*
    1. *If a thumb nail is off, compensate with 3 shillings.*
    2. *If a person strikes off the shooting-finger, compensate with 9 shillings.*
    3. *If a person strikes off the middle finger, compensate with 4 shillings.*
    4. *If a person strikes off the gold-finger, compensate with 6 shillings.*
    5. *If a person strikes off the little finger, compensate with 11 shillings.*
55. For each nail a shilling.
56. For the slightest disfigurement of looks, 3 shillings and for the greater, 6 shillings.
57. If a person hits another in the nose with his fist, 3 shillings.
58. If it is a "dint,"²² a shilling.
    1. If he receives a "dint" [from] a raised hand, pay a shilling.²³
59. If a "dint" is black outside the clothing, compensate with 30 sceattas.²⁴

60. If it is under the clothing, compensate with 20 sceattas for each.
61. If a stomach is wounded, compensate with 12 shillings.
    1. If he is pierced through, compensate with 20 shillings.
62. If a person undergoes a cure, compensate with 30 shillings.
63. If a person is badly wounded, compensate with 30 shillings.
64. *If a person destroys the generative "limb" (OE lim), he shall pay to him three wergelds.*
    1. If he stabs through, compensate with 6 shillings.
    2. If he stabs into [it], compensate with 6 shillings.
65. If a thigh is broken, compensate with 12 shillings.
    1. If he is crippled, then friends must arbitrate.[25]
66. If a rib is broken, compensate with 3 shillings.
67. If a person stabs through a thigh, each stab 6 shillings.
    1. If over an inch a shilling, two inches two, over three 3 shillings.
68. If there is a welt wound, compensate with 3 shillings.
69. *If a foot is off, pay 50 shillings.*
70. If the big toe is off, pay 10 shillings.
71. For each of the other toes pay half as much as stated for the fingers.
72. If the big toenail is off, 30 sceattas for compensation.
    1. For each of the others, compensate with 10 sceattas.

To the novice the laws give the impression of Kent as an abattoir, as a kind of Kentish Chainsaw Massacre without the more advanced and equally messy technology. Why such a schedule? What does it mean? How was it put to use? Was it ever put to use? What does it say about law itself, about the idea of legislating, if this is in fact legislating and not merely restating the oral law? Are the prices of body parts, the slices and dices, what they understood to be the very core of law, that there was no better way to get at the ideas of entitlement, value, exchange, harm, and compensation? And if body parts it must be, what sense can we make of the relative valuation?

It is not as if these provisions are out of whack with the first thirty-two provisions, or the final eighteen, that make up the entire code. The schedule of prices for personal injury just presented follows upon sections devoted to compensation amounts for theft, the value of which depends on the rank of the owner of the property stolen. One notable scholar has argued a crucial nexus between price-setting, mutilation, and primitive legislation dating back to early Mesopotamia.[26] The primal form of a law may not take the form "thou shalt not," but has instead the form "for X pay Y," where X is a body part or body and Y is some money-like substance. Our worker's comp schedules still have the same look.[27]

Æthelberht's laws are nothing if not a schedule of evaluations: of property and of property in bodies. Thus the first provision (§1): "God's property and the church's, 12-fold compensation; bishop's property, 11-fold compensation; priest's property, 9-fold compensation," and so on. Subsequent provisions deal with harms to the king's rights, then harms to the rights of *eorls*, then to *ceorls*. We are given the wergeld of a *ceorl*: "If one person kills another, compensate with the standard wergeld of 100 shillings" (Kent had a different scale than the 200–600–1200 of Wessex). And should you kill his "loaf-eater," (*hlafæta*), his dependent, you owe the *ceorl* who heads the household 6 shillings (§§21, 25). Everything has its price.

Once the personal-injury section concludes with toenails the laws move on to marriage, which in the diction of the time is discussed in terms of "buying" wives: "If a man buys a maiden for a price, let the deal stand as bargained for, if there is no fraud" (§77).[28] The code concludes with servants and slaves, whose being commoditized does not surprise us. The slave might not have a wergeld, as I indicated, but he surely had value, so if a servant loses both his eye and his foot the injurer owes the master "his entire worth." No differently from free men, a severed eye and foot add up to the value of the whole person: 50 shillings for an eye plus 50 for a foot (§§43, 69) = 100 shillings, precisely the amount of the ordinary wergeld for a free man in Kent (§21) .

It is not hard to discern a cogent ordering to the personal-injury provisions:[29] with some minor deviations they run not just head to toe but head to toenails. Even some of the apparent deviations make sense. Thus after various injuries to the head have been completed and we descend to the collarbone we go down the arm to the hand, beginning with the thumb and through the fingers in order and ending with the nails. But how to get back to the body after having reached the end of the arm? By raising the general issue of disfigurement, which takes us back up to the face for punches in the nose and the various bruises and marks of a brawl before starting straight down the trunk to the stomach, to the genitals, to the thigh, to the feet, and ending with the toes and toenails. The provision on the rib, §66, is clearly out of place, and as often is the case, we will blame it on some weary scribe at some stage in the text's transmission. All in all, it is intelligently organized, something the later and less substantively and grammatically primitive codes often fail to match.

The same top-to-bottom ordering organizes the entire code. It moves from the highest-priced free men to the lowest – from clerics, to kings, to *eorls*, to *ceorls* – then to parts of them, then to women of varying ranks (with an indication that the parts of women were to be compensated for as for men (§74)),[30] and finally to servants and slaves. The final provision makes a gesture of coming full circle, by taking up the subject of recompense for theft by a slave, theft being the subject of the first provision: "If a slave steals, compensate with 2-fold payment" (§90).

When slaves steal, however, certain principles get inverted. In the first provision of the code the cost to the thief was the value of the stolen property multiplied by a multiple geared to the status of its owner; but in §90 it is the slave status of the thief that determines the multiplier. The free thief who steals from a priest pays ninefold the value; the slave who steals from a priest pays twofold. But twofold what? Two times the value of the object, or twofold what a free man would owe a priest, that is, eighteen times the value of the object? The answer could only be of theoretical interest anyway. The slave would be hard-pressed to make any reparations beyond returning the stolen object. He can't even pay with his body, for it is not his to make amends with. One suspects that most all these multiples are the stuff of hierarchical ideology or fantasy, because ninefold damages are too stiff unless the object was trivial or unless the thief were a lord, already well-heeled in ill-gotten and coerced gains. And that kind of thief was hard to bring to justice.[31]

In the personal-injury section, one can also discern two substantive principles at work that help determine the price of the damage: one is utilitarian – eyes are much harder to do without than a middle finger or a molar. It makes perfect sense that the hand, eye, foot, power of speech, and hearing should be highly valued. The other principle of valuation is about "looks" and thus directly about honor and shame. To have one's front teeth knocked out or a bruise or a scar that showed outside the clothing made not just for ugliness but for stories about how you got the crap kicked out of you, especially when the other guy was unmarked. Only some scars and bent noses conferred honor, and even honorable scars had still to be cool-looking honorable scars, like nineteenth-century German frat dueling scars. As a rule the benefit of an honorable scar gained in a fight could hardly compensate for its dishonor once it reached a certain level of ugliness.[32]

This code and the other Anglo-Saxon codes have prompted scholarly work of the highest quality.[33] Rather than reiterate or tackle larger questions regarding the purpose and function of such codes, I want to stay small and bring Æthelberht for a ride on my value-measuring-body-parts-revenge-payback-blood-and-money hobbyhorse. It is the laws' view of fingers and toes, strikings off, and gougings out that I mean to deal with – §§33–72 just quoted.

Picture a barroom brawl, or the seventh-century equivalent, a mead-hall brawl – which was enough of a problem to take up three of the sixteen provisions in the Kentish code issued by Æthelberht's descendents toward the end of the seventh century[34] – in which about ten people go at it pretty good. Some lose a few incisors; some get their ears bit off, an eye gets poked out here, an arm broken there, a scalp lacerated, and a lot of cuts and bruises. In honor societies such occurrences are fraught with all kinds of disruptive possibility. There is the legal morass: every injured party, or the kin of any who got killed, has a claim for the harm he suffered and liability for what he inflicted. Even self-defense will generally not spare one from having to pay up something.[35] As many as ten different legal actions could be commenced, each party suing to recover for his tooth, arm, eye, and so on. And there is a strong impetus to sue, or to take revenge, because in honor cultures it takes a lot of real work to let bygones be bygones.

We are thrown back on the evidence of the Icelandic sagas to fill the gaps in the Anglo-Saxon sources. What it shows is that the many lawsuits that might grow out of a single affray seldom got processed in the courts beyond commencing the action, if that. The sheer amount of time that would be consumed processing the legal claims drove people to easier and more effective procedures. The more numerous and messier the claims, the more likely it was that the whole incident would be submitted to arbitrators who would dictate a settlement. Instead of ten or more suits, they would all be joined in a single arbitration. And the noteworthy thing for our purposes is that very little coin or sheep needed to pass hands as compensation. The effective medium of exchange was the blood, body parts, and wounds themselves. To trust the saga evidence, arbitrators would declare Æthelwold's gouged-out eye to be balanced against Wulfhelm's sliced-off foot; Helming's broken arm to be balanced by Aldhelm's lacerated ear, and so on. And then the injuries that were left over were paid for in conventional money substances.[36]

If one side had come away lightly injured and the other side bore the brunt, then the winners would have to scramble to come up with funding to pay the bill for their success, because they would lack offsets arising from the affray. The sagas show people in the heat of a battle actually keeping a running account of the damage they were inflicting, deducting the damage they were suffering. This is a cold reminder to us who feel that passions must suspend certain types of rationality. A pretty dumb thug could be fighting like a berserk, glorying in how well it was going for him, and still keep count (think, if you resist the thought, how much calculating you are capable of right in the midst of the most passionate act of darkness):

"Let us pursue them," said Kolskegg. "Bring your bow and arrows..."

Gunnar said, "Our purses will be empty enough by the time we have paid compensation for those who lie dead here already."

Or says another character, though in a cool moment:

And as soon as I estimate that you have killed off as many of them as you can afford to pay compensation for . . . I shall intervene with all my men to stop the fighting.[37]

But the sagas show that even in the cases where one side had a steep bill to pay, compensation was not always paid in conventional money or property but rather by finding unprosecuted claims that third parties had outstanding against the victims and getting those third parties to assign their old claims to the defendants, who then paid them over to the victims as offsets.[38] Legal claims were themselves a kind of money, traded back and forth, given and sold, in the way debt instruments are among us. (And in sixth-century Frankish Gaul we find that when the bill of one side was more than they could pay the church might step in to make up the rest of the compensation award.) [39]

There was a poetry to such awards, an art to balancing who against whom, whose what against whose what. A lot of social capital could lie not just in how many corpses you were thought to be worth – or in one famous saga case, of how expensive your finger turned out to be[40] – but in whom you got paired with in the offset game. That the saintly Hoskuld Hvitanesspriest in *Njál's saga* is declared to be worth the enormous sum of three wergelds means one thing, but that it was actually paid, not by a transfer of silver, sheep, or land, but by being balanced off against the corpse of his killer, the ominous Skarphedinn, means another. Each is thus honored in being paid for by the other.

Think back to that purse of silver in chapter 7, which memorializes much as a bloody token does. That purse, remember, can finance the return blow, the breach of the very settlement it was meant to conclude. By balancing one corpse against another, we simply wipe out the silver as a middleman scurrying back and forth between the feuding camps. Practical and efficient, yes, but also productive of subtleties of meaning. What were they saying about competing cultural values when they equated the saintly man of peace, Hoskuld, with the perversely intelligent and werewolfian wisecracking killer, Skarphedinn? There was a real poetic possibility in the art of declaring what was to offset what. Conventional money substances, silver, sheep, and the like, had only variances in the amounts for the arbitrator to play with; bodies and their parts had so much more poetic possibility because they came laden with the value of the honor of the person to whom they once belonged. When it mattered, such complex media of value could be exploited to give a judgment a sense of its own rightness precisely because it had a compelling poetry to it. You want an "expressive theory of value?"[41] It need not be all sweetness and light: for expression to carry a punch, it must sometimes carry a punch.

Æthelberht's schedules might have served more as an aid to arbitrators, if, that is, they could read, giving them a way of selling their decisions as having struck an acceptable balance, than as a directive to judges, if they could read. The numbers assigned for each wound, each body part, lent a colorable precision to their awards. It allowed the arbitrators to declare that the sides were even and then prove it to be so. OK, Eadhelm: it says here the loss of your little finger and goldfinger is not quite balanced by your smashing Edgar's jaw to pieces. Pay him three shillings and we are quits.

But maybe the schedules were not really meant to be used. Felix Liebermann, the great editor of the Anglo-Saxon laws, considered these body-part schedules "wohl nur juristische Theorie," a lawyerly fantasy of precision and order.[42] The Icelanders had no schedule of body-part prices and yet were masterful at balancing injuries and wounds. They had rules of thumb and developed customs of what people would accept as fair for the loss of an appendage. As a practical matter, then, it is not clear what such a formalized schedule gets us. If all Æthelberht was doing was giving customary rules of thumb and rough rules of practice a faux precision, is anything gained?

Well, yes and no. Part of the need for the schedule is that Æthelberht was extending his power beyond Kent and perhaps this was a way of introducing clarity where competing customs might lead to chaos, for the value of body parts was not the same in Kent as further west. There is also a kind of magic even in spurious precision that could benefit Æthelberht as a king: precision, even the claim of it, lends a kind of majesty to majesty. It might even lend authority to the judgments of judges and awards of arbitrators, if these needed extra bolstering. Bolstering they could probably use, given the fragility of many such settlements or the difficulty of making legal judgments stick as *res judicata*, as final, when people reopened judgments again and again as their feuds moved from the battlefield to law courts and into arbitration and back again. Says one exhausted and frustrated litigant in a letter to King Edgar regarding a lawsuit King Alfred, Edgar's father, had already been involved with: "And, Sir, when will any suit be closed if one can end it neither with money nor with an oath? And if one wishes to change every judgment which King Alfred gave, when shall we have finished disputing?"[43]

Let me saw off the limb I am on by suggesting this: the market in body parts is just the kind of market where a formal price list might be more insulated from the pressures of supply and demand than the royally promulgated price lists for more routine items such as we see King Ine attempt: "A ewe with her 'young sheep' is worth a shilling until 14 nights after Easter."[44] Prices could look stable in the blood-and-body-parts market, though even here there must have been pressure to sell at a discount during especially violent times. Getting the parts list all down in writing makes for some psychological order if nothing else.

Or psychological disorder: I remember offers of dismemberment insurance that were given to us as grade-school children that we were to take home to our parents. These listed what our parents would get in dollars if we lost an eye or a leg on the playground. The schedule looked much like Æthelberht's laws. And we ten-year-olds, for whom the idea of a thousand dollars might as well have been a million, were made dizzy by the sudden knowledge that we, who were forever being told how useless or worthless we were by the older kids and our parents too, could be so valuable, even if it meant we had to be carved up to cash in on it.

Flipping the Bird

Lurking in Æthelberht's schedule of payments is a gold mine of information. Consider the hand, which unlike the foot in §69 is not dealt with as a whole, but as the sum of the thumb and fingers:

54. If [one] strikes off a thumb, 20 shillings.
    1. If a thumb nail is off, compensate with 3 shillings.
    2. If a person strikes off the shooting-finger, compensate with 9 shillings.
    3. If a person strikes off the middle finger, compensate with 4 shillings.
    4. If a person strikes off the gold-finger, compensate with 6 shillings.
    5. If a person strikes off the little finger, compensate with 11 shillings.

How do we account for the relative ranking of the digits?

a. thumb (*þúma*)
b. little finger (*lytlan finger*)
c. index (*scytefinger* "shooting-finger")
d. ring (*goldfinger*)
e. middle (*middelfinger*)

Easy case for the thumb in our view and theirs too. The opposable thumb is, along with laughter and language (if we let in a few other primates and a dog or two), a signature of our humanity, and not least, it is functionally crucial to gripping and having a useful hand. Montaigne devotes an essay to the thumb, alleging as proof of its importance the number of generals who cut them off their defeated enemy.[45] But the little finger next highest in value? And the middle finger last? After the thumb, function seems to play either a smaller role or almost an antirole. We cannot even fob off our confusion on scribal errors, which are especially frequent when it comes to copying numbers. But here the numbers add up, and I mean add up: $20 + 9 + 4 + 6 + 11 = 50$. And 50 is the value of the foot and the eye, a distinguished club to which the hand properly belongs. The numbers cannot be explained away as a mistake.[46]

Not until I broke my little finger pretty near off trying to tackle my then ten-year-old son and let it heal itself back up as a crooked, useless appendage, rather than visit the doctor for something as shameful as a busted pinkie, did I realize the functional value of the little finger. Much of the gripping force of the hand depends on it, and I received a stern lecture from the doctor when I finally complained about it to him after it was too late. The job the index finger does can be assumed by the middle finger should the index finger be cut off. The ring finger cannot, however, substitute for the baby finger. Join the cast of real tough guys, the doctor said, building-trade guys, who out of embarrassment to see me for a baby finger have to go on partial disability. Said I, putting on a show of cool nonchalance to confirm I properly belonged with the tough guys with whom I had just been cast, "But will I still be able to type?"

The little finger, because it is the little finger after all, can play a symbolic role too. Thus King Edmund provided that if a group of slaves were caught stealing, though the ringleader was to be hanged, his followers were to be spared their lives and whipped instead, scalped too, and then "*truncetur minimus digitus in signum*," have their little finger truncated *as a sign*. No need to destroy nearly all their economic value by amputating the whole of their thieving hand.[47]

Let us grant, though, the little finger its functional value, and so too the "shooting finger" (not guns, obviously, but drawing a bow-string or guiding a javelin). The ring finger was also their ring finger, as its name – goldfinger – indicates, a bearer of ornament precisely because it needn't be kept free for anything else, being pretty much useless. But the middle finger? Why so low? Could it be that it was a taboo finger back then too? Valued low because it was routinely available for nonreproductive sexual work and not much else, and thus also for flipping the bird? I always thought so, but where to find the proof?

Proof of a sort was forthcoming from a text five hundred years later than Æthelberht's. A collection of laws known as *Leges Henrici Primi*, representing in substantial part a translation into Latin of the earlier Anglo-Saxon laws, renders the schedule for finger payments not from Æthelberht's laws, but from Alfred's.[48] We find the four fingers named as follows:

a. *index*
b. *impudicus*

c. *anularis*

d. *auricularis*

Index is index, *anularis* is ring finger, and *auricularis* is "ear finger." Here is a crucial function of the little finger to be added to its gripping force: we need it to work about in our ears. I find more common humanity with a seventh-century person scratching inside his ear in no less a comical fashion than I must confess I do myself than when I think of him using his middle finger to insult such a one as I. Yet look at the name for the middle finger: *impudicus*, the shameful finger, named for its shame, known for nothing else, but being in the middle parts, in Hamlet's suggestive idiom. There we have our proof, such as it is.[49] Not quite "the bird," but then one knows that that bird is not a sparrow, or a hawk, but a cock, located on the hand in such a way as to reproduce the looks of the penis in its natural setting.

The middle finger is priced the lowest because it is a dirty finger. It is a finger of insult. It can curse. Why should that lower its value, though? As a weapon of insult it has great value. Why not put a high price on the cursing finger? Yet that is precisely why it must bear a low monetary value. It has power, the power to contaminate, and that very power is a function of its low value. It contaminates and devalues because it is already itself devalued.

Value plays itself out at both extremes when it comes to penis symbols like *impudicus*, the cheapest of digits, at one end, and a real penis, the most expensive of members, indeed of whole persons, at the other:

> 64. If a person destroys the generative limb, he shall pay to him three wergelds.

Three wergelds! Here the "little man" is worth three times the man it is (or was) attached to. Will ironies never cease? The middle finger is devalued because it is a symbol of a penis, a symbol that keeps trying to pretend it is the real thing. It is forever finding itself in awkward places, doing after a fashion what the real thing should be doing, after a fashion. And for its disgracefulness it is put last among digits. But the real penis is not satisfied to remain real; it quickly becomes symbolic too by garnering to itself a value that is suprahuman, three times supra. The overevaluation is the stuff of fetish, the part not merely standing for the whole but transcending the whole by several magnitudes. More than the man, more than the penis, it is manliness itself. This is plain old symbolization in a classic and up-front manner, conventional and not all that surprising, except perhaps for how much it costs. You can kill a man in Kent for 100 shillings but if you castrate him it costs you 300 shillings.

Is this serious? A whim of the legislator? A whim of a cleric for whom bodily wholeness (more than holiness) was a prerequisite for office? "He whose testicles are crushed or whose male member is cut off shall not enter the assembly of the Lord" (Deut. 23.1), though priestly bodily perfection inhered in ears, eyes, and fingers no less than testicles (Lev. 21.21). Or is it another example of Kentish exceptionalism and weirdness, usually blamed on its being settled neither by Angles nor Saxons, but by Jutes? Alfred's code, in Wessex, speaking of injuries to the testicles rather than to the penis, values the male generative capacity at 80 shilling, or 40 percent of the standard West Saxon wergeld of 200 shillings. In Kent you are better off killing a man than mutilating him and letting him live. You are also better off killing him than taking his two eyes and a foot or a hand, for the price of the parts is much greater than the price of the whole no matter how you cut it.

How are we really to understand that triple wergeld? Is the humiliation worth three times your life, an admission that a life in such shameful circumstances is worse than death? Or is it rather a stricture against corpse mutilation? The latter does not seem to be the case, for this law is one of the very few in Æthelberht's code that includes the pronoun indicating to whom the payment is to be made or mentions the payee directly: "*prym leudgeldum hine man forgelde*," "with three wergelds a person shall pay *him*." He is clearly not meant to be dead. Nor can it be a stricture against Judaicizing the body – circumcising it, that is. Jews did not seem to be a noted or feared presence in seventh-century Kent.

The schedule gives a fairly clear image of the valorized, in this case, male body. Genitals stand alone at three times a man: then come the eyes, hands, and feet, at half a man each, then shoulders, then hearing, and so on. Did you not play the game – of course you did – one of the many ranking games we play, about which sense you would least rather lose? Vision always won. Or which of your limbs? We dismembered ourselves imaginatively quite frequently, and the story was manifestly not just a way of talking about castration or displacing it. Eyes, as the Oedipal tale makes clear, matter as much or more than anything else, and, as previously noted, men share them with women too.

There is a refreshing tale of gender equality here. Women's bodies have in many times and places been figuratively divided into parts, each part functioning less as a symbol of the whole than as a thing desired for itself: thus the fetishization of breasts, thighs, lips, eyes, brows, hair, feet, it being understood that the sum of the parts is significantly more valuable than the whole, just as the schedules of body-part prices make the sum of the parts of both men and women greater than the whole. It is hardly surprising to see this fetishization articulated in terms of price. A tenth-century Icelandic skaldic poet values his love's eyes at 300 apiece, her hair at 500, though he does not tell us what the unit of account is, whether silver – ounces or marks – or ells of cloth.[50] Andrew Marvel, more tastefully, makes years the unit of account, rating his coy mistress's eyes at 100 years for the pair, but 200 for each individual breast, that is, were there "but world enough and time." (The prices quoted by both Viking and Puritan are so overstated as to make them hypothetical, the men, not without some wit, paying their respects in unpayable promissory notes.) But hyperbole was not just poetic license: the laws purported at least to mean what they said. Another Germanic code, for instance, was no less vehement about protecting a woman's reproductivity than Æthelberht was about protecting men's. The Frankish *Lex Salica* (§§32–33) provided that if someone kills a free woman who is fertile one must pay three times her wergeld; but if she is beyond childbearing years, a single wergeld.[51]

If the reproductive capacity of both male and female is worth more than the whole, the same is true of any number of sums of various parts. Two eyes or two feet are already a whole man or woman. It is not surprising that that should be the case. Although fetishization is clearly needed to explain the hyperevaluation of *one* part as three times greater than the whole, we need not resort to fetishization to explain how two eyes and two feet might add up to more than a person. The price of each part is only partly a price of that part; it is mostly a measure of the loss of value to the whole occasioned by its removal. If a mere loss of a finger or toe can disqualify one for the priesthood, then the part lost that so lowers the value of the man takes on a higher value excised than it, in and of itself, had while a part of the living body.

Amidst this carnage let me add an uplifting tale of hacking and hewing: one saga tells of a Viking named Onund. His skill in a battle against King Harald unfortunately drew the attention of Harald's men. "They said, 'Let's give that man in the prow who is doing so well something to remember us by, to show he has been in battle.'" These warriors were on the same page with Nietzsche. Memorialization, memory creation, is intimately linked to severed flesh and spilled blood. Onund loses his leg just below the knee. He is dragged to safety, but thereafter "he walked with a *tréfót*, a tree-leg. The wooden leg not only gave him support, it gave him a new identity, for he was now known as Onund Treefoot. Onund's missing limb does not deter him from more Viking activity, and he acquires quite a name for himself. Eventually he settles in Iceland, where it was said that "few could stand up to him even though they were whole." And when he died he was considered "the bravest and most agile of all the one-legged men in Iceland."[52] (So deep runs the comparative and ranking impulse that there is even a scale ranking one-legged men.)

The suggestion is that the class of such one-legged men was not of negligible size, nor is there the least sense that such men were not to be reckoned with. When it came to fighting on ships Onund was not at much disadvantage, and the treeleg might function as something of a life preserver if he tumbled over the side. On land, his wooden limb served as a threat to those he met in combat, for like burning one's ships or bridges, Onund's wooden leg meant there was no point in his fleeing; Onund Treefoot was rooted to the ground and he would fight to the death. People were honored to trace their descent from him, and in the saga in which he appears he is the root of the tree that produces the saga's main character, Grettir, who, recall, was known, among other things, for being avenged in Byzantium.[53]

NINE

Of Hands, Hospitality, Personal Space, and Holiness

IN OUR POST-KANTIAN WORLD we are much given to pious talk about dignity, the dignity of the person. Everyone has it; it cannot be lost; it inheres in being human, like opposable thumbs (which, however, can be lost). Dignity is sometimes contrasted to honor, which can be lost or simply not acquired, there being no special presumption you were born to it unless your parents had it, and which, even if they did have it, was yours for the losing. Honor, unlike dignity, was also there for the taking; it could be captured from others. Kant himself opposed dignity to price: "In the realm of ends everything has either a price or a dignity. What has a price is such that something else can also be put in its place as its equivalent; by contrast whatever is elevated above all price, and admits of no equivalent, has a dignity."[1] Our talionic peoples, though, had a different way of talking about something very closely akin to dignity, and it had a price.

We have seen that pretty near everything – the body, life, and even more abstract goods like honor – had a price, for even though you could not quite buy honor, you could surely buy honor *back*, or redeem it. In fact, the surest way of proving you were entitled to it was to reacquire it when it got taken away. And you could sell your right to buy back your honor in blood by accepting wergeld or compensation payments instead, which as we have seen could also be an honorable outcome, though with its own attendant ambiguities. Those tough-minded people of honor who populate the Icelandic sagas recognized a principle of maximal negotiability: "Everything is compensable." The saying occurs in a setting too rich not to reproduce more fully. A certain Asbjorn has just killed Atli. Asbjorn then quickly rides to the farm of

Thormod, the dead Atli's brother, and has Thormod seized. Thormod asks him for an explanation:

Asbjorn said he would know soon enough and then told him his brother Atli had just been killed. Thormod asked if it was worth making an offer for his own life. Asbjorn said there was no point to bother since he had already killed his brother which meant he could never trust him after that. Thormod said, "everything is compensable" to which Asbjorn replied that tricks would not avail him. Thormod made his last confession and prepared for his death.[2]

They killed poor Thormod, because Asbjorn expected him to avenge his dead brother.

"Everything is compensable" speaks to several issues. It represents Thormod's desperate attempt to buy his own life back from Asbjorn, who means to strike a preemptive blow by taking it, but it is also a reminder that if Asbjorn lets him go, money can surely settle the claim he, Thormod, has for his dead brother whom Asbjorn has just murdered. Money, says a desperate Thormod, can settle anything. Asbjorn doesn't buy it. He suspects that, even though everything may be compensable in theory, such purchases and sales are not quite final. The person might want to return what he bought for an exchange or seek later to redeem the sale. That is why Asbjorn rejects Thormod's offer. Life means hope. And Asbjorn can predict very well what Thormod's consuming hope will be should he live. In these kinds of cultures, hope is the hope of getting even.

Hospitality and *Mund*

Despite a willingness to talk about the deepest matters as compensable, redeemable, or priceable, honor cultures, from the North Atlantic to the mountains of Yemen, had something very much like a dignity principle. Although they steered clear of the hyperbolic diction of pricelessness we feel compelled to employ, they too felt that there was something suspicious about being too eager to take money in place of accepting payment paid out in more honorable specie, like blood and corpses.

Q: But priceless? A: "Everything is compensable." Their notion of dignity has a very different feel to it, and it lacks the fundamental Kantian quality of not being available to everyone upon being born human. Still, if we limit ourselves to free male (and female) householders, we see something comparable, in the Germanic world at least, that is worth discussing; it will bring us back to the body and its parts.

The idea is embodied in the Germanic word *mund*. It means "hand" and derives from the same Indo-European root that yielded the Latin word for hand, *manus*. Fairly early on, as early as our earliest written records in the Germanic languages, *mund* had already acquired a legal sense, which ended in pushing its root sense "hand" to poetic uses. Though it still served to mean plain old hand in *Beowulf*, even there *mund* is not used as much as *hand* or *hond* is.[3]

In its legal sense *mund* is usually translated as "protection" and is compared to the authority of the Roman *pater familias* over his household members. It contains within it the idea of guardianship, thus the modern German word for guardian: *Vormund*. *Mund*, in this extended sense of protection, protector, guardian, figures as the second element in names like Edmund, Sigmund, Gudmund. Æthelberht's laws set a value on the *mund* of the various social ranks, which then must be paid to the person whose *mund* is violated. The king's *mund* is worth 50 shillings, a churl's is 6, and a "best widow of the 'eorl' class" has a *mund*, like the king, of 50 shillings, special upper-class widows qualifying as queens of a sort.[4]

How are we supposed to understand Anglo-Saxon *mund*?[5] It is not wergeld. It is not what is paid to your kin for your death. Instead, it partakes of several notions, such as sanctuary, personal space, jurisdiction, quarter, protection, and "peace,"[6] as in the king's peace. Even certain selected uses of the idea of hospitality are invoked. In Clint Eastwood's *Unforgiven*, Little Bill, the tough sheriff of Big Whiskey, Wyoming, after having savagely beaten William Munny, mocks a nearly unconscious Munny as he struggles to crawl out of the saloon: "Let that man out, WW, he is desiring to leave the hospitality of Big Whiskey behind him." Here *hospitality* bears more than its usual sense of generous entertainment of the stranger; it also means a jurisdictional space that the host controls and in which certain breaches of behavior, such as bearing arms, are a breach of the host's hospitality. In Little Bill's sense *hospitality* means more the space one is invited into, rather than being treated to a fine time; the hospitality of Big Whiskey is Little Bill's *mund*.

In the Berber world we can see the same notion embedded in the idea of *h'urma*, or in the idea of honor itself among Yemeni tribesmen.[7] Thus the grim jurisdictional aspect of the case of the Levite's concubine, mentioned earlier, in which the host assumes the prerogative, without consultation, to put his guest's concubine out of the safety of his house, with obligations of hospitality to a male stranger trumping the safety of any women, even the host's own daughter.[8] And although the guest ultimately puts out his concubine himself to spare the host putting out his daughter, the host assumes from the start the right to offer the Levite's concubine:

> As [the Levite and his host] were making their hearts merry, behold, the men of the city, base fellows, beset the house round about, beating on the door; and they said to the old man, the master of the house, "Bring out the man who came into your house, that we may know him." And the man, the master of the house, went out to them and said to them, "No, my brethren, do not act so wickedly; seeing that this man has come into my house, do not do this vile thing. Behold, here are my virgin daughter and his concubine; let me bring them out now. Ravish them and do with them what seems good to you; but against this man do not do so vile a thing." But the men would not listen to him. So the man seized his concubine, and put her out to them.
>
> (Judg. 19.22–25)

This is grim stuff, yet even here we see an instance of bodies doing money-like work. The Levite's poor concubine finds herself offered as a means of payment, and, like a coin, she is a symbolic substitute for a deeper value she represents. She is not enjoyed by the base fellows as a woman but as a substitute for the man they wanted and asked for. The woman stands in the place of the man, her vagina passing for his anus, the less valued being substituted for the more valued in much the way sheep or money replaces the more valued blood as a means of payment in revenge.[9]

133

The Levite's host exercised considerable power in his space. In the Germanic world this hospitable power was *mund*. But it is not just about the powers you assume; it is also about the duties and liabilities that come with it. Granting someone admission to your space alters legal and quasi-legal relations, in a way that is somewhat similar to the permitted admissions that are the substance of sex.[10] Once persons or things enter the domain of your *mund* you end up responsible for them, as the host for a guest. In other words, there are liabilities, not just benefits, that attend this version of "dignity," the dignity of being entitled to an inviolable space that is your own. Is it not the case that the ability to incur liabilities that are your own is a sign of a deep respect for you as a person, a fully legal person?[11]

We can get an idea of how magical the space of *mund* is from this law issued by Kings Hloþhere and Eadric of Kent (c. 680 A.D.):

> If a person entertains a visitor for 3 nights in his own home – a merchant or other person who has come across the border – and he gives him food, and he [the guest] does evil to any person, that man [the host] shall bring the other to justice or do justice.[12]

This gives new meaning to the old saying about fish and guests who stay beyond three days. If a stranger by invitation comes within your space, the domain of your *mund*, he has three days for it not to matter – three days in which your youness will not rub off on him, or his hisness on you. But combining the spatial magic of *mund* with the temporal magic of three days metamorphoses the social and legal identities of you and your guest. He becomes part of you. You become liable for his wrongs, chargeable and even killable for his offenses; if he is killed you are to avenge him or undertake legal process on his behalf.

But it is not only space and time; it is also about eating together. The magic also depends on a hospitable mini-communion. How nicely our prior themes come back to haunt and to assist: sharing food binds one person's matter with the matter of others, making guest and host – just as they are etymologically cojoined, being different forms of the same word[13] – into a cojoined person. He took food from your hand, he becomes you. This is hospitality with a bite.[14]

The Kentish laws give us more mundane matters of *mund*. If a man kills someone on the king's premises he owes the king his *mund* of 50 shillings independent of any wergeld he may owe to the kin of the victim; if he kills someone at an eorl's residence he must pay the eorl his *mund* of 12 shillings. Similarly, sexual relations with the householder's serving women are violations of the householder's *mund* and cost 6 shillings.[15] Suppose you invite some people over for a party and one of your guests insults the others or punches one of them: in such cases not only does the person directly insulted or assaulted have a claim against the unruly guest, but you, as the owner of the place where the incident took place, have one against him too.[16] Your space has been violated, your hospitality, your peace, your honor. It is an affront to you to the extent that a certain holiness of your space has been desecrated; your space is accorded a certain sacral quality that has a price: the *mund*.

Hands and Reach

From whence this holiness? I like to think that *mund* is still present with us in the idea of a sacrosanct personal space upon which intrusions give rise sometimes to legal offenses, as in rape or assault, but mostly, among us, to social offenses and moral demands. The moral body does not really stop abruptly at the skin; there is an ever-weakening force field that extends out from it that establishes a space we claim by moral right as our own. Think of the body proper as a point surrounded by a gray zone of shifting but reasonably predictable shape. In some cases the zone is very small, not even including all our skin, as in particularly crowded presses as we try to get into the stadium for a game. In other cases, the zone can expand to include our office, even our whole house or yard. Our *mund* asserts itself in that domain; in one sense it *is* that domain. It is the space in which we justly feel that others must reckon with our demands for certain treatment or stand in a relation of formal offense toward us; it is a space in which we also owe duties of protection, those duties often subsumed under notions like hospitality, when we allow others admission.

In a crowded elevator I cannot complain about your standing in space I would never admit you to but for the fact that we both must curtail our claims under these special circumstances. I cannot even deny you the physical contact of standing shoulder to shoulder, although should we both be in short sleeves and of different sexes the problem gets, pardon the tastelessness, hairier. Imagine, though, if it were just you and one other in the elevator and he chose to stand right next to you. Even when we must press up against each other in a crowded space, there are mutual duties owed one to the other to avoid certain parts of us pushing against certain parts of them. In the broader spaces of my home I have certain claims on your behavior to me and to others who are invited in. You had better not be rude to the other guests, at least in such a way that cannot pass for comical and entertaining. It is a violation of my *mund* if you offend another there.

One can see a good portion of the writings of Erving Goffman to be devoted to parsing the parameters of one's jurisdictional immunity, one's *mund*. He notes that we are not quite at the geometric center of our jurisdictional space. It extends out in front of us, for instance, considerably farther than it extends out from our backside, or laterally. Certain parts of the body function as spacers and are meant to come into contact with others so as to ward them off from more sacred domains: the elbows are the best example, but shoulders and the butt also play this role. Some body parts can never play this role: lips, penises, breasts, except for those big-bosomed middle-aged British matrons who employ their breasts as battering rams.[17]

Probably no two parts of the body have a more complex role in this jurisdictional game as protectors and assertors of our jurisdictional bubble than the hands and the eyes. The eyes ward off with a glare, which is manifestly not a stare and which is often the hostile response a stare elicits. Eyes intrude and give offense not only by the kind of look they give but also by how long they look and by what they see. They also ward off offense; they tell the intruder to back off, just as they signal permission or invitation to a desired person to get closer. We wear a special look when we are trying to recognize a person we have never seen before whom we have arranged to meet, and so subtle are we in reading that special look that we seldom have to scan more than a few faces before we correctly identify the person. The person so scanned will also be wearing the look of looking for someone he has not met, and those people who are incorrectly scanned will take no offense at having their eye caught because they too will recognize our purpose and that we mean to violate no *munds*.

Like the eyes, hands work as defenders and offenders, qualified for defense because so well qualified for offense. The hand defends by warding off and pushing off; it also protects and defends by assuming the offensive with grabs, throttlings, and punches. Unlike the eyes, which can work across space and can be cast – a glance can also be thrown – the hands are more limited as to their reach. To let them get more than an arm's length away either we must resort to throwing stones and spears, pulling triggers, or we must give them more expansive powers by metaphorical interposition. Such is *mund*. The hand of *mund* extends itself into real space with moral, social, and legal force beyond the physical range of the enfleshed hand attached to the body. Because the hand can claim things by grabbing and holding, it comes to be able to grab and hold by ritual and metaphorical extension. That is why I can still be understood to possess the things I own when I leave them on a chair I mean to return to; that is why I still possess the contents of my home when I am away on vacation. They are still in my hand's grip, or *mundgripe* as the *Beowulf* poet would say.

The *mund* extends itself morally and legally to protect and claim its jurisdictional space. There are thus handshakes, handclasps, handsels that bind, accept, transfer; there are *manu*missions, *eman*cipations, *manu*captions in Roman law; and *main*prises in French and the common law, even mort*main*, the dead hand of control from beyond the grave. The hand in every one of these rituals extends itself, now to grant, now to grasp. Hands are implements of possessing, of having and holding, of grasping and seizing, giving and "handing" over. The hand's work of seizing and grabbing is the stuff of asserting a claim and then protecting and defending it. It means the hand becomes the image of possession and protection of what it possesses. It thus symbolically controls children and hands them over in fosterage and marriage. And the *mund* is that space to which my hand so conceived extends, the space in which I claim a right or an interest in all that happens. The *mund* then is more than just my turf; it makes no very clear distinction between my space, my things, my self, and my honor.

Does this not look like post-Kantian dignity that is more than a hope and a prayer? It has teeth. So serious is dignity conceived in this way that it grants you the rights of a king. You can exact fines for breaches of your peace; your jurisdictional power gives you the right to mulct those who do not respect the hospitality of your domain. This is a serious way to give some backbone to the notion of respect. The *mund* also embodies a basic no-harm principle, but even more expansively than ours, for it recognizes affronts to dignity as compensable in silver to be sure, but in blood too.

A lot of moral and figurative force grows out of the hand. A king can extend his hand, his *mund*, by alloying it with his word.[18] Thus Æthelberht (§2) claims for himself his 50-shilling *mund* if anyone interferes with his men riding to attend him after he has summoned them. The word of summons carries with it a virtual hand, claiming to protect those within reach of a word. I can even use my word, my writ, my letters patent, to suggest that my hand is where my seal is. And although it is unwise to lump Anglo-Saxons together with continental Germans and see them as part of one big happy Germania, I find it a bit uncanny that among the Franks the notion of the *verbum regis*, the word of the king, meant quite simply being within the king's special protection, within his *mund*.[19]

Wholly Holy

A couple of pages ago I likened the jurisdictional bubble of *mund* to a sacral space, to a holy place. In medieval Iceland the idea of *mund* was largely subsumed into the notion of *helgi*, the word being cognate with English *holy*.[20] *Helgi* (like *mund*, prominent as a name – Helgi, Helga) is the immunity a person has not to be intruded upon. It embodies the no-harm principle and it is the possession of every free man or woman. Even slaves and dependent people had some version of it. In Iceland you were not within your rights to have sex with your own female slaves if they were married to a slave; indeed the slave husband could rightly kill you if you did.[21]

The idea of *helgi*, like *mund*, marks off a space with the body at its core, a real defended space that extends socially, morally, legally, and physically beyond the skin. How far it extends beyond the skin is a function of power and honor and varies by age, gender, and juridical rank. Do not tread on someone's holiness lest you lose your holiness as against the person whose state of *helgi* you violated. She or he can kill you for it. Violation of it comes at a price. *Helgi* sees the person as his own sanctuary, a place where he resides free of harm, and a space within which he grants protection to those admitted, a space not even insulting words have a right to enter. Now we are talking respect.

Helgi, unlike *mund*, makes no reference to a body part, with the part standing for the whole; *helgi* is about wholeness, not parts at all. The holy, *helgi*, and the whole have a common philological origin. *Holy* and *wholly* are not a bad pun, a fortuitous homophone; they come from the same root. One can tease out the constellation of values that generate both the idea of holiness and the idea of wholeness: the holy is an inviolate wholeness, hale (also a member of the same family of words) and whole. Interesting too is the connection across many cultures that requires the holy to be whole; thus sacrificial animals must be perfect before they are split up and ripped apart and eaten to make the recipients healthy and whole. The very idea of wholeness suggests vulnerability to partition, suggests it horrifically at times: "When Hyrcanus [the high priest]," writes Josephus, "fell down at his feet, Antigonus, with his own teeth mutilated his ears, in order that he might never again resume the high priesthood...for a high priest must be physically perfect."[22] We are never far from blood and guts in these kinds of worlds, even in ours, especially when it comes to matters of *health* and *healing*, both words also deriving from the same Indo-European root as *holy*, *whole*, and *helgi*.

TEN

Satisfaction Not Guaranteed

GETTING EVEN – repaying one's debts and getting repaid when owed – is legally and technically a matter of satisfaction. Debts must be satisfied. It is still perfectly normal English to speak of claims, debts, and obligations as being satisfied. The church also employed the notion of satisfaction to represent the retributive and punitive phase of the sacrament of penance, and we still speak of making satisfaction, or a bit more archaically of receiving satisfaction regarding a point of honor. Although its earliest recorded sense in English relates to debt discharge and repayment, *satisfaction* very soon extended its semantic range to indicate a feeling, the sensation of being satisfied, of having desires fulfilled.

Release of Pressure, or Filling the Void Up Full?

Satisfaction thus became a key idea in various conceptions of the emotions, drives, and passions. The underlying metaphor of debt discharge seemed to fit sexual passion so aptly that we have not yet succeeded in breaking away from the metaphor.[1] But before satisfaction applied to sexual fulfillment, it applied to sexual obligation; it was about not begging off via headache or lack of desire; it was about the claim another had to your services and duties. It's an old story. Wyclif's fourteenth-century translation of the Bible renders Paul's First Letter to the Corinthians (7.3) thus: "The hosebonde ȝelde [must yield] dette to the wijf, and also the wijf to the hosebonde." The Wyf of Bath expounds upon this in her brash style:

> Myn housbonde shal it have bothe eve and morwe
> Whan that hym list come forth and paye his dette.

> An housbonde I wol have, I wol nat lette,
> Which shal be bothe my dettour and my thrall,
> And have his tribulacion withal
> Upon his flessh . . .[2]

She sounds something like Shylock, taking her debts out on the flesh of her debt-slave husband, with flesh, recall, being a euphemism for penis.[3]

We think of discharge in sex, though, not as being discharge of an obligation but of built-up pressures we call desires or maybe, preferably, appetites, given that the word *desire* has become a cant term in academic writing in the humanities. Not only appetites, such as sex, hunger, and thirst, could be satisfied, so also could passions, like fury and hatred, and many other motivating sentiments that were caught up in the world of both love and enmity.

But satisfaction was more than the fulfillment of a desire or the discharge of an appetitive urging; it came to name an emotional state of its own, indicating something like contentment, which was supposed to be a more positive feeling state than merely the absence of the urgings of the desire now satisfied, recalling the "peace" that discharging a debt was to buy. Presumably the discharge of that initial desire left one better off than merely back at the status quo ante, emptied of passion. Yet the exultant avenger seems something more than merely satisfied and perhaps less than content; he is, by one common view, ecstatic, glorying, pumped up, all hepped up. But after ecstasy then what? The inevitable depression of the letdown? That is rather less appealing than quiet exhaustion or languid serenity. To the pessimistic soul, exultant glorying is nothing but a setup for a letdown, if not a crash.

One would think the satisfaction of contentment a simple matter, but the notion of satisfaction soon admitted all kinds of shadings, some of them vaguely ominous or threatening as in, "Are you satisfied?" which can barely be said without a sneer; other shadings indicated a minimal idea of having passed muster, as in, "He satisfied the authorities as to his competence" or of "being satisfied with an explanation"; and some contentments were the forced "contentment" of resignation, approaching Dickenson's quartz contentment like a stone, as in

Shylock's "I am content." Satisfaction thus comes to mean the second-, third-, even tenth-best option, or worse in Shylock's case, where it represents defeat and the acceptance of dictated terms, as content as Lee at Appomattox.

"I am satisfied" is so tainted with mediocrity that we feel it necessary to restore its positive sense by coupling it with modifiers like *perfectly*, *completely*, and *very*, and accompanying it with appropriate tonal markers and facial expressions. (*Satisfaction* is tarnished by association with *satisfactory*, the grade no one could possibly be satisfied with.) Because many cases of those begrudged admissions of satisfaction – ya, OK, I'm satisfied – are in response to the settlement of a misunderstanding or of a hostile claim, the expression of satisfaction need be nothing more than the ritualized statement of agreeing to accept an apology one is not quite sure is sincere. Yet even in these settings the expression of being satisfied with the outcome is meant to mark a shift of motivational state from enmity to truce, war to peace, with an illusion of evenness and balance restored if nothing else.

It is hard to see how any term used to indicate the discharge or satisfaction of a debt, or the settling of accounts, could have avoided taking on secondary emotional meanings that would soon dwarf its creditor–debtor senses. Payback, discharge, getting even are itching to burst the bounds of returning a borrowed ox. The language of debt and obligation is also the language of enmity and friendship, because it is the language of exchange, giving and taking, of being bound and released. Such words cannot have a sociology without soon acquiring a psychology; they develop an inner life in response to their outer one.

Satis in *satisfy* means "full" in Latin. The idea of filling a void – not the idea of discharging or emptying out a build-up of pressure – is another way of conceiving of satisfaction. It is about eating and drinking, filling up the emptiness that is hunger or thirst, not about fornicating and discharging fluids or energies. Get the image of ejaculation and orgasm out of your head and substitute – where I grew up – beer and brats. Thus too the Germanic word *fulfill*, which gives us a double dose of filling up, for both the *ful* and *fill* go back to the same root. To fulfill is "to fill up full," leading to satisfaction, fulfillment, fullness.

Amidst our present cultural panic attacks about obesity there lies, however, a reminder, a rather ugly reminder at that, that fulfillment and satisfaction come with associated costs. If satisfaction is about filling up full, then there is no way to avoid the uncomfortable feeling of satiation, the heaviness of being sated, the torpor and indigestion, which in turn bring on desires to be relieved: thus enter the pleasures of defecation and urination.[4] Satisfaction as discharge comes to the rescue of satisfaction as filling up full. (Some cultures, from the Roman to the Kwakiutl, find discharge pleasure in vomiting too.)[5] I suspect that the idea of satisfaction as discharge did not first arise with sexual pleasure but with those secondary pleasures of evacuation that ameliorate the unpleasant sensations of having sated ourselves with food and drink. Even the Freudian scheme puts oral and anal satisfaction, at contrasting ends of the alimentary canal, prior to, developmentally at least, genital satisfaction.

In Old English the word *sad*, as in, "I am sad to see you leave," meant "full." An Old English translation of Psalm 78.29 – "So they did eat, and were well filled" – is rendered "Swiðe ætan and *sade* wurdan," or to translate the Old English more precisely, "They ate a ton and were full."[6] *Sad* is cognate with Latin *satis*; they come from the same Indo-European root. The history of *sad* subsumes the whole sad story of the dissatisfaction of satisfaction: from having a good meal in abundance, to the heaviness of being full, to gravity of disposition, to suppression of laughter and smiling, to plain old modern English sad, which already could mean sorrow by as early as the fifteenth century.[7] And that is only the depression that comes in eating's wake; we have not even gotten to the depression of satisfying sex: *post coitum omne animal triste*, which captures both the sadness at the cessation of intense pleasure and the sense of feeling a bit foolish and befuddled at having invested so much effort in the whole thing.

As with sex and eating, so too revenge. It is a pleasure; perhaps there is no greater. But it is as equally fraught with the problems of letdown, rebound, befuddlement, anxious doubts, and purposelessness. Says Inigo Montoya in the *Princess Bride* after he has finally succeeded in fulfilling his lifelong mission to kill the killer of his father, "You know, it's very strange – I have been in the revenge business so long,

now that it's over, I don't know what to do with the rest of my life."
Such, too, W. H. Auden's comment on what he calls the Romantic
Avenger Hero: "My injury . . . is not an injury to me; it is me. If I cancel it out by succeeding in my vengeance, I shall not know who I am
and will have to die. I cannot live without it."[8] This is Captain Ahab,
clearly, but it applies to Hamlet too.

Satisfaction is tricky business, and what I want to get at in this
chapter is the emotional side of getting even, the sentiment of paying
back what you owe, which ties up with our themes of justice, its scales,
meting and measuring. Just how is one to be satisfied? What kind of
payback really restores the spirit? What variables are there to consider?
Are there as many different types of satisfaction as there are individuals
to be satisfied? Or unless there is a big dose of poetic justice added in,
is all satisfaction a bit dissatisfying? That there is not agreement on the
matter is hardly surprising. In some cultures the proverbial wisdom is
that satisfying revenge is a cold dish, for others it is best achieved in
hot blood, or for still others, waived or denied while one proclaims
that true satisfaction lies in denying all injury, as among the Stoics,
or in forgiving admitted injury, as among Christians; these latter two
purported to be ways of being above it all.

How much is the avenger's satisfaction dependent on what his adversary's mental state is at the time he takes revenge? How tied up is his
mental state to what he imagines or knows the other's to be? And what
is the observer supposed to feel? Is all passion to be spent? Or are we
and the avenger meant to glory and to crow over the victim, as the
Greeks, and now gangsta rappers, were and are wont to do? Or do
audience and avenger split responsibilities, the audience indulging a
sense of triumph, the avenger a sense of relief, exhaustion, or emptiness, his very sense of self disappearing with his sense of purpose, as
in Inigo Montoya's case? Or are we all meant to have an inkling that
the ending was not quite right, that something more was required, that
there is an ineffaceable incompleteness to the story, that our enjoyment
and the avenger's too are imperfect?[9] So much revenge does not end the
tale but simply means that it is your turn to play defense, as when one
exults in a touchdown in the first quarter, only to lose the game in the
fourth. The discussion this time will draw from sources less medieval,

less biblical, than in the previous chapters. We will go to the movies for a few minutes.

Serving Up Revenge: Bitter or Sweet

What makes for a satisfying revenge? There are, it seems, style points as well as substantive points, issues of quality and quantity, of timing, of courage and cunning. Some cultures favor the openness of a duel or face-to-face encounters at even odds or even at unfavorable odds to show off one's courage (European upper-class dueling);[10] others prefer cunning, poison, stabs in the back, or ambushes (Montenegro, Albania, Renaissance Italy, the Mediterranean in general). And in many cultures the rules have enough play in the joints so that much is left to the particular competence and artistry of the avenger.

Revenge, says Homer, is sweet; Aristotle even thinks it a pleasure in the contemplation as long as you truly are willing and able to take it; but how best to serve up the dish?[11] Cold or hot? And might not sweetness cloy or leave a bitter aftertaste? Poor Satan, his dignity suffering by having to transfigure himself into a serpent, felt twinges of bitter shame even as he felt compelled to carry out his vengeful and honorable duty:

> Revenge, at first though sweet,
> Bitter ere long back on it self recoiles...
> (*Paradise Lost* 9.171–172)

But Satan's response shows he has been affected by the antirevenge discourse that postdates him.

In present-day Montenegro the ideology is that revenge is sweet, a pure fulfillment of the soul, and with cultural support like that, who is to doubt that many feel nothing but satisfaction in their revenges? Christopher Boehm reports that a certain Savo Todorovic, a seventy-year-old man, "explained the meaning of osveta (vengeance) thus: 'Osveta, that means... a kind of spiritual fulfillment. You have killed my son, so I killed yours; I have taken revenge for that, so I now sit peacefully in my chair. There you are.'"[12] Todorovic may be reporting what he feels he is supposed to report, or what he has been taught to tell himself he feels, although that does not mean he does not feel as he says he does or as he has been taught to feel. But he is an old man who has discharged his duty; there is nothing more to do in any event.

How did others understand the sense of a vengeful ending? Here are some things to consider. Must the avenger feel the costs of taking revenge? Must it come hard so that the sense of achievement is greater? Or do we prefer the easy revenge effected in an almost blasé confidence of cool and power, with a flick of the wrist? What is the emotional state of the avenger ideally supposed to be? Is he best motivated by anger, by grief, by hatred, by a sense of duty, by the sentiment of honor, by pity and compassion for others, or by simply going with the flow of the cultural script with no clear sense of how he is to be moved, either because the script leaves that up to the avenger or because there are several competing ones?

Our best-known revenge tale – *Hamlet* – is largely about the inability of the avenger to find any motivating sentiment, or at least one that is capable of satisfying him. And in the end he botches the revenge badly, because in fact he avenges his father only as an accidental by-product of avenging his mother in a moment of mindless fury. One hardly senses that Hamlet is satisfied. And neither are we by how he concludes matters. Instead of true vengeful justice we get a partial poetic justice and a rather dissatisfying one at that, where Claudius and Laertes die more by their own plots recoiling on their heads than by Hamlet acting as an avenger. And what satisfaction we experience is one of cathartic exhaustion, in the Aristotelian sense, at the sadness of it all, but not because of satisfying revenges; we are drained, wiped out.

The Mind of the Vengeance Target:
Regret, Remorse, Cluelessness

Satisfying revenges, beyond the simple triumphant yahoo-like "yeah" with raised fist – even this response is embarrassing to you within an hour – are hard to come by. But one problem of considerable difficulty is what you as the avenger want the mental state of your victim to be when you are avenging yourself on him. This problem has come to be something we moderns think of as a crucial one, eager as we are to reform the evil mind, to bring home ideas of repentance and improvement to the wrongdoer, to justify our vengeance as "teaching a lesson even as he is about to die." Feuding cultures cared less about this for several reasons, one of which will suffice for now: they were as likely to visit the revenge on a relative of the actual wrongdoer as on the wrongdoer himself; hence the state of mind of the expiator, other than seeing he feared you, if even that, was pretty much beside the point.

Let us approach the problem by considering a scene from Clint Eastwood's *Unforgiven*, one of the few films in my sentient life that actually deserved the Best Picture award it won at the Oscars. William Munny (Clint Eastwood) is standing with a rifle pointed at Little Bill (Gene Hackman), who lies bleeding to death from a wound to his chest inflicted a few moments earlier by Munny. Bill is about to die; he shows no fear, but he does take a moment to lament the injustice of the cosmic order:

> *Little Bill*: I don't deserve this, to die like this. I was building a house.
> *Munny*: Deserve's got nothing to do with it.
> *Little Bill*: I'll see you in hell William Munny.
> *Munny*: (barely audible) Yeah.

And then Munny, without batting an eye, shoots Little Bill dead.

Bill shows no fear; he does not grovel. He is impenitent for having killed Ned Logan, Munny's friend. No remorse at all. He does, however, express a regret, a wistful wish that his life should not end before he can finish and enjoy the house he was building.[13] But regret is a rather different sentiment from remorse. Remorse in the Christian moral scheme of penance is *the* central self-directed moral sentiment; call it guilt if you will, though the Freudian baggage borne by that sentiment demoralizes it somewhat, making it banal. The idea embedded in the word *guilt* is one of debts owed, and in Old English it was used to render Latin *debitum* (debt) in translations of the Lord's Prayer, all of which puts us squarely back to the idea of reciprocity and revenge lying at the core of our moral sensibility.[14]

Regret, though, seems to occupy a largely amoral ground, the world in which, quite simply, our luck went bad. I don't feel guilty when I wager double or nothing after winning a few hands and lose, but I sure have regrets about having done so. I may not be very remorseful about killing your brother, but now that I have been caught and am facing the electric chair, I surely have regrets about the whole thing and wish I could at least turn the clock back to sometime before I got caught, if not before I killed your brother.

But would Munny or we, the viewers, prefer Little Bill to grovel in remorse for having whipped Ned to death? Or is there more pleasure in snipping him off in his impenitent defiance; or do we feel frustrated and defeated at our inability to break his will even at the point of a gun? Don't we want him to show fear at least? Or do we recognize the imperfections and moral complexities in the world of revenge and take some small solace in his impenitence, gaining thereby the benefit of knowing that we avenged ourselves on an incorrigible reprobate, that is, on someone who had it coming, or contrarily, that we avenged ourselves on a real man, no coward he, and thus a worthy object to balance against the corpse of our good friend?

Do we want Bill's apology? Munny doesn't want Bill to be sorry about killing Ned, really sorry, except in the regretful way I am now claiming. Regret for now having to pay a price he did not anticipate, yes; regret at having his life's projects terminated, fine. Were Little Bill truly contrite, though, his contrition would undo any meaning in Ned's death. It would be like announcing to a dead soldier's parents that their son died by friendly fire. Sorry, all a big mistake; the forward observer called in the wrong coordinates. A sincere, but not excessively abject, apology would throw the whole vengeance drama into confusion; a defiant enemy helps us steel ourselves to kill him. Make him truly apologetic and all of a sudden our pity strings start vibrating; surely those of the audience would, and the avenger would feel the chagrin of knowing his public support for his vengeance was being badly eroded by his target's contrition. And then suppose Little Bill were to say, "I don't deserve to die like this, I was abused as a child." It wouldn't make for much of a movie, but it would throw the payback story into all kinds of confusion.[15]

What would Munny gain if that regret were about killing Ned rather than not completing his house? Nothing. But wouldn't Munny prefer Bill to show a more broken spirit? A little less defiance? Munny doesn't seem to care. He did take care to inform Bill beforehand why he must die: "for what you did to Ned." He has done all that he can and must do. And Munny is not a glorier or a gloater. The movie kills or humiliates all those who gloat and glory: before Little Bill (even Bill in his cynical way is a gloater), there were the comical Schofield Kid and English Bob.

But why wouldn't it still be a mini-vengeance of sorts if the apology were motivated by genuine contrition? Don't we think of authentic remorse as deeply painful for the remorseful person? Don't I gain by plunging you into a state of excruciating contrition, thereby making you your own punisher as you eat yourself alive from the inside? There is an easy answer to this that I discussed more fully in *Faking It*: you might be faking your remorse, it being so easy to fake. And should I feel reasonably confident that you are sincere, we never quite believe that people are as hard on themselves as they should be; we fear they may actually be pleasuring in their guilt, feeling rather self-congratulatory about it, and oh so moral, proud that they have such sensitive consciences. We suspect they know that they are also being prudent, that by feeling truly guilty they are getting their life back. And their present sincere guilt gives us no certain assurance that they will not offend again. The prospect of feeling guilty was not enough, obviously, to have kept them from wronging us in the first place.

There is yet another reading of Little Bill's regret that might make regret, imperfect as it is, the best we can hope for from the person we are about to blow away. This is not my idea, but one a colleague offered with whom I was discussing taking revenge for having been jilted by a boy- or girlfriend. Yes, she wants him to want her back and then for him to suffer her rejection when he tries, not exactly with either regret or remorse, but – and here is the insight I mean to call attention to – that, in her words, "there would be a certain admixture of cluelessness, a sort of resurfacing of his core stupidity in the moment of his being rejected, the very stupidity that led him to wrong me in the first place."[16]

Here, then, is another possibility: we may want our victim vaguely baffled, wondering, hey, what the hell is going on here, duh. Isn't this part of what Munny is in fact extracting from Little Bill? The cluelessness of what is happening to him and why: I was building a house. Leave it to Nietzsche to have stumbled upon this insight earlier, though he finds it already present in Spinoza. He suggests that the hardened wrongdoer simply felt his punishment to be like "a piece of fate" and that he "suffered no 'inward pain' other than that induced by the sudden appearance of something unforeseen." "Mischief-makers overtaken by punishments have for thousands of years felt in respect of their 'transgressions' just as Spinoza did: 'here something has unexpectedly gone wrong,' not: 'I ought not to have done that.'"[17]

Contemporary philosophers – for example, Robert Nozick – insist that the wrongdoer needs to know why he is dying or being punished and that the avenger must take care to give him that information.[18] What satisfaction could there be in not letting your target know what hit him and for what reason? But this view depends on seeing revenge mostly as a one-on-one affair, say, of two warring spouses or ex-friends, whose behavior is exclusively concerned with its effect on the other, the avenger being wholly obsessed and consumed by the other and not giving a damn what third parties might think; getting to the mind of the other is all. Some avengers in the Jacobean drama concur. Thus Vindice in the *Revenger's Tragedy*:

> Oh, shall I kill him a' th' wrong side now? No.
> Sword, thou wast never a back-biter yet.
> I'll pierce him to his face; he shall die looking upon me.
> (2.1.376–378)

But honor-based feuding cultures, model payback cultures, did not always operate this way. Views differed. Nozick's view simply assumes away the various forms of group liability of many a revenge culture, in which getting anyone of a certain dignity on the other side is all that matters. Do you really need to inform John that the reason he is dying is that it was his misfortune to have a cousin, Bill, who could not keep his zipper zipped? John knows full well what the risks of having a cousin like Bill are. Will that improve your satisfaction? A related matter: well-known experimental psychological evidence from the 1960s showed that "we feel better when we see that the person who had angered us has been hurt" and that "we do not have to hurt our frustrator ourselves in order to experience this pleasure."[19]

Recall too that for all the myriad worries our archetypal Jacobean avenger, Hamlet, manages to come up with, the one he evinces absolutely zero concern about is whether the vengeance target must know why he is about to die. When Hamlet forgoes his perfect chance to stab Claudius in the back while the latter is praying, it is because, Hamlet says, he might send Claudius to Heaven by killing him in the midst of his prayers. Hamlet couldn't care less about stabbing him in the back unawares. In fact, the perfect death he imagines for Claudius is taking him fully unawares as he sleeps or as he is engaged in sex, to kill him "When he is drunk asleep, or in his rage, / Or in th' incestuous pleasure of his bed, / At game a-swearing, or about some act / That has no relish of salvation in't."

Revenge was seldom, if ever, a two-party affair; it was invariably played before an audience, and much of the satisfaction one took in one's own revenge was "caught," like a disease, or like laughter, from the response you observed in others to your actions. If they liked your performance, then you most likely would like it too; if they did not, it would be like ashes in your mouth. They scored your performance, and there was no reason you could not get a high score for dropping your target completely unawares with a single shot that took considerable marksmanship. Remember Grettir's avenger, Thorstein, who gained honor for avenging Grettir out in Byzantium. The person who got his head sliced off by Thorstein did not know who or what hit him or for what. No matter; it was a glorious revenge.[20] Informing your victim of why he is about to die is not a necessary component of a perfect revenge.

Killing Him or Keeping Him Alive for Scoffing, and Other Fine Points

If there is no perfect and completely satisfying way for the vengeance target to act – groveling, apologetic, defiant, regretful, clueless – then what is one supposed to do with him? Kill him? Or prolong his life in order to make him feel his inferiority for the rest of it – not physical torture, mind you, merely daily humiliation and chagrin? Both options have a list of virtues and vices supporting them. And it is not always clear that we, the consumers of the vengeance tale, will agree with what the avenger decides to do. We in the audience often want more aggressive paybacks than the avenger sees fit to give. How often when some vile rapist is dispatched by the avenger's bullet does the movie audience feel that it was insufficient to repay the motiveless harm he inflicted on his victim? And if that is unsatisfying, the indication that Iago will be turned over for prolonged torture after the play ends satisfies us not at all. It is as if he got saved by the bell.

Shakespeare has a way of not satisfying our sense of justice in the ends he visits on the villains in *Lear*, *Hamlet*, and *Othello*; he seems too lenient. But in *Twelfth Night* he is too harsh in his revenges on Malvolio. Is that because it's a comedy? Does the comic license excessive revenge? *Macbeth*, though, works to take stunning revenge on Macbeth, but the sense of its perfect ending has little to do with how satisfying Macduff's revenge may or may not be for him or for us (for by that time we are rooting for Macbeth in spite of his having murdered his lord and guest and Macduff's children) and much more to do with the stunning uncanniness of those weird prophecies homing in on him. Might it not be that Macbeth's obsession with the prophecies, and being lulled into complacency by them, makes his inner state partake of that cluelessness my colleague desired to witness in the guy who had jilted her?[21]

Perhaps the perfect Shakespearean revenge takes place in a play that denies that revenge is taking place, and there the culprit is given his life but is systematically humiliated and unmanned, kept alive to suffer his shame, all in the name of mercifulness. When mercy unites with the excesses licensed by comic vengefulness, watch out. I have already belabored that theme in my discussion of *The Merchant of Venice*, a play that shows that mercy may be the most satisfying of revenges precisely because it keeps its victim alive to let him suffer his degradation for a lifetime.

Mercy offers other perverse pleasures to the avenger, such as the extra chagrin your enemy suffers when you deny that your most excellent revenge is revenge at all, the very denial being part of the revenge. St. Paul and the Stoics long ago recognized the brilliance of this move: "Beloved, never avenge yourselves, but leave it to the wrath of God; for it is written, 'Vengeance is mine, I will repay, says the Lord.' No, if your enemy is hungry, feed him; if he is thirsty, give him drink; *for by so doing you will heap burning coals upon his head.*" (Rom. 12.19–20).[22] Paul does not mean to leave God much work to do, for if Paul is not quite advising killing your enemy with kindness, he surely means you to torment and frustrate him, indeed he means you to drive him crazy.

There are other kinds of endings. Some of our vengeances are necessarily private, so that no one knows, especially the victims, that they are objects of revenge. Anyone who has been a waitperson and dealt with obnoxious customers has enjoyed knowing that they will soon ingest various bodily fluids of your own with perhaps an occasional succulent addition from members of the kitchen staff. How does that make for a satisfying revenge, you ask? One must catch what satisfaction one can, and this is not bad as satisfactions go. The powerless must make do within the constraints their lack of power imposes upon them. But there are pleasures to be had in such revenges, as many of you well know, not just for the avenger but for whatever audience you choose to enlighten. It is the pleasure of putting something over on someone, of outsmarting him, of having him look ever so foolish, for it is usually left to the powerless to have to resort to low cunning in their revenges. The powerful can just hack and hew. And yes, those obnoxious customers are utterly clueless.

If you don't like such lowly revenges you can blame them as small-minded, effeminate, slavish, and you can employ all the Nietzschean machinery to dismiss them. Yet even such secretive revenges are not always very secret. It is not as if the waiter doesn't gain status with his coworkers for striking a blow on their behalf. Some of the most cunning of revenges are still played out before an audience. No, we will not play the part of Atreus and let the patron know what horror he has supped upon, but we will regale our workmates and friends with the tale of our wondrous revenge.

In our unheroic, utilitarian world we may even contemplate a different form of revenge, a perfectly rational prudential form of revenge in which we do not have to cut off our nose to spite our face. Edith Wharton puts it this way: "The civilized instinct finds a subtler pleasure in making use of its antagonist than in confounding him."[23] The pleasure must be very subtle, for this kind of revenge is not much different from a business deal in which one party comes off slightly better than the other. Wharton's world is one in which true revenge has been redefined so that it largely disappears into a multitude of petty revenges while all cordial relations are maintained, no single act of vengefulness ever rising to a level that it cannot be denied to be what it is.

So which is it? Does our sense of an ending require death, or only humiliation? This shouldn't be an either/or. One crucial consideration is just how we understand the avenger himself to be motivated. Is he motivated by anger, as Aristotle believes he is, or by hatred?[24] Anger is understood to be assuageable, hatred less so. Anger exhausts itself too quickly to see some important matters through to their conclusion, or it is too susceptible to being undone by apology. Anger can be satisfied. Hatred, too, in Hobbes's view, misses the delicious subtleties that are available to the proper avenger. Hatred and revenge seek different outcomes, he says: "Revenge aimeth not at the death, but at the captivity and subjection of an enemy . . . To kill is the aim of them that hate, to rid themselves of fear; revenge aimeth at triumph, which over the dead is not."[25] Hobbes argues for a strong link between drawing things out and revenge.

Time figures in revenge in some key ways. For instance, revenge is not properly the instantaneous slam back at the person who slams us; that is mere reflex or a barroom brawl. A boxer does not avenge each jab he takes, although he might be understood to avenge an earlier loss to the same opponent.[26] True revenge contemplates some passage of time – for stewing, for fantasizing, for plotting, for terrorizing the other. As the Viking proverb had it, "Only a slave avenges himself immediately, though a coward never does."[27] The sense is that the slave is too stupid to be strategic; he is all anger and fury and hits back in dumb reflex. Still, his stupidity is morally superior to doing nothing; that is the coward's way, unless you can sell your doing nothing as a grand gesture of forgiveness granted from a position of strength. So even though Hamlet engages in paroxysms of self-loathing for deferring his revenge, in fact his delay is his best revenge against Claudius, for he succeeds in making Claudius a nervous wreck. The point is that a skillful avenger wants more than to kill or to make his enemy suffer a lifetime of misery if kept alive: he wants him to experience the torment and terror of anticipating the revenge that eventually must come.

In Hobbes's scheme, killing your victim is a sign of hatred and not of what he calls vengefulness, which aims at humiliation and domination. Such drawn-out humiliation and domination are possible in a closed, aristocratic society or in a closed honor group out in the middle of the North Atlantic, where exit is not much of an option; but in the American West, how is William Munny to gain the benefits of walking about town forever crowing over an abject Bill? In this newfangled big country Bill would simply pick up and leave and start fresh elsewhere, the same as Munny was to do in the movie's epilogue to avoid any of Bill's avenging angels, if he had any. Hobbes's view that the best revenge is to keep your adversary alive for a life of abjection is hardly suitable for all occasions. Too many people and cultures have decided that it is best to go for the kill.

There is something awfully final about killing. Even though people who engage in bloodfeuds know that killing is a move in a continuing exchange of corpses, killing still provides dramatic closure in a narrative that limits its story to one offense and one payback. There are practical matters, too, not just matters of narrative closure, or of crowing and glorying over a humiliated foe. People don't like being humiliated, and they will avenge their humiliation if they can. To avenge their degradation is about the only way they can ever recover their moral and social worth. So it might be better to kill your foe as a practical matter, even if less satisfying, especially if he is kinless and you do not have to worry about his brothers or sons.

In saga Iceland, among those true aficionados of feud and revenge, the perfection of revenge lay less in its aesthetic characteristics than in whether it worked; practical issues trumped aesthetic or emotional ones.[28] Whether anger or hate was being indulged, neither should be indulged to the extent that it was stupid. The hard practicality of opting for killing rather than subjugation led Montaigne to argue that it is cowardly to kill the object of your revenge, because to do so is evidence of your fear of his reprisals.[29]

Our movies tend to side with the Icelanders on this issue. It is movie bad guys who want to humiliate enemies and keep them alive too long. When they decide to kill they draw out their killings and linger over them so as to terrorize and humiliate. The James Bond movies turn this into high camp.[30] The extra time the villain needs to orchestrate his perfect revenge provides the hero with the opportunity to escape. Unwise in Hollywood, unwise in saga Iceland. But is Hobbes even right about hatred? Does hatred seek to kill, as he says, or can't it be rather well satisfied with making the other hurt, forever and ever? The hater might in fact need the hated one more than any angry man needs the object of his anger. Our very identities are often intimately dependent on our enmities and hatreds, no less than on our loves; they not unusually involve the same people.[31]

One problem is that the enemy has only one life to give, and one little life may not be enough to satiate the thirst or hunger driving the avenger if his satisfaction depends on satiation, or to discharge the hate or fury, if his satisfaction depends on release. Such an avenger does not just want to kill his enemy, he wants to *keep on killing him*. One death is not enough. No wonder the Greeks kept stabbing and dragging and mutilating the corpses of the enemy. So too Othello: "O that the slave had forty thousand lives! / One is too poor, too weak for my revenge" (3.3.445). And later, "Had all his hairs been lives / My great revenge had stomach for them all" (5.2.73). But neither is Othello sure whether it is not preferable to make the one death a long slow torturous one: "I would have him nine years a-killing" (4.1.175). Killing your foe was insufficiently satisfying, and not killing him was not satisfying either; you wanted to destroy his being, but resurrect it so as to destroy it again, to visit upon the foe the image of his own corpse. Yet the desire to bring back the enemy so as to kill him again and again can, with just a little tweak, become the subject of a horror film, where no matter how many times you kill Jason, Michael, or Freddy, he will return in the sequel to haunt you and be killed again. No satisfaction there, but a nightmare of eternal recurrence, and not just on Elm Street.

What satisfies observers may not always be what satisfies the avenger; the former may sometimes achieve a nearly perfect enjoyment, but the latter? Observers have it pretty easy. From safe seats in the audience, or watching TV back home, they may lust for a lot more than the guys at the sharp end see fit to give. The avenger often has his desires for a perfect revenge compromised by the fact that he is the one who must do the dirty work. World War I memoirs indicate with some frequency, for instance, that the soldiers in the trenches might hate their counterparts in the opposing trench less than the people back home hated them, less even than they themselves came to hate the people safe, warm, and dry back home for whom they were supposed to be fighting.[32]

The avenger is constrained in his revenges by his need to keep his legitimacy intact, to operate within limits that still make him, if not quite a good guy, at least not a villain. There is thus a small paradox here: the avenger must do less than the audience wants him to do or the audience may abandon his cause. The audience will have to sate itself on the endless supply of the villain's henchmen, whose distinguishing traits are their inability to hit anything with their weapons and their serviceability for dying by the dozens at the excellent marksmanship of the good guys. Even in those Jason, Freddy, and Michael horror films, the heroine's desire is to save herself first, to get the hell out alive, and only incidentally to kill the offender. The moviegoers, on the other hand, want to see her destroy her tormentor in the most gruesome way possible.

If there were a perfect satisfaction, we expect that it would put an end to matters. But we do not even know how to envisage perfection: what our anger wants may not be what our hate wants. Our sense of justice is not even sure how we want the victim to think about what we are doing to him. We are not sure how much of it is up to us and how much up to the wishes of others, or to expectations the culture has erected that we seem never quite to attain or never quite to feel the sense of their rightness when we do attain them. Why should revenge be different from sex? In the end practicality takes over. You do your duty, or you get mocked for not doing it. Or cultivate a stoic style and suffer the mockery with nary a blink.

Return now to Munny standing over Little Bill.

Bill: I don't deserve this, to die like this. I was building a house.
Munny: Deserve's got nothing to do with it.
Bill: I'll see you in hell William Munny.

Even as the movie is ending there is not quite closure, though it is hard to find a movie with a more powerful and fitting end than *Unforgiven*. There is still a disagreement as to whether the balance has been struck. Bill claims that his desire to complete his house should figure into the accounting. He refuses to accept that the end of the movie is a final resolution. He promises Munny to continue the dispute in the afterlife. Munny himself is not even sure that the matter is over in this world, let alone the next. He thus must holler out threats into the stormy night to cow any would-be continuers of the feud and the movie. Munny rides out of town threatening to come back, like Jason or Freddy, if these people mistreat the whores or do not bury Ned properly. One is never sure in the revenge world whether the end is the end, unless no one lives to tell the tale. Munny was concerned enough, as I noted, to disappear further west lest Bill have avengers unaccounted for.

Munny's line "Deserve's got nothing to do with it" seems to remove his whole revenge story from the idea of debt and repayment. But that is not what he means to do; he takes care to let Bill know why he is about to die: "for what you did to Ned." It is all about paybacks. To Munny's mind deserve's got nothing to do with it because he knows that had the movie started back when Munny was blowing up women and children, Little Bill would be the avenger tracking down a villainous Munny. Where we start the story will determine who owes and who is owed. Desert is a function of an arbitrary decision as to when to start the camera rolling, or of what state of affairs to declare the initial equilibrium position.

The genius of this movie is that it owns up to the imperfections and impossibility of perfect revenge even as it knows that blood revenge is the only satisfying way it can end. Imagine how limp and tawdry the story would be if Munny, moved by a penitent Bill, decided to hug and reconcile – the blockbuster: *Forgiven*. No, the revenge is not perfect, though it is hard not to thrill to it, and it is infinitely more satisfactory than had there been none. Munny is not Hamlet, of whom Hazlitt said, "Because he cannot have his revenge perfect, according to the most refined idea his wish can form, he declines it altogether."[33] And a special satisfaction is to be had from the film's smartness about knowing that for all its hand-wringing about the ambiguities of revenge, a revenge story must end in revenge. Even Hamlet finally comes to realize that he must accept the demands of being cast in a revenge drama, resist it though he tried.

If art and philosophy have this hard a time in attaining perfectly satisfying revenges, then we should tip our hats to the genius of the oddmen, the judges, and the elders at the gate, who manage in the real world to substitute satisficing ends for satisfying ends, as well as real avengers who simply did their duty. That is why it is so important that there be wiggle room in the idea of balance and evenness: it allows finality to be something more than a mere aspiration or an elaborate cultural self-deception. Not every act of violence generated an endless cycle of tit for tat. The oddmen made sure of that, and sometimes the principal players accepted that in fact a "rough" balance had been achieved.

ELEVEN

Comparing Values and the Ranking Game

WE STARTED WITH THE SCALES OF JUSTICE and returned to them when Shylock had them in hand to collect his forfeiture. Our discussion has never been far removed from settling accounts, determining the price of wrongs and the value of debts and obligations incurred. The notion of getting even, of restoring balance, so crucial to the idea of justice, necessitates measuring. The metaphors are insistent. Thus justice is "meted" out, which is the Germanic word for "to measure." And "measure for measure" is but another way of stating the law of the talion, abstracting it from its biblical concrete eyes and teeth and generalizing it. And the talion loses none of its ominousness for such generalization; it even hints at ever more dandyish ways of striking the balance.

Justice required measuring and meting that was meet, but meetness meant accepting a certain practical roughness. Portia was overprecise and picayune expressly to deny justice. Rough justice can thus be rough in more than one sense. To us "rough justice" means unofficial revenges taken out on the body; that kind of justice was rough because it contemplated pain, fear, and blood as part of the payback, the roughness serving as both a just means and a just end. But justice also meant that *roughly* getting it right was to get it right plain and simple. The demand for excessive precision could lead to perverse cruelty if it were achieved, or to paralysis at the near impossibility of meeting the demand of an overprecise precision.

The Politics of Comparing Values, or What's Eating the Incommensuralists

In the late 1980s to the late 1990s, there was a bit of a brouhaha over the issue of commensurability, or comparability, of values, engaged in mostly by philosophers and certain philosophically oriented law professors. More than a few of the philosophers who made the most important contributions to the debate also had partial appointments in law schools.[1] Although the precise issue at stake often varied from writer to writer,[2] the core dispute pitted two groups. One believes that significant values or goods cannot be compared or measured one against another. Each value is good in its own special way, and so reason cannot aid in deciding between one such value and another. (I will refer to those who hold this view as apples-and-oranges people.)

Those in the second group believe that one can make a reasoned choice among values by ranking them with respect to some criterion, in short, by comparing them. But what folksy name can I give them? None suggests itself. To refer to them as commensuralists is to cheat by putting Latinate gravity up against mere fruit. (You see we can even compare the word *apple* and the word *commensuralist*.) To use "the everything's-got-a-price people" would be unfairly negative, and not quite accurate, as we shall see, in that it suggests (1) that money is the sole, best, or even always a possible measure for making these comparisons or (2) that something more precise than a defensible and sensible ranking of better, same, or worse need be demanded for commensurability, or comparability, of some sort to obtain. Both 1 and 2 are false. Commensuralists will have to do.

The value of a walk in the park cannot be measured against reading a Trollope novel, say the apples-and-oranges people; nor can the value of a life as a clarinetist versus a life as a lawyer (the example is a leitmotif in this literature owing to Joseph Raz).[3] Reason cannot settle it. But others make a fairly strong claim that if the choice is presented in a little more detail, reason surely can settle it.[4] The flurry of debate has petered out, but nevertheless I want to add a few points of my own to the commensuralist side in this and the next chapter, mostly by calling attention to our deep compulsion to rank and compare everything from quarterbacks to old loves. I mean to add to points already on the table in these debates the telling force of the premodern materials I am comfortable with. Talionic cultures, feuding and revenge cultures, made difficult comparisons all the time; people knew they had to justify their choices in a manner convincing to others or suffer a significant increase of risk to their life and limbs. There was no way to avoid complex trade-offs, especially in matters of social and moral worth, in a world of honor and feud. A culture of honor required that actions (and mere states of being too) be valued with respect to honor; no easy matter, but that did not stop them.

Meting and measuring, law and justice, depend – still today, but more starkly then – on balancing what at first sight appear to be apples against oranges, such as you against me, my eye against your hand, my honor against your cow, your daughter against my beached whale, even your faith against mine, as when Iceland officially abandoned paganism in the year 1000 and converted to Christianity by putting the matter to the decision of an oddman named Thorgeir. His decision was remarkable for the sophistication of the trade-offs it made and the reasons given to justify them. He balanced a new requirement of baptism and public confession of Christian faith, which his decision implemented, against a continued right to expose children, eat horsemeat, and sacrifice to the old gods in private. Thorgeir invented the public–private distinction to make the necessary trade-offs. None of his reasons went to the truth of the competing faiths.[5] These people were good at articulating complex compromises that required trade-offs of what we often dismiss as noncomparable.

My suspicion is that the apples-and-oranges people in these recent debates – who, by the way, outnumbered the commensuralists by a considerable margin in the symposia and essay collections given to the topic – were less motivated by a deep belief in incommensurability than by prior political commitments and matters of taste that they felt to be imperiled by certain forms of cost–benefit analysis. Some of them fear that commensuralism jeopardizes liberal pluralism. Others have been goaded by sheer vexation at the dominance of a certain kind of economistic literature, often in service of market-oriented political conservatives, coming mostly from adherents of the law-and-economics movement rife in the law schools in which many apples-and-oranges people work.

One can hardly blame them for getting aggravated by economists who assume away almost everything that is interesting, complex, and playful about human motivation and use a flattened theory of rational and self-interested motivation to "explain," without shame or modesty, absolutely every aspect of psychic, social, and moral life and to recommend policies on the basis of such oversimplified explanations. My own annoyance with this easy economizing drove me to cheer on the apples-and-oranges position at least to the extent it annoyed the economists, until I heard the still small voice: what would Skarphedinn (my favorite of favorites among saga characters and indeed any character in all heroic literature) say?

There are in this literature several issues in play, which though kept formally straight do not always get kept emotionally and spiritually straight. One, the big question: whether values are comparable or commensurable. Two: whether it is moral or proper to make the comparison even though it is possible to make it. And in three we introduce dollars and market exchanges: even if it is possible and moral to rank values, whether ranking them in units of dollars is possible and, if possible, whether moral. And as a corollary to ranking them monetarily, an issue I might make point four: whether it should be permissible to trade or exchange these things in the market for dollars, or whether we rather should make them inalienable, that is, prevent their marketability.

In other words, one can be an everything's-got-a-price person and still be horrified that there be prostitution and markets in human flesh; such a person can without any incoherence argue that such sales are best prohibited.[6] Even a pro-marketeer might think that the market doesn't always get it right. He will admit on occasion that there can be market failures, as when Amazon.com has his book, with its tenure-awarding, even Nobel-Prize-winning arguments, listed at 478,464th on the "best-seller" list two days after his mother bought three copies no less.

But if the free-marketeer finds his own emotions and feelings at odds on occasion with his professed beliefs, so too, it would seem, do the apples-and-oranges people. Thus, a commitment to incommen-surability of values never seems to prevent its adherents from taking and rationally defending strong political and moral positions that they believe are superior to the positions they reject. To the extent that the apples-and-oranges people are motivated by a concern to protect cul-tural pluralism, it would seem that they draw a line as to some cultures; they are not relativist all the way down. A culture might have to satisfy what Joseph Raz would call eligibility criteria, which can be rationally determined: that is, the cultures must be good enough to make the team, at which point we can say, well, each is good in its own way.

Raz or Elizabeth Anderson – the two most formidable and sophisti-cated proponents of various types of incommensuralism – hardly would think the Taliban just another culture incommensurable in intrinsic value as against liberal democracy. Neither would have a hard time proving that it is a defective moral system, significantly worse for human flourishing than any number of other possible social and moral arrangements. And they would have no trouble showing me why the culture of honor and payback I so admire is inferior, at least from the point of view of weakling academics like me, to democratic liberalism.

Anderson has little patience with honor culture, mostly on the grounds that its denizens are commensuralists with a vengeance.[7] Their insistence on determining the relative worth of people, wergeld itself, is an embarrassment to apples-and-oranges people; merely to measure life in terms of dollars is fraught morally, though they, like most all of us, have made their peace with such measurements operating in restricted domains. For instance, they would accept that life insurance no longer raises the grave moral issues it raised in the nineteenth cen-tury, when its opponents argued it should be made illegal as nothing more than blood money.[8]

We academics are familiar with a weakened form of honor culture. In our world, rank – where one stands in the esteem of peers – is much of the game. Pure pursuit of knowledge motivates all but the most ardent scholars only intermittently. One craves some recognition – not that much, mind you; a hair more than what one's colleagues get will do. Even more upsetting is that this esteem sometimes comes to be expressed, although imperfectly, in dollars. Other times, the currency is the size of your office, the number and quality of your outside speaking engagements, your popularity with students, whether your writing is attended to and where, and things too pathetic even to own up to privately, let alone mention in public.

But for now let us focus on dollars. It is not that salary is the clearest measure of what economists would call your marketability; that is much too thin and bland a way to see it. Your salary is more aptly thought of as your wergeld, a number that indicates your rank. Salary is not a private matter in public universities. The salary schedule does not reduce esteem to dollars; dollars, rather, are commandeered to reveal the mysterious ways of esteem. Mean deans have been known to raise one person $100 more than a colleague he had heretofore been even with to please inordinately the one, and to shame inordinately the other. The $100, I need hardly belabor the point, is not working as money in that instance, not at all. The apples-and-oranges people, much better than the economists, understand that money can often be more than money.

Would it not be a better world if we could get out of this exhausting and often demoralizing competitive moral economy? Good luck, I say, for it is impossible to avoid judging the quality of one's own work and where one stands, and the work of one's, to use a loaded term, "peers" and where they stand. Even if we moved to a pure seniority salary scale, some other coin would do the work of determining who gets to look down on whom. And that is precisely the problem. It seems one deep motive pushing the apples-and-oranges people does not go so much to ranking values per se; rather, it is that by so doing, what usually ends up getting ranked is people. And they are for the most part sincere believers, as I am, in the virtues of a fairly strong form of equality – political equality to be sure, but also more equal distributions of goods, although policing any equality worth the name necessitates commensuration to see whether some people are not getting more than their fair share.

Funny, though, as I have noted earlier, is that honor societies, so hated by the apples-and-oranges crowd, require rough egalitarianism. Honor is a game played by players understood to be roughly in the same league. People in honor cultures jealously police others who may be getting so big that they no longer belong on the same field of play. They employ all manner of leveling mechanisms to knock them back down. Among these, envy-laden gossip and ridicule play an important role, and if that doesn't work, harsher methods, killing or exile, may be employed. Yet, at the other end, they do not want people getting so contemptible that they fall out of the game, either; hence the endless shaming of the slacker to motivate him to get his act together so that he will be able still to play the game.[9]

The apples-and-oranges people are also revolted by the vulgarity of monetizing rank; if rank there must be, let it be marked in more tasteful coin. Instead of dollars we can rank values on how well they promote dignity, or merely on how well they *express* a commitment to human dignity. But that merely rewrites the whole ranking game in another register (though it does avoid monetizing it in dollars). How are we to determine that one position is more expressive of human dignity than another? Whose interpretation of the meaning of an act of Congress or a social custom or a religious practice is to prevail? Why do the apples-and-oranges people take one political position rather than another, and how do they come to the decision? They do not flip coins. No way are they willing to concede that those positions are mere rationally unjustifiable preferences even as against a smaller group of options they deem rationally eligible. They believe their moral and political commitments to be justifiable, as well they should.[10]

The apples-and-oranges people, in other words, have no trouble ranking, taking political positions that they defend as better than the alternatives, or taking moral positions they defend as better than the alternatives, and of trying to convince others they are right. Their anticommensuralist position is itself a *moral* position in some of the versions in which it is presented, not merely a formal one about the limits of rational decision making. But one also suspects that their position is equally an aesthetic one, to the extent one can distinguish the moral and the aesthetic. Mostly it is money talk that offends them; it is the crass reduction of everything to dollars, the dollar as the unit of all values, which vulgar talk, they argue, not without reason, coarsens us in serious ways. It is the language of trade-offs that the economists use that irks and offends them, the discourse of indifference curves. They believe it reveals or in fact creates an insensitivity to certain sacred values. The hucksterism, they feel, of everything for sale, everything tradable for something else, is no less offensive for coming from academics and policy wonks than from snake-oil salesmen.

Indeed it is one of the few positions in which academics of left-liberal views are likely to find themselves in the majority, with the red states solidly behind them. There is more than good reason to be annoyed with some aspects of the unabashed economic evangelizing that goes on in economics departments and law schools. Some wonder at the unapologetic blitheness with which economists shrug off the nontrivial descriptive failures of their theories of human motivation and instead train their students to behave as economic theory says they should. Students who once bought beers and maintained conviviality amidst drunkenness, making sure everyone took his turn getting a round, are now trained to calculate their advantage, to pursue it, to see what they can get away with in order to grab as much of the gains of a trade that they can buffalo others into agreeing to: it is a world of markets and trade-offs, hard bargaining, operating, and threat advantage. A law school teacher sees the results. Those of my students from econ, political science, or business backgrounds will shamelessly argue that a 90–10 split in the split-the-pie bargaining game, with its take-it-or-leave-it offer, is rational to both parties because each is better off than he would be were there no pie. Only an economist could be surprised, or dismiss it as irrational, that the person offered the 10 percent cut refuses it with indignation, greatly preferring zero.

Such is the complacent security of the ivory tower that the people who argue this way run no risk of getting beaten to a pulp. You could not make this kind of offer in the talionic world unless you had either might or right on your side, but you had better make sure you had one or the other, and in the long run it was safer to rely on right rather than might, because even the mighty had to trust enough to the good will of others that they could close their eyes and go to sleep without being axed in their beds, as some indeed were. The business schools have an answer; they will say these kids have taken only the intro course on bargaining theory and still have not gotten all the riffs down involving side bets and precommitment and signaling strategies; they will also talk about bilateral monopolies and transaction costs, bloodless terms that miss the power and pull of honor, manners, emotions, insult, disrespect, and fair play.

Some of the law-and-economics people who have recently discovered social norms will actually discuss the merits and demerits of things like not leaving a tip when you know you will never return to a particular restaurant. And the reason they devise for leaving a tip? It is even more chilling than their having almost succumbed to the temptation to stiff a minimum-wage waitperson they will never see again because it might be economically rational to do so. Ready? You couldn't guess if you tried. You will be pleased to know that the reason you tipped the waitperson you will never see again was that you were signaling to those accompanying you your willingness to follow social norms, so that they could trust you not to rape or kill them if you thought you could get away with it.[11] Makes you want to shut down the universities, does it not, or at least the law schools? But would this kind of silliness drive you to the apples-and-oranges position?

The Ranking Game

No wonder humane sorts are driven to careless fury and to throwing the baby out with the bathwater, a dead metaphor that is partly revivified by the themes of this book. The baby they throw out is our deep compulsion to rank, to rank almost anything and everything. Is ranking not the very stuff of sport and life? What are the standings? Who made the playoffs? Who won the playoffs? And we make everything a sport in this way, matters trivial and matters serious. Who is the prettiest in the class? Who is the ugliest? Who will get the A's that the curve restricts me to?

But you say that these are not measuring incommensurables, but commensurables? Well, maybe that is because we suspect that there are always commensurables or else we wouldn't be playing the game. You don't see us playing the game of which insurance policy tastes the best or which square root you find the most sexually attractive. Some things are indeed noncomparable; it is senseless to rank and compare them. That it makes no sense to rank square roots by their sexual attractiveness hardly casts doubt on the general comparability of values, but only on some aspect of the particular instance.[12] When we play a ranking game a good part of the game is to find a sensible basis for the ranking. Much of the game is thus taken up with proving the justifiability of the game itself, or there is no point in playing it. And we always find a point in playing it; it is the stuff of lying awake at night, the stuff of entertaining conversation, the stuff of grim triages.

If you insist that playing who is the prettiest is not a fair example, let us take one Anderson uses. How about comparing works of art, not just one genre at a time but all genres together? Anderson derides not only the silliness but also the impossibility of rationally ranking the ten billion greatest artistic works of all time. Those who insist on doing so are nothing more, she says, than "philistines, snobs, and prigs, precisely those least open to a free exploration and development of their aesthetic sensibilities."[13] Philistine I own up to, but not priggishness, though I do get a bit sniffy if someone ridicules the Icelandic sagas. I love nothing more than having arguments with friends, admittedly sometimes in my cups, about which are the ten greatest lyric poems, the ten best novels, the ten smartest writers of all time, the ten best movies, the ten best comic movies, the five most overrated actors, the ten biggest frauds in the academy. The point is that it is fun, and fun because it is not the least bit senseless and not the least bit easy. The very difficulty of the ranking is not a sign of the failure of comparability at all, but a challenge to our discernment and reason-giving abilities.

It may indeed be foolish to take the list to ten billion and this seems in fact to be Anderson's point; but the top one hundred or one thousand? It is true that once we get to the mid-ranges of any large array, like any bell curve, things clump. And as any teacher who grades tons of papers knows, one B+ (formerly a C) looks very much like another on any scale you care to put them. But once we get to the very bottom of the heap, we can surely get back to sensibly listing the ten worst, no less than the ten best. And even those clumped in the middle are not incomparable; they are equivalent in their mediocrity.

Incredible how many of us seem driven to rank bests and worsts, and it is more than a contest over who can shout his preferences the loudest. Inevitably someone disagrees with your rankings; and when she does, you do not answer, "Well, you have your views and I have mine," at least not initially. You defend your rankings; she defends hers. You come up with reasons; you sometimes admit error and change your mind when she presents better reasons for hers than you did for yours; you seek, in other words, to convince others of the merit of your rankings. Initial positions are altered or abandoned as a result of argument. Someone will end up teaching you why you missed what was attractive or appealing or ironic in this particular novel or movie. When all alone, you argue with yourself and probe to explain why you find this novel better than that one, better in what way, how important are the different ways, and so on. The entire thrust of these kinds of discussions and arguments is to get into the other's mind, to solve the intersubjectivity problem, and these very arguments and the effect they have on our views and tastes are proof that we do get to one another.

Such arguments are inseparable from what reflection is, what critical appreciation is, what education is, what teaching is, what the experience of an artistic work at least partly is. Admittedly some go in for it more than others. The ancient Greeks were compulsive rankers. Did they not make evaluating their playwrights an annual event? Did not some of the greatest tragedies get written because of the competitive ranking game? *The Divine Comedy*, in the estimation of many the greatest work of literature, is an homage to ranking exactly what the apples-and-oranges people say, at least once you satisfy Raz's eligibility requirement, is unrankable: moral merit. There is perhaps no more nuanced and complex a ranking, as well it must be: for you had better be able to justify convincingly why some people are condemned to various circles in Hell, while others get to work off their sins ascending the levels of the mountain of Purgatory, while others reach their stopping point at the differently ranked spheres of heaven.[14] Even our funding agencies for the arts are forced to play this game, and across genres too. The National Endowment for the Humanities does not ask would-be grantees to buy a lottery ticket, but to write an application and provide samples of work. We cannot avoid ranking in conditions of scarcity, in conditions, that is, in which we cannot fund everyone or give everyone first place. And it is remarkable how rarely we resort to lotteries even in areas where one would think taste reigns supreme.

Could that be because we suspect that we should have to give reasons even for our tastes? Well maybe not for matters of food or sex – but then, even then, how many times have you found yourself explaining to yourself or others why you now have come to prefer blueberries to raspberries because of the looks of disbelief on their faces when you declare for blueberries? Or when you fancy Mary rather than Jane, or Bob rather than Mary? When Pascal says *le coeur a ses raisons que la raison ne connaît point* (the heart has its reasons of which Reason knows nothing), he seems to be arguing the irrationality of certain affections of the heart, but he is subtler. He does not say the heart is irrational *tout court*. The wit of the saying is that the heart too must develop means of knowing and ordering the claims made upon it; the heart has reasons. It too ranks its affections, and not only by intensity but also by quality. The heart does not say, though Reason might, well, I love Mary and I love Jane, so I will flip a coin. The heart does not flip coins except as a joke or out of despair. Should it come down to deciding for Mary for the inarticulate reason that she has a special something, then the heart must have adjudged that she has more of that special something than Jane.[15]

I asked my seminar students how many times in the past week they had found themselves playing ranking games. Almost all could recall that they had. Theirs were not the ten greatest novels or the five best Shakespeare plays, though one had ranked the best American rock bands of all time, but were more of the ilk of who was the smartest or dumbest in the seminar, who was the last person you would sleep with in this bar, who the first, who was the last in this class, who the first? But the prize was won by a woman who said that she and her friends had ranked world leaders by their hair. We were all flabbergasted, yet within nanoseconds of her mentioning it we all understood perfectly and started playing the game.

Do not object that these games finesse the problem of finding a single scale. One must always find a single scale, or a metascale. That is what is difficult and the substance of the game itself. Who was greater – Gretzky or Jordan? Jordan, you say? But would Jordan do as well on skates as Gretzky would in a pickup basketball game? Who broke more records in his relevant sport by a greater margin? You mean you think Jordan because basketball looks cooler? Did you factor in how poorly hockey translates to TV, how little relative exposure you have had to hockey compared with basketball? How does your reverse racism figure in, so that no white, especially one who looks like Gretzky, could be as great an athlete as a black, especially one that looks like Jordan? I am not ready to say apples and oranges yet or ever, are you?

If questions like these are how sports lovers refine their understandings of sports, consider the pop music scene. My fifteen-year-old daughter, Eva, with whom I was disputing the five most overrated songs, repaired to her room to retrieve a magazine she had recently bought: *The 150 Greatest Rock Lists Ever.*[16] How about that? A ranking of rankings. In her view the lists are meant to get you mad, to provoke you into proving them wrong by coming up with a better list. What do you mean that "A Hard Day's Night" is ranked number 1 among Beatles' songs? Could it possibly be better than "A Day in the Life" or "I Am the Walrus"? But the magazine gives reasons: "Where their earlier singles were reassuringly sweaty, this anthem to post-work shagging is far cooler. The guitars virtually invent the mid-60s jangle. That moment just before the final verse when Paul McCartney's climatic 'Yeah' overlaps with John Lennon's incoming 'Mmm' is the single most life-affirming moment in their career." And now we are off to ranking competing life-affirming moments. There are rankings of the ten greatest rock songs about cars, the twenty most forgettable follow-up albums, and more. How could the incommensuralists be so wrong, at least on the issue of reasoned comparability?

No, these games are manifestly not about simply declaring preferences. Even games about who is the most or least sexually desirable lead to argument. People give reasons, seek to convince others of the rightness of their decisions, and people are led to change their minds. If it is largely a matter *de gustibus*, it is hardly for that reason not worth disputing. Quite the contrary. Tastes change; they develop; they can be formed, by becoming informed, educated, cultivated, trained. Why bother with these rankings, these cultivations, if we do not think some tastes are better than others? That is what "having taste" is all about.

Such disputes are proof of sorts that tastes can be disputed; the point is whether it is good manners to do so. These arguments are the very stuff of determining merit and demerit; it is about honing critical capacity and justifying decisions. Greatness of a song, specialness of hair, are hardly simple matters, but are compounded of several values and features that mix and bond in various ways. Some of these compounds have no name. Yet that does not mean we cannot use that nameless value to make reasoned comparisons. It only makes the comparison harder to make or harder to articulate, but it does not make it impossible to make, though out of sheer exhaustion we might often say: "OK, OK, I guess it's just a matter of a taste."

Examine that statement. How likely are you to say it in a tolerant tone of welcome at the wondrous richness of diverse views and desires, or in a respectful tone full of appreciation of the other's unique subjectivity? It is ever so likely that we resort to the language of incommensurability – I guess it's just a matter of taste – out of frustration or boredom. When we say it's all apples and oranges we do not mean to make any grand philosophical statement about the incommensurability of values; we mean only that we are tired, frustrated, fed up, or have finally determined that our interlocutor is an uneducable knucklehead, snob, or sicko. There is no reason liberal pluralists should find solace in incommensurability. Intolerance is also a risk of accepting the apples-and-oranges way of looking at it.

I confess that some might find many such ranking games morally offensive. And that claim suggests that those who make it hardly think these ranking games are trivial. The claim is partly that such comparing and measuring disparages human dignity, that it does not treat sacred matters with sufficient respect. In short, these games often have serious stakes. But this is a very different claim from the claim that the ranking game itself is impossible to play rationally. An everything's-got-a-price person may not like these games either and may justify his dislike on purely utilitarian grounds: that the psychological and social gains achieved by those ranking above average do not offset the pains of those ranking below average. But those kinds of judgments need to be made on a case-by-case basis.

What is wrong with ESPN choosing a play of the day, or the plays of the week across some ten different sports, ranging from golf to football, hockey to tennis? What is wrong with grading your students' essays? And it is not just a matter of taste. There are standards. Remember that Onund Treefoot was declared to be the deftest of all one-legged men in Iceland, but the saga took care to provide the basis for the plausibility of the claim; and recall, too, the Icelandic legal expert who ranked outlaws by their greatness. He gave reasons to justify his selection of Grettir. Let those who finished second or third come up with competing criteria: had they held out as long as Grettir? Had they been avenged in Byzantium?

Ranking at a Viking Feast

Recall the Old Norse word for even, *jafn*. The Norse combined the word with the word for "man" thus: *mannjafnaðr*, literally, man-evening, man-balancing, man-comparing. It was used to describe two distinct actions.[17] One: it referred to the balancing of dead bodies in arbitration settlements discussed earlier, the offsetting of the dead Hoskuld against the dead Skarphedinn.[18] Two: more crucial to our present discussion, it was the term for a quasi-formal contest, a kind of slanging match, which seemed to figure regularly at feasts, especially when people were in good spirits with drink. The game was to choose the best man in the district, town, or hall; it was, in short, our ranking game of who's the smartest, prettiest, sexiest, coolest, best athlete, least sexually attractive. Arguments were made and reasons were given, for honor was a complex matter. Honor could inhere in physical toughness, to be sure, but not in that alone. One got credit for belonging to an honorable family, credit for being a successful and generous farmer, a good poet, a great athlete, a brilliant scholar, a cagey lawyer, a wide traveler. No matter. It was all ranked and compared. It was not easy to do, but people did not fold their intellectual tents by declaring impossible what is merely difficult.

One may still wish to argue that it is not good to play man-evening games, and the sagas will give some good reasons to take that position. These ranking games could get tense, much tenser than the debates in the 1990s about commensurability. Reports one saga:

> There was a lot of ale drinking. They spoke of "man-comparing," who was the greatest man in the district, the foremost chief. And there was no agreement, as is often the case when there is a man-comparing. Most went with Snorri the Priest as the greatest, but some named Arnkel. There were even some who named Styr.[19]

Snorri's response was to have Arnkel killed. Yet another saga mentions a *mannjafnaðr* in which Erlend claimed no one to be as courtly or as brave as Kalf, while Illugi claimed that that prize belonged to Thorgrim. "The tale ended this way: Erlend killed Illugi for no other reason than that."[20]

Even the risk of dying in the enterprise could not keep people from ranking men according to their worth. Do such disagreements suggest that what they have stumbled upon is incomparability? Not in the least. These games never end in someone saying it's all apples and oranges, that man-comparing is pointless. No one says that Kalf cannot be compared with Thorgrim or vice versa. There is no judgment of noncomparability. The disputes are over the criterion and getting the measure right, or arise over simple frustration at another's refusal to be convinced by your arguments. There would be no point in playing these games again and again if people were not mostly in accord on the principles and standards of judgment. Above all, these very games were a way for people to think about the norms of merit and demerit, to acquire and to advance an understanding of the standards of excellence, the norms of right action, in their society.

A lot depended on these competitive rankings, just as it did when they were made in high school years ago or does in your workplace now. More tense than the *mannjafnaðr* game was the feast itself where the ranking games were played, for the host had to seat his guests and the seating arrangement was its own man-comparing game. The seat in the center of the long table was the seat of honor, and the proximity of your seat to that seat indicated that the host considered you higher than the man one seat further down. The arrangement was not just that farmer's whim, unless he was nuts. His decisions had to be reasonable and defensible. Everyone generally had an idea of who belonged where; they would also make allowances for the host having to favor certain people to whom he had special obligations of kinship or clientage. Still, fights broke out, as you might guess.[21] The most famous and bloody of saga feuds had its origins in the anger of one woman who was forced to move to a less honorable seat in deference to another.[22]

To compare small things with great: one of my uncles ceased talking to my mother for years because he felt he had been seated too far from the head table at my sister's wedding, and I have more than one colleague who has gotten huffy about the office he was assigned, believing it to be inappropriate to his dignity even though we have a seniority rule for assigning them purposely to avoid correlating offices with merit. But even though you get the office that was available at the time solely by virtue of being older than any of the other claimants, the size of the office nonetheless works some perverse magic. A student comes by for office hours and says, "Hey, Professor Miller, nice office." To which I reply with false moroseness, "It is a sop to my getting old and nothing more." Yet I cannot deny that I feel honored. And though the glow lasts but a second or two, to be fast replaced by my feeling foolish about the depths of my vanity, about the very profoundness of my shallowness, I am more pleased than displeased, way more in fact. Lord, what fools we mortals be.

Montaigne plays the game too. One of his essays – "On the most excellent of men" – gives his top-three list: Homer, Alexander, and Epaminondas, the great Theban general who defeated the Spartans at Leuctra, whom Montaigne names the greatest of them all. The essay provides the reasons, not just among those three but why other worthies did not make the final three. He thus feels obliged to explain why Epaminondas is superior even to Socrates or why Alexander beats out Caesar, who Montaigne admits gives Alexander a run for his money. It is worth quoting if only because the imagery of weighing and balancing human value so reinforces the themes of this book: "Even if Caesar's ambition were more moderate [than Alexander's], it was still disastrous: it had as its vile objective the collapse of his country ... so that when all is put together and weighed in the balance, I cannot do other than to come down on the side of Alexander."[23]

It is not impossible to rank people against each other as to their worth with respect to a given value or with respect to their worth in general. The very lie to the proposition that we can't rank them is that we do it all the time, not only teenagers and sports nuts but also Vikings and geniuses like Montaigne. It might, as I said, not always be wise or nice to do so. That the rankings might involve many different plausible and crosscutting, even conflicting, reasons does not end the matter; it only increases the degree of difficulty. We develop and argue for weightings and give reasons for the weights we assign to the reasons.

Independent of concerns about whether such rankings are too often beset with error to be of use, there is the widely held belief, as I mentioned earlier, that ranking demoralizes losers more than it exalts winners. Some have even argued that if commensurability is true it is best to disguise the fact, even when the issue is not about rankings using a dollar metric.[24] At my children's grade school there are no longer races in gym class because parents complained that their kids weren't winning or were feeling depressed about losing. Soccer was banned at recess – I am not making this up – because some kids complained to their parents, who in turn complained to the principal, that they were not being passed to enough or were not scoring.

Although this might spell the end for America as a world power, do not worry: these same parents are buying their children after-school tutors to catch up and paying for summer camps to train them in soccer as well as in taking the SATs. Much child's play now takes place in uniforms, in leagues with referees, so it seems that most everyone, independently of their commitments either pro or con on the commensurability issue, are nonetheless highly competitive man-comparers and man-measurers when it is crunch time for their kids. Cheating has been renamed training and has become its own virtue, and if some feel justification is necessary, that can be readily found in solicitude for the self-esteem of the child.

Do not assume that honor societies, however, were any more virtuous on this score: stacking the deck in one's own favor is as old as Jacob stealing Esau's birthright and as the chariot race at the funeral games in the *Iliad*. Nary a Viking drinking bout goes by without someone accusing the other of cheating, with the frequent outcome that a short sword or an axe settled the matter.[25] But then they were not committed as an official matter to the discourse of dignity, so though they may come off as big babies, they do not come off as hypocrites.

Let me add a point in clarification. The issue of ranking might be perceived as different from the issue of commensurating, this latter requiring a precise metric so that we can get to the even point in matters of debt, revenge, and justice. One is about ordering with respect to a value, such as honor, worthiness, coolness; the other is about paying back what you owe, finding an amount that compensates correctly your harms or satisfies debts of justice and commerce.[26] Though arriving at an initial ranking is hardly an easy matter and leads to the kind of evaluative arguments we have described, it can usually proceed without having to answer "how much" with any precision; categories like "a little bit" or "a lot" do just fine. Sometimes, however, the need for greater precision is forced upon us, as when I kill you out of envy and am killed in return by your brother. Are the sides now even? Do I equal you in death, if not in life? Not if all agree you were the better person. What will it take to make up the difference?

This kind of question is standard fare in the sagas and in feuding cultures in general. And the how-much-better-or-worse question need not be very much harder to answer than it was to provide the justification for the rank ordering in the first place; in fact, it often seems easier, for the very reasons adduced earlier regarding the play in the joints of measurement and evaluation and the general expertise people developed in resolving disputes of this sort.

I have already mentioned in passing an Icelandic story in which a man, Thorstein, is casually introduced at the story's start as such a hard worker that "it would take three men to work as hard."[27] This looks like the stuff of a tossed-off, stale comparison, meant to be taken loosely as a way of praising Thorstein's industriousness and showing that he ranked high on the scale of workmanly virtues. But when Thorstein kills three of Bjarni's servants, such loose talk hardens into a tough-minded and ironic literalness. The dispute is settled on terms that

Thorstein pay himself over to Bjarni to compensate him for the three men he killed. Everyone thinks it a just, an even, settlement, because, after all, everyone knows Thorstein was worth three standard-issue guys. The transition from ranking talk to equilibrating and balancing talk was handled with aplomb.

And is it not telling that their word *mannjafnaðr* describes both the action of *ranking* men in the slanging match and of *evening* men, balancing men as equal, in arbitrated judgments, in which they showed no hesitancy in making up the difference between one man and another by adding silver, sheep, or land, or exiling one of the parties? To their mind the notion of *mannjafnaðr* was equally serviceable to mean ordering or to mean evening. And it makes perfect sense that it does, for the information needed to decide evenness is the same needed to decide greater than or less than, and in some cases it also resolves the how much question, which never seemed to bother them much anyway, for they knew how to get it right.

TWELVE

Filthy Lucre and Holy Dollars

THE MAN-COMPARING CONTEST was not about reducing the value of men to money. It was about ranking them according to honor; material wealth was only part of the equation. Commensuration does not require coin, though some types of trade-offs are easier to make when there is a ready way to monetize values. The difficulties talionic cultures had in pricing life were not moral or conceptual; they were practical. Their problems with pricing what we think of as priceless were the inevitable problems of finding a workable medium of exchange.

Coin, as I noted earlier, may not yet have been invented and once it had been, it was in chronically short supply. One had to select among various kinds of money substances, some providing the measure of value, others acting as the means of payment. Thus it was that people, pigs, silver, grain, peppercorns, cloth, hides, blood, or oxen could now be a measure of value, now a means of payment, some more likely to play one role than the other. Even when there was coin, the exchanges were hardly much easier, for coins, with their varying weights and silver content, presented the same problems of quality that sheep or humans did when they served money-like functions. Just as some animals and some humans are more valuable than others, so too not every silver shilling was in fact a silver shilling. That is why merchants did not abandon scales as a tool of their trade until quite recently. It behooved the careful merchant to weigh and assay the legal tender. Yet if exchanges were not always easy to make, they were still made. People had rules of thumb about setting values and exchange rates even when markets were distant or held infrequently; they looked to respected members of the community who had reputations for getting appraisals of value right.

Setting prices on the most sacred of things was not a dirty notion among them. On the contrary: a high price was how best to express something's intrinsic value. But, as I have observed on more than one occasion, there was still something less honorable about taking silver than taking blood. Does this show that for blood there was a certain incommensurable *je ne sais quoi*, a certain moral virtue to it that was beyond compare? Hardly. There was no disputing that prices could be set on anything. The problem was not in measuring value. The problem was in the more specialized money function of finding the appropriate means of payment. Their moral qualms about blood versus money were over which of the various types of moneys used as a means of payment was best suited in any given situation. And sometimes blood was quite simply the best money, the best means of payment, and they understood exactly that to be the case. One did not even have to transport it to the place of delivery. The vengeance target carried it there with him. But even though blood had its special virtue, that too had a price; it could be traded off. Remember what Thormod said: "Everything is compensable."

Here is the crucial point: might it not be that these people were so much better than we are ("we" means to include economists as well as incommensuralists) at commensurating what the apples-and-oranges people claim are incommensurables *because* they did not have ready access to a single standard currency or plentiful coin? Talionic peoples were used to making difficult and complex calculations because there was no single easily available money substance, and for some – the biblical Hebrews, the Germanic medieval north – not even Arabic numerals. All transactions, I reemphasize, involved negotiating not only the price but also the means of payment. They were not lulled into analytical laziness by thinking that if dollars or shillings couldn't work to measure the differences in value then nothing could. They were startlingly resourceful and intelligent. Recall in this light the sophisticated homily and charade in chapter 5 that solved the problem of comparing the pains felt by two men by putting their pains on an index measuring the mutually acknowledgeable *frustration* of their not being able to take revenge for their pain.

Our ready markets and ready dollars may have made us intellectu-
ally less skilled at comparing and commensurating than these tough-
minded peoples, no less than growing up with calculators has made
our children a lot slower at doing sums in their heads. At least kids still
know that sums can be added, multiplied, and divided in human heads;
they have not declared that it cannot be done because they have a hard
time doing it. Not that the let-the-market-solve-it types are any better,
for they try to make everything a matter of dollars when a smart elder
at the gate, or a village wiseman, or a saga oddman would know that
dollars are not always the best or only measure of value or even always
a possible measure, and surely not the only or best means of payment.
Sometimes blood was better at being dollars than dollars, body parts
better than silver, a marriage into your family worth my undertaking
to teach your kid law.[1]

This last example shows that it was not only in matters of corrective justice that talionic peoples evaluated and priced astutely. Most
marriage and fosterage arrangements, hostage exchanges, and slave
trading – transactions, in other words, involving humans – were not
corrective. True, these people were not faced with the complexity of
the allocative decisions of the type the government of a modern nation
makes as it decides what to fund and how much, the stuff of policy
wonks. Yet closer to home, few of us have lived in such conditions of
scarcity that forced you to slaughter a good portion of your herds each
fall because the fodder you had managed to harvest could at best get
only half your animals through to the time when the grass started to
grow again in the upland pastures. Should you discover in February
that you had not culled enough animals in November, you will now
have to kill off more than you would have had to had you got it right
in the fall; and you feel the anguish of having wasted the fodder eaten
by the beasts that you now have to kill. You pray for an early spring.
People who were good at making these kinds of calculations had a skill
other people would hire them to exercise. The same tough decisions
were often made at the birth of a child.

For us, the problem is much more an anxiety about the relation
between money and certain things felt to be sacred. This is surely the
chief anxiety of more than a few of the apples-and-oranges people.

The concern is not just the unseemliness but also what is claimed to be the immorality of the idea that everything has its price, and if it has a price then that must mean everything is for sale. Remember the points we need to keep straight. One is that it is impossible to compare values; on this point the apples-and-oranges people are wrong, both as a matter of fact and as a matter of psychological and social practice (the ranking game). Two is whether it is moral or proper to rank even though it is possible; the ranking game again. Here views are mixed. It depends for what end and in what context. Three (combining points 3 and 4 noted in chapter 11), does that mean we subject some of these values deemed special to market-like exchanges – if, that is, they are of the sort that are measurable in dollars – or do we decide to make them inalienable?[2] Let us consider the third point further. Our social practices and our moral sentiments in this domain are fraught with ambivalence and confusion.

Dirty Dollars and the Making of Pricelessness

In her unfailingly interesting book *Pricing the Priceless Child*, Viviana Zelizer traces the history of damage awards for accidental death of American children. In the nineteenth century, damages were based on the loss of the child's wages to the household; and the awards as a result were low. Children were not worth much when their value was a matter of their economic contribution, especially if they had not been working. The sacralization of children changed that. They became too precious to work. But with child labor laws preventing all but certain types of proper kids' work – selling newspapers, babysitting, acting, and farm work – the price of a dead child dropped to almost zero. Jury awards of $50 or even $1, the classic slap-in-the-face award to reflect a technical harm too trivial to value, were not unknown. But now the low valuation started to scandalize a public that felt that damages should reflect a child's new moral value. The "useless child" (Zelizer's mischievous phrase) became the "priceless child." The useful working child of the nineteenth century went cheap. But that changed: "Unlike the nineteenth century when price determined value, value would determine the price of a sacred child."[3]

Even Simmel, who detailed the ways money became a universal solvent rendering everything tawdry, promiscuous, undistinguished, and undistinguishable, had to admit that money could also bless certain things with sacral value – not just confirm an intrinsic value already there but actually create the sacral value.[4] To the chagrin of the economist, numbers have different values independent of mere mathematical difference. Certain amounts are magical and can change the essence of the object to which they are appended – really high ones, clearly, but really low ones too. Numbers ending in zero, especially a lot of zeros, have a different feel to them than numbers ending in other digits. Large numbers can be as sure a sign of the sacred as there is.

Some may lament that a Picasso is put up for sale, but that it fetches $104.1 million means it occupies a place of flabbergasting ineffability.[5] It sets the boundary of the "priceless" way beyond our understanding of sacral "pricelessness." Zelizer is right; "priceless" does not mean no price, but rather a special price in which the number of dollars makes the dollar mean something more than mere dollars. If the sacred must be sold for money let it be for a price "beyond compare," for what in wergeld cultures would qualify as a "king's ransom."[6] The sacralization of the child, it could be said, changed the status of a child from slave to thegn, to a modern avatar of the 1200-shilling man. Contrast this with the ham-fisted attempt to gain a modicum of sacralization posted on highway construction sites in Michigan in 2004: "Kill a worker, $7500."[7] Just as some sums can exalt, so other sums can insult.

A Picasso already is conceded to qualify as sacred, even priceless. But how sacred and how priceless? One way of finding out is to have our owner refuse a $104.1 million offer; some would cheer him on, but the painting wins either way – whether he sells or refuses. The Picasso is now sacred-plus for having that stratospheric price pinned to it. And is not clear whether we credit the owner with very much virtue for refusing to sell; plenty of art lovers, and even some apples-and-oranges people, might either find him crazy or else know him to be so rich already that $104 million here or there is no test of his virtue. Suppose, though, that the Picasso owner has become tired of his sacred Picasso but still primly refuses to offer it for dollars, exchanging it instead for a Rothko. This exchange simply does not add anywhere near the same sacral power to the Picasso as would either refusing or accepting $104.1 million for it. Not unless the Rothko can show it is playing in the same priceless league: the league of paintings that fetch more than $100 million. Both paintings, in other words, have to be roughly the same value as measured by some more vulgar medium. Barter does not quite avoid the issue of dirty dollars.

Such swaps can also lead to the ridicule of the one who got bested in the trade, as when Homer remarks on the stupidity of Glaukos exchanging his gold armor for Diomedes' bronze in an access of friendship on the battlefield: "Zeus son of Kronos took Glaukos' wits away from him."[8] It seems that crass, mercantile thinking was a quality epic heroes had better have too, along with berserker-like recklessness, but not such recklessness that it might lead one to make a fool's exchange of his precious armor for standard-issue fare. As we saw earlier, Icelandic warriors calculated in the heat of battle the costs of the injuries and deaths they were inflicting. You needed both a hot head and a cool head within nanoseconds of each other in these kinds of violent encounters.

If there is a moral problem with translating things into dollars and thereby leading them to market, sellers, as an historical matter, have come in for more of the blame than buyers; whereas those who buy back, redeemers, are cast as moral heroes. (I will return to redeemers in the next section.) Sellers continue to be perceived as morally inferior to buyers. The drug and prostitution laws take this attitude, as do consumer protection laws, in which the assumption is that sellers will be knaves and tricksters unless otherwise restrained and that buyers are inevitably fools who need all the help they can get (unless they buy to resell, which means they are really wolfish sellers in sheep's clothing). Throughout history those who sold goods for money were often hated and mistrusted outsiders or treated as outsiders if they were insiders; they were dirty and polluting: Jews, Armenians, Chinese in Southeast Asia, Germans in the Slavic east.[9] They traveled across seas and deserts or floated down the Mississippis of the world like so many Kings and Dukes who needed to skip town before their unwary buyers became aware of the shoddy wares they had bought.

You cannot, however, sell without buyers; nor can you buy without sellers. Each brings the other into being; nonetheless it has been hotly disputed who rightly should bear the blame as first cause of the evil. The conventional Marxian Frankfurt school adherent, many a Christian moralist, and a slew of left-of-center academics see consumerism and excessive cupidity as mostly the fault of purveyors creating false demand, generating needs, fomenting addictions and false consciousness that create markets for unneeded goods. Others, contrarily – namely, Mandeville and later Sombart[10] and those following them – have argued that demand generates production, that if demand was not quite the necessity that mothered invention, then surely our endless vanity for trinkets, amenities, and markers of status was mother enough. Producers were spawned by the vices of vanity, luxury, sexual display, and emulation that motivated would-be purchasers. The sellers in this theory are innocent. Though fathered by vice and vanity they in fact acquire virtues by catering to the vices of consumers: industriousness, inventiveness, mastery, and self-control, among others – real social and moral virtues that are blamed sneeringly and tiresomely as bourgeois and capitalist by artistes and such.

In barter-like situations it was never clear who was the buyer and who was the seller. Whom do we blame then? When one of the bartered goods could also be thought of as money, the seller was the one who received it. A person who went house to house with a pack was clearly an S, even if he took his payment in cakes or turnips. A person was also labeled S if he traveled across a desert or a sea with a cargo to unload, even though he bought goods at his destination and took back another cargo with him. People who lent money were S's of a particularly loathsome breed, selling that which should not be sold. It is one of the great ironies of the Christian West and the Islamic East that for much of their history, to sell money raised more moral hackles than to sell people.[11] And it is an even greater irony that such an anti-usury rule ends up, perversely, sacralizing precisely that which it meant to blame: money. Like the crown jewels, it cannot be sold.

Among sellers, habitual sellers of goods – merchants and traders – were more suspect than occasional sellers, although they too suffered, mostly by being considered pitiable, because Fortune must have played rough with them to reduce them to selling or pawning that which even they held sacred. One thinks of the feckless aristocrat who must sell the family jewels or patrimonial estate to pay his gambling debts at one end and, at the other, the dutiful daughter of a poor family who prostitutes herself to earn enough to keep her parents and siblings from starving.

Buying, though it has tended to fare better at the hands of moralists, is not given much moral grace either unless it is necessities that are being bought: nongluttonous amounts of food, modest drink, and modest shelter are OK. Anything more than that is considered to be in the service of vanity, gluttony, luxury, sins of the flesh and spirit. Reconsider the $104.1 million Picasso. Do we loathe the seller more than the buyer of that painting? Could it be that when the price paid to acquire something gets high enough we think the buyer to be a self-indulgent fool? Sacred as a Picasso might be, actually to shell out that kind of money for a painting strikes us as frivolous, self-aggrandizing, and a total misprision of values. I am not sure we would feel that much different if it were Ernst Gombrich buying it so as to commune with it, or Bill Gates so as to improve the décor of his bedroom for whom it would be a mere drop in the bucket. Actually, a consortium of investors who mean to turn it around for a higher price in a few years but display it in a museum in the meantime will strike us as considerably less foolish and self-indulgent. Big numbers work their magic again, though not always in a positive way. Sometimes they are an indication of how crazily out of whack our values have become.

Since when does sacralization require that kind of number? Hell, shouldn't $10 million be enough sacredness? Poetry and music, at least since the age of print, do not present the kind of moral problem painting and sculpture do. Shouldn't we penalize painting and sculpture a few points in our ranking of the thousand greatest works of art? By their being confined to a single artifact, they invite extortion, selfishness, and all kinds of hucksterism. They get the benefit of being scarce as a consequence of our comical beliefs regarding "authenticity." My beat-up paperback of *Hamlet* is just as good a read as your hardbound copy, but a perfect knock-off of a Vermeer or even a high-resolution color reproduction of it is somehow thought not to give me the visual

187

and contemplative pleasure of your authentic and hence priceless Vermeer, to which I cannot get close enough to see the brushwork anyway.

Hamlet is pretty near a public good. The Vermeer is given both property- and liability-rule protection in the nine digits' worth of dollars. And sorry, even a Vermeer, by that most perfect of painters, cannot match *Hamlet*. Though each is perfect in its own way, we can rank perfections. One is perfect in its Vermeerness, in its restrained intimacy, the other perfect in its infinitude, in its sheer mind-boggling grandness, a composition in which every line is its own Vermeer, where a mere freezing sentry at his post can answer, "For this relief much thanks. 'Tis bitter cold, / And I am sick at heart." Priceless, but it could not bring $104.1 million because I can download it for free or memorize it. So we can rank works of art on the quality of their perfection, even if dollars are not the appropriate measure; we mint better moneys to do it. And *Hamlet* may not even be Shakespeare's greatest play.

Buying Back and the Sacred

Anthropologists have described primitive economies in which there are several different "spheres of exchange." The classic example comes from the Tiv of central Nigeria, who have three such spheres.[12] The point is that money is not a general solvent equating all goods, but there are different monies appropriate to different spheres; only things within a sphere are to be exchanged for each other. Among the Tiv, the first sphere is for purely utilitarian daily items: food, goats, chickens, baskets, pots; the second is for prestige goods: cattle, slaves, and certain ritual offices, which are exchangeable for brass rods; the third is for rights-in-people: wives, children. In fact, though, despite the ideology, it is possible to move items up and down the spheres by means of exchanging them for brass rods, or even by some clever bargaining in out-and-out swaps, like Diomedes and Glaukos. It is the rare object that does not get diverted or seep through the permeable membrane that separates the spheres. The ideology of incommensurability and nonexchangeability is one thing, the reality of porous membranes another.

Igor Kopytoff has shown that, for all our moralizing about making some objects strictly inalienable and others effortlessly alienable in the marketplace, all objects vary in their degrees of susceptibility to transfer for a price at different points in their life cycle. Objects have biographies; and alienability and inalienability are parts of the life cycles of most all objects, though clearly in significantly varying degrees. In the course of an object's life it will experience different levels of interaction with the market. Although some things are produced solely for the purpose of market exchange they need not forever be mere commodities. Some things are bought and then consumed. End of matter. Others are bought and then may become favorite objects; they may even become heirlooms. Yet these too might be recommoditized should times get hard or tastes change.

Kopytoff uses the slave as an example. Though a pure commodity when captured or bought, a slave nonetheless takes on a new identity as he is "resocialized and rehumanized" in various degrees into the host society. He may even become a household favorite and end up running the show, a Mameluke of sorts, no more sellable than the master whom he now "owns."[13] And if a slave might start as a commodity and end up inalienable because too valuable to alienate or too powerful, a free man's market inalienability, as I noted earlier, was always at risk among raiding, warring, and feuding peoples, or in a society that required a person to pledge his body to secure his debts. Though he started out free, he might spend part of his life not only as a commodity but also as a means of payment, as security for his own debts.

As among the Tiv, objects in our sphere of the sacred – the sphere that we consider to be comprised of inalienable objects – can be diverted to other spheres, spheres in which their inalienability is compromised or suspended.[14] Not all objects are born sacred; some are upwardly mobile. Take old mason jars that become collectibles, or nineteenth-century farm implements that are put up on walls as décor. Once on display in a museum a commodity from the eighteenth century is rather differently on display than it was in the milliner's shop where it was first sold. Display in one means "for sale"; display in the other means "Show respect, feign interest, and do not touch." But tastes change and some objects are downwardly mobile; those antique tools on suburban walls may not retain their stylishness and then they might find themselves priced as junk rather than art. Once secured in a glass reliquary in a museum, the now sacred object should have found a permanent resting place free from the germs and vices of the market, but it can still reenter the market in an emergency or as a plunder of war, or it can circulate by reclamation, a special kind of redemption, if the legality of what is collectible, such as Indian artifacts, changes. And what of those saints who were decanonized as not having existed? What of their relics now?

Any sacred inalienable – a Torah, a saint's relic, a person, a family photo album – can immediately enter the world of price when it is stolen or held hostage. We do not sell our children, but we will surely buy them back if they are kidnapped, or collect the insurance we took out on the sacred objects the thieves got away with. Buying back the sacred and inalienable when it has been captured or held hostage is a sacred duty. It is about redemption, the very stuff of obligation fulfillment, the sign of love, the moral imperative behind revenge, the ultimate promise held out by God to the poor and to the faithful. Though selling degrades, buying back exalts.

Could it be that the insecurity of possession in rough-and-tumble stateless societies, in which debts were secured with bodies and hostages were taken to secure peace agreements – could it be that the obligation to buy back was always too much a part of their revenge or honor world ever to indulge the talk of pricelessness? Buying back, not selling, was the primal transaction; reactive yes, but constitutive of their moral world. Redemption was first among duties, and it meant that anything that mattered had a price.[15]

Yet even buying back has its limits beyond which we today feel the price in dollars is too high and it becomes necessary to pay in blood instead, the kind of redeeming that leaves the kidnapper dead rather than rich at your expense. And you make blood the specie not only because meeting the hostage taker's crazy demands encourages more hostage taking, but also because the price the villain is asking in dollars is just too high, even if you are good for it. Asking a "priceless" sum indicates that the hostage taker has no intention of being paid in coin; blood is his argument. Should he be holding Picasso himself hostage and asking $104.1 million for his release, I bet we would send in the SWAT team if negotiators couldn't get the price lowered.

It is crucial to recognize the moral distinction between putting up for sale and buying back. A society may not deem everything that is "yours" to be entitled to property-rule protection; certain things may be declared inalienable, unsellable no matter what someone is willing to pay you for them. That, however, may not stop a thief from stealing your inalienable object. And then society will have to come up with a value, a compensatory price, or else there is no protection worth the name for precisely those items it declares too sacred to be exchanged. Judges and legislators cannot escape it. Set prices they must, and unless they are in a talionic culture, they set a rather low price, the price of liability-rule protection we discussed earlier. Remember those scales of justice.[16] The iconography of Justice represents a commitment to an ideal of commensurability, of setting a price on things taken from you against your will. That is why she is provided with scales. And that is why most societies have trained or recognized a class of people who are very good at making these kinds of evaluations.

Everything for Sale

I have suggested that what is driving the apples-and-oranges people in part is not the truth, if there is any, of the incommensuralist position, but rather their horror at the idea of selling the sacred, of putting prices on that which dignity demands should not be sold, or valued in such common and unseemly ways, as certain of the more over-the-top market priests are known to do. This is a much narrower claim than the larger one about the incommensurability or noncomparability of values, because, as I have noted, one can believe in the commensurability of values and still believe that certain things should not be sold.[17] The story is an old one: the seller and his quest for money was believed to dissolve values, status, and dignity into a soup of tawdry slop, one spoonful as bad as the next. The trader disrupted certain useful illusions; he created and fed cravings. He offered everything for a price; he was a pimp, a go-between, a purveyor; money went a-whoring or made everything and everyone a whore; nothing meant anything because everything was for sale.[18] Selling for a price polluted the thing bought and sold, the person buying and the person selling.

The imagery is familiar and I need not rehearse it at any great length. But this view is hardly an objective view of money or of the people who deal in it. This view keeps bad company with lazy aristocrats and energetic anti-Semites, those who looked down for various reasons on trade and the trader. This is an irony that should give some pause about the company one keeps: the antimarket, antitrader, anticommercial, antibourgeois spirit of the PC left academic makes him or her the heir of the old aristocratic distaste for working in trade, whether that view is embodied in the person of an Achaean warrior, a sixteenth-century English duke, or a nineteenth-century impoverished habitué of St. Moritz looking for a rich American heiress to fund his uselessness. The people? Hoi polloi? They higgle and haggle, or in more successful guise they were the fathers of those rich American heiresses, men who hawked their daughters to old European blue bloods at fancy watering holes to gain grandchildren who would soon learn to be ashamed of them for having been in trade.

It should hardly need to be pointed out that money is as money does. The antimarket people want money, too, but they want it to know its place and to be devoted to purposes deemed dignifying, or paid out indirectly via various subsidies, just as aristocrats wanted it via inheritance or by marrying rich spouses and felt it should be devoted to the glorifying, because wasteful, purposes of sumptuous display. If through its history money has been demeaned as barren metal or filthy shit – it is never quite clear whether sterility or fecundity is what makes it revolting – at least as excrement it can fertilize schools and the arts.

In addition to the claimed moral revulsion at putting the sacred up for sale is the serious concern that the producers for many such markets would be overwhelmingly poor people whose kidneys, wombs, or babies might be their most valuable and readily tradable assets. A few noticed an even more ominous cost.[19] Rather than money and the market reducing everyone to indistinguishable commoditized cloned mass-produced units as Simmel and others have argued, it would do quite the opposite: it would rank, categorize, and distinguish with a vengeance.

A market in babies would discriminate powerfully among babies. Some babies – healthy white ones – would go for very high prices, and others – not white or not healthy – would have lower prices, some even having negative prices because there would be no takers unless the babies came with a subsidy. The image of such a divorce between price and "value" would be a truth we would not wish to see so starkly revealed. The market would rewrite the wergeld ranking system on infants. It is pretty much that way now, although adoption agencies veil the ugly truth a little better than markets would. These are the kinds of things better kept obscured, swept under rugs, in the name of dignity. So what if it is an elaborate deception, or a secret everyone knows; it may be, the argument goes, that we gain so much more from the deception even if we have to pretend to be deceived.[20]

In other words, the moral claim, the beneficial moral claim that dresses itself in the idiom of the pricelessness of human dignity and human life, risks being made a joke were we to see just how cheap most of us are in dollars – kill a worker, $7500. How do we keep up a belief in the dignity of each individual human when most of us go so cheap? It may be that the unseemliness resides less in putting the sacred up for sale than in the horror at discovering the ease with which the market values it. The so-called incommensurable and priceless stripped of its pretenses turns out often to command the price of a low-end widget.

In the end it may be a good idea not to force upon us the knowledge of just how much cheaper we are in a dignity culture than we would be in honor-based talionic cultures – if, that is, we managed to lead middlingly honorable lives. As long as a few jury awards reach a magical multiple of a million for a wrongful death action here and there, the illusion of pricelessness continues to be nourished.[21] One wonders whether the discourse of human dignity, its commitment to pricelessness, is itself a new coinage designed to compensate us for the failure of the dollar value of our lives to confirm our moral beliefs as to their "true" value. We cannot bear to see price so completely unhinged from what we think is "true" worth.

In conclusion, recall the issues of the preceding chapter. The apples-and-oranges position is one of partial luxury; it is parasitical on wealth, a certain level of material well-being. It is telling that the standard dilemma used to show incommensurability in this literature is whether to pass life as a clarinetist or as a lawyer, or whether to read a novel or take a walk in the park. Given our general level of security and wealth it makes it much easier to say, well, each choice – clarinetist or lawyer, novel or walk in the park – is valuable in its own incommensurable way. But introduce serious scarcity and suddenly some of the nicest of people start talking trade-offs. John Rawls thus concedes the justifiability, for instance, in limited circumstances, of postponing civil rights in favor of economic development in order to get to a certain threshold of prosperity in which such rights and liberties actually can be enjoyed, can be something more than paper rights.[22]

Let's get society to the point of sufficient economic well-being so that hard allocative choices can be pushed off into a remoter political sphere inhabited by professionals and not be a feature of the daily lives of individuals who have not enough food to feed all their children and so must send some to fend for themselves, nor enough fodder to winter more than a quarter of their herd and so must slaughter three-fourths.

Although my tone may be too harsh at the expense of the apples-and-oranges crowd, and my respect for talionic cultures sillily excessive, the benefits of pricelessness and dignity talk, despite its hypocrisies, may be worth the price. And we may rightly feel that something has gone terribly wrong when economists can undertake to measure in dollars the implicit value of a young child's life to its mother on the basis of her decisions about buckling the kid up in the car; this is commensurability gone mad, undertaken by people who do not recognize the proper limits of their field, or what it means to be a rushed and harried mother, or who cannot understand love (though they may indeed feel it); or if they do understand these things, they do not let that knowledge lead them to a critique of the rational limits of their enterprise and methods.[23] "There are more things in heaven and earth, Horatio,/ Than are dreamt of in your philosophy." An Icelandic oddman, a village wiseman, consummate commensuralists both, would run the risk of losing a lot more than reputation if they were ever this out of touch with how properly to measure value or what kinds of coinage to mint (fastening seat belts for measuring a mother's love?). Even economists, it seems, might wonder what has gone wrong with their enterprise that it should be this unhinged from human experience, human motive, and human understandings of value.

So it is more than a pious fraud to talk pricelessness and find clever ways to disguise the fact that dollars might have to figure at some point in our notion of pricelessness (though it is more than dollars that make it appalling to use seat-belt-fastening behavior as the means to come up with a dollar value for mother love). Talking pricelessness talk might bind us to behave in ways that are kinder, gentler, more mannerly, more consistent with some form of a belief in a rough equality (remember that honor cultures, too, were fiercely egalitarian within the honor group) and at no great cost either.[24] But maybe we should also, when we talk this way, be mindful of how much richer we are because of the work of those "moral menials"[25] – the actuaries, social planners, and politicians – who must keep their heads and put a price on how much we are going to shell out for the various "priceless" values we hold. Someone has to decide how to allocate limited resources among things like cancer research – whether prostate or breast – AIDS research, highway construction, national defense, rescue missions, firefighting, police protection, performance art. You get the picture.

But the discourse of hard-nosed economists, the faux toughness of the marketeers, of those economists who wish to measure commitment and caring by a "willingness-to-pay-in-dollars" standard, is no less parasitical on dignity talk than the apples-and-oranges position is parasitical on fairly healthy amounts of filthy lucre. The everything-is-about-self-interest crowd, the market priests, the willingness-to-pay guys, know that their game is played for pretty safe stakes, not just because they make a living by flattering and being serviceable to the rich and powerful, but for the very reason that no one will kill them for their tastelessness and bad manners, for letting money speak with a megaphone in our ears, for telling us that we are motivated by nothing more than a painfully risible view of human behavior as driven solely by self-interest, because, well, the life of a person who argues that the reason to leave a tip is that it signals a willingness to abide by social norms has a priceless dignity independent of the views he articulates.

And as long as he follows the social norms he does not have a clue to understanding, and even comes up with dollars-and-cents reasons that he thinks are motivating him to abide by the norm, we will not put him in jail or even beat the living daylights out of him. But should he deem it cost-effective not to leave a tip and cease faking being a member of civil society...[26] Well, then: thine eye shall not pity.

Conclusion

I HAVE TALKED OF SCALES, of talionic equivalence, and of getting even, of revenge and redemption. I thus introduced "oddmen" (the arbitrators) and "unevenmen" (those who refused to submit to arbitration and refused to pay for their wrongs); we have seen how people equilibrate, commensurate, evaluate, and price pretty much everything when called on to do so. Redemption, the foundation of their moral edifice, requires no less. We have seen them mint coin in the strangest of substances: in living flesh, dead flesh, animal or human, parted or whole, in blood, grain, and peppercorns, as well as in what we have come to think of as traditional money substances like silver and gold. I have spoken of the play in the joints of actual instruments of measurement, and the play, the ambiguities, in the conceptual joints of payback and redemption so that peace and "satisfaction" could be achieved, at least for a while.

Justice and obligation are treated by political, moral, and legal philosophers so abstractly. They lose sight of the fact that matters of justice and matters of obligation are concrete, practical, and homely: justice was first a matter of paying back, of buying back, of determining the amount of the obligation owed or the value of the thing or person to be redeemed. In the end it was never far from being a matter of blood, flesh, and bone. Remember: "peace" and "paying back" – whether from Latin *pax/pacare* or Hebrew *sh-l-m* – were part of the same constellation of values. There was no separating the determination of value – prices and payment – from peace and justice. Peace worth the name meant getting even, settling accounts, and that was their description of justice too. Justice meant creating the conditions of peace, debts quit, accounts settled.

The seminal imagery of peace and paying, of justice and getting even, does not allow for separating, practically or conceptually, things we think of as being as diverse as revenge, justice, obligation, debt, blood, bodies and parts thereof, measuring, meting, meat, eating, hospitality, *mund/helgi*, honor, and inviolability. These things shared so much genetic material that each partly contained the others and was in turn contained by them.

Ideas of balance, evenness, and justice led us to the talion, and the talion to ideas of commensuration. One smart character in an Icelandic saga written eight centuries ago came up with a remarkable way of solving the problem of commensurating pain. The talion, I have suggested, was a way to teach fellow-feeling. If I can take your eye in payment for your having taken mine, then I know you will feel my pain, as we are wont to say in our New Agey way, and we will be able to put a just price on it. I then, in an effort to set a good example, have shown how much fellow-feeling I could generate on behalf of Shylock, my brother, in hopes that you too would cheer him on.

We saw too how remembering was a necessary addition to the tough family of obligation, redemption, and debt repayment. Memory was never the mere recollection of prior mental images but rather was about the discharging of obligations of flesh and blood. Recollection necessarily meant debt collection; remembering, as the ghost of old Hamlet knew, meant revenge.

Again, let me emphasize, this is not so much academic overinterpretation and false drama. Very little interpreting was necessary: the ancient and medieval sources were so up-front about the linking of bodies alive and dead and their body parts to the measuring of value that even an academic could not miss it. The early Germanic laws, especially those of King Æthelberht of Kent, brought home the point in cold detail. The first laws in English did not begin with a preamble about abstract rights; they got right down to the business of pricing harms to people and their property. Price-setting did not demean some prior conception of human dignity but instead provided the force to notions like honor and their versions of dignity. *Mund* was not an abstraction; it was the jurisdictional power you wielded in your space, your domain of sovereignty. It started with the real hand and emanated outward, along with the glance of an eye and the sound of a word. And it had a value and a price.

I then took a psychological turn. The language of debt discharge, of getting even, of being satisfied, we saw, got internalized in the strangest of ways, when the idea of satisfying a debt supplied more than one language and culture with competing theories of the emotions. What was satisfaction? Was there agreement as to what the most satisfying payback was? No. It was not even clear whether satisfaction required discharge of built-up urges and tensions so as to let off steam and restore us to a relaxed equilibrium, or whether satisfaction meant filling up a void. Was the satisfaction of payback more akin, that is, to fornicating, or to feeding?

And finally when arriving at our own day we confronted what it meant to talk tough about valuing and pricing. I took what was something of a plague-on-all-their-houses position, going after, on the one hand, those who are wary of the moral costs of making comparisons of values – the apples-and-oranges people – and, on the other, those, mostly associated with a simplistic theory of motivation at the core of much legal economic literature, who think that a robotic notion of self-interest makes making comparisons no harder than breathing, but who are so mind-numbingly wedded to valuing things in dollars that they can't hold a candle at playing their own game to those oddmen in the sagas and elders at the gate in the Bible, who knew how to value moral matters in something other than dollars – they measured and traded in honor and blood, eyes and teeth, as well as silver.

Against them both I offered an account of how complex is our strong desire to rank and order, how inventive we are at devising measures to justify our rankings, and how inadequate dollars are for measuring value in most of the rankings we engage in, though the values at stake are no less comparable, and thus rankable, for that. It is by means of the very process of devising measures to rank the bizarrest of things that we hone our critical sense, that we teach ourselves and others how to appreciate what makes things what they are. It is how we educate our tastes, acquire them and change them; it is how we forge our judgment and our critical capacity.

I sing the virtues of honor cultures long since dead that left literary remains to die for: the Hebrew Bible, the *Iliad*, *Beowulf*, the Icelandic sagas. When closer to home in space or time I see not much to admire in urban ghettos or in the Islamicist Middle East, which are sometimes declared to be honor societies in the same breath as they are declared models of dysfunction, as if it were honor and the talion that made them so. But these are not dysfunctional because of their views of honor and justice, but because they deviate in some important ways from the model of the well-functioning talionic society one sees in the sagas, in other heroic literature, or in the ethnographic accounts, say, of the Bedouin.

The inner city has no old men *with property*, who have the means therewith to threaten, bribe, and control the aggressive young males who hold their communities captive. These communities are bereft of the class of elders who have the power to keep the violence of the young within responsible, because compensable, limits. In a well-functioning honor society the young men were not allowed to run the show; they did the bidding, within some fairly broad limits, of their elders. And the community was in complete agreement that "unevenmen" were not to be tolerated; either they learned to live by the rule of "even" or else. The pastors and the grandmothers in the inner cities, try heroically as they do, are simply outgunned and lack the resources.

The Islamicist Middle East introduces a religious ideology that comes close in some of its more extreme versions to devaluing life on earth to the zero point, thereby undoing much of the compensatory force of the talion, whose thrust, recall, was to make life on earth expensive. The problem is not just young men, who are a problem for the structures of social control in any society. The problem is the old men, the clerics and political leaders, who welcome the resource that the young men provide them. The young are thus used not only as human bombs against the enemy but also to gun down the young men of other factions with whom they are competing to blow up the enemy. This can be seen as a way of controlling their young men, too, for at the end of the day they will have gotten rid of quite a few of them. The problem need not be intrinsic to Islam as a general matter. Contrast the Bedouin, whose commitment to Islam was once such that it blended very nicely with the assumptions of their classic honor culture. Will the culture of jihad disrupt their internal equilibrium too?

But in functional honor societies, the clerics, or whoever occupied the status of wisemen, were the class from which the society drew its mediators and arbitrators; these were the people who were counted on to have a talent for peacemaking, for engineering imaginative compromises. And a talent for peacemaking, recall, was inseparable from a talent for pricing, for knowing how to value harms to property and harms to honor, within the constraints of what people could actually be expected to pay. The Islamicist clerics might well answer, "We meet your description of the skilled wiseman to a T. Our followers quarrel and feud among themselves; they come to us to judge their disputes, and we come up with a price that buys peace. We strike the balance and even up accounts – *within our group*. But outside the group we do not feud, nor quarrel, we *war* unto the death. Compensation and balance is a principle to be applied only within the honor group; Jews and Christians – and even in certain matters a Sunni to a Shi'ite, a Shi'ite to a Sunni – are outside the rule of balance, the rule of equal. We owe them nothing, for the principle of holy war means that the offense of the Other is his mere existence."

Can they possibly be surprised that the Other might object, even find such a view an offense not to be borne?

The well-functioning honor society elicits admiration, if not quite nostalgia. The conditions in which such societies thrived are not available to us, nor would we want to make them available to us if we could. Honor societies tended to be small and poor, and the cost of the tough virtue I so admire was in part their poverty; they seldom generated enough surplus to support lordship, let alone expensive governmental institutions. And they made sure that no one did too well for too long because that way lay serious inequality. Remember: they clipped the wings of those who were getting too big for their breeches. And prudent people might keep their talents and ambitions within limits that would prevent eliciting murderous envy from their jealous neighbors. This tough policing of the conditions of rough equality comes at

.nous social cost – to innovation, to experimentation, to certain .ms of productive ambition.

The value that our material wealth provides is not to be sneezed at, though the moralists always feared it would lead to softness and a kind of moral laziness, and, as is often the case with moralists, they have a point. But honor and a modified form of talionic justice still are with us in restricted, roughly egalitarian domains: on the playground, in school, at the workplace, in church (yes, there too). In these domains we still recognize as the core principle of justice, the central moral principle that one "good" turn deserves another, the quotes indicating that good means both bad and good. Reciprocity, paying back what you owe, means everything to your moral standing, to your character. And the fuel that maintains this moral economy is the desire to have a bit more honor than your neighbors; the pleasures of looking slightly down upon them seem to match those of being mildly deferred to – nothing untoward, mind you. Both the desire for deference, and the looking-down upon, must always be deniable; that is, they must be indulged in tastefully so that the large principles of rough equality and of treating honorable people honorably are maintained.

There is one smaller point on which I have no ambivalence whatsoever: though we have progressed in certain domains of knowl-edge – science and technology, for instance – it is not obvious to me that we are better psychologists and social psychologists than humans were in centuries past. Indeed it is obvious to me that we are not. Nor are we better educators and scholars. And with no irony I can attest to my belief that when it comes to understanding human motivation – no less than to understanding justice and what it means to get even – we are not as smart now as we were when people worried more about their honor than about their pleasure.

Notes

One. Introductory Themes: Images of Evenness

1. For a history of the blindfold, see Kissel, *Justitia* 82–92; Jacob, *Images de la justice* 229–237; also Jay, "Must Justice Be Blind?" For the sixteenth-century depiction of two-faced Justice, with one side blindfolded and the sword-drawn side fully sighted, see Jacob, 230, illus. 125.
2. See Evans, "Two Sources for Maimed Justice"; also the discussion in Groebner, *Liquid Assets, Dangerous Gifts* 75–78.
3. The image is taken from Acts 9.18.
4. Under older rules of contributory negligence the defendant had to be much more negligent; under newer comparative negligence regimes, only a little bit more.
5. *Iliad* 8.69–70; 22.209–213 (where they tip); 12.430 (as an image of the evenness of the opposed forces).
6. See Kane, *History of Dharmasastra* 3.361–370. It is not always clear in these ordeals whether you win if the pan goes up or goes down; see Jacob, *Images de la justice* 221; Kissel, *Justitia* 96. It depends on what is being weighed against what; see also Daube, "The Scales of Justice," for the ordeal-like notion of the scales "symbolizing things standing on a razor's edge: the slightest deflection spells triumph or ruin." But see my later discussion of the play there needs to be in the joints of the scale.
7. Bianchi, "The Scales of Justice," 8.
8. Daube, "The Scales of Justice," 113.
9. See the collection of depictions of the psychostasia from Egyptian books of the dead collected in Kisch, *Scales and Weights* 30, fig. 4.
10. See, for example, http://members.tripod.com/mdean/justice.html.
11. Christiansen (*Norsemen* 19) takes the view, contra Stalsberg in "Women as Actors in North European Viking Age Trade," who understands them to be merchant's tools, that the scales are symbols of good housekeeping and compares them to the keys, often found in female graves, to the locked pantry or treasure chest. There are certainly domestic uses for scales beyond the symbolic, but I accord Stalsberg's view credit.
12. See Kissel, *Justitia* 97–98.

13. I thus find Simone Weil's "The search for equilibrium is bad because it is imaginary. Revenge. Even if in fact we kill or torture our enemy it is, in a sense, imaginary" glibly pious and strangely confused, as it vacillates between the quest for publicly verifiable balance and whether or not such balance is psychologically satisfying to an avenger (Weil, *Simone Weil* 198); discussed with terse penetration by Kerrigan, *Revenge Tragedy* 10–11. As we shall see, the whole impulse of the talion is rather brilliantly to equilibrate fellow-feeling via imagination; see chapter 5.

14. The compulsion to commensurate can even be made the subject of jokes, as when Aristophanes at the conclusion of "The Frogs" has the decision as to who is the greater between Aeschylus and Euripides determined by weighing their verses against each other.

15. See Bloch, "Natural Economy or Money Economy," 236.

16. *Hrafnkel's saga* ch. 2; this passage is my translation, however.

17. See *Grágás* II 279; Dennis et al., *Grágás* II p. 355, which they translate as "decider."

18. The Norse phrase literally translated was "to stand at odds" (*standask í odda*).

19. Even skilled arbitrators could not always make all those who felt they had a claim happy. It was not uncommon to find people chagrined by what they felt was inadequate compensation or by having received nothing when they felt entitled morally, but were without a strictly legal right to compensation: for example, Lyting or Amundi in *Njál's saga* chs. 98, 106.

20. On stasis, see Cohen, *Law, Violence and Community* 25–33.

21. Consider in this light the saga peacemaking practice in which the peacemaker orders the combatants to cease fighting or he will join the first party that listens to him, thus threatening to fight immoderation by creating an imbalance in favor of the other side; *Guðmundar saga dýra* ch. 3; *Eyrbyggja saga* ch. 9.

22. Aristotle, *Nicomachean Ethics* 5.1133a–b.

23. Burnett, *Revenge in Attic and Later Tragedy* xvi–xvii; so too the Chinese, where the character for "even" is combined with the character for "public" to yield the character for "justice."

24. Vlastos, "Equality and Justice in Early Greek Cosmologies," 173–174n158, citing *isa essatai, Odyssey* 2.203–204, as getting the equal; also discussing the passage in Anaximander, where winter is described as paying back summer for its hot aggression. See also Burnett, *Revenge in Attic and Later Tragedy* 50.

25. And in Hebrew, too, an arbitrator is understood as an oddman: thus the hithpa'el of the root for three, *sh-l-sh*, means to be appointed an arbitrator; see Klein, *Etymological Dictionary* s.v. Sh-l-sh, 3.

26. See generally Aijmer, *English Discourse Particles*, particularly ch. 4 on *just*. Schourup, "Discourse Markers"; Fraser, "What Are Discourse Markers?" On *just*, also see Lee, "The Semantics of *Just*" and "Categories in the Description of *Just*"; Wierzbicka, *Cross-Cultural Pragmatics* 350–354.

27. For *jafn* as a discourse particle doing identical work to English *just* and *even*, consider this dark-humored quip: "You don't need to look; it is just/even as it seems. Your leg is gone" ("Eigi þarft þú að líta á, *jafnt* er sem þér sýnist, af er fóturinn"; *Njál's saga* ch. 63).
28. See OED s.v. even adv., II.6–8; on *even* see Kay, "Even."
29. *Hamlet* 3.3.135–136; Gen. 10.9.
30. Note too that *equal* joins the *just/even* group. The Revised Standard Version of the mid-twentieth century renders Ezekiel 18.25: "Yet you say 'The way of the Lord is not just.'" The Authorized Version of the late sixteenth century has "Yet ye say, 'The way of the Lord is not equal.'" Also see Shylock's reference to an "equal pound / Of your fair flesh" (1.3.145).
31. I do not want to push this too far because the pervasiveness of the use of juristic notions of *just*, *even*, and *right* doing such discourse particle work, though present in other languages I have some familiarity with, may not run as deep. Cf. German *eben* or French *juste*. For studies of so-called focusing adverbs and then the narrower domain of exclusive focus adverbs, see Nevalainen, *But, Only, Just*.
32. British usage has *straight* do discourse particle work synonymous with *right*: straight away, right away.
33. OED s.v. quit, quite, a. and quite, adv.
34. For *merely* as an exclusive focusing adverbial see Nevalainen, *But, Only, Just* 147–149, discussing *merely*'s function as an intensifier and its development as an "exclusive" (cf. "solely," "only") between 1570 and 1630.
35. More than a few aspects of Indo-European semantics attest to a fundamental norm of evening up accounts, of balance and reciprocity. Thus the root notion of "to take" is inextricably bound up with the notion of "to give." See Watkins, "New Parameters in Historical Linguistics," 786–788, who discusses the idea of reciprocity implicit in IE *nem, yielding Germanic *niman*, "to take," and Greek *nemo*, "to give," "distribute." He also notes that English "to take" can possess antithetical directional senses. When paired with "to give" it indicates direction toward, but contrast the idea of *taking* an object *to* someone as in "I took the book to Joe." But mostly consult his discussion of *ethnos* and its semantic origins in notions of reciprocity. Consider too the frequently cited example of *host* and *guest* as reflexes of a common root.
36. See Daube's masterful discussion in *"Lex Talionis,"* 134–146.
37. *Piers Plowman* B.19.188ff; Langland takes the tag *redde quod debes* from Matt. 18.28, and imbues it with significantly more force than it had in the parable.

Two. The Talion

1. See Vlastos, "Socrates' Contribution to the Greek Sense of Justice," praising Socrates for the moral innovation of rejecting the then dominant principle of the talion; but as I indicate in the text I suspect that antitalionic

arguments were always available to people who were about to get paid back in blood. Indeed Vlastos cites the passage from Thucydides I reference in n. 3 of this chapter.

2. Poe, "Marginalia," *Southern Literary Messenger*, June 1849, *Essays and Reviews* 1461.

3. Thucydides, *History* 4.19; see my *Bloodtaking* chs. 6, 8.

4. Our sentencing guidelines are more than matched by early medieval penitentials, with their complex ranking and gridding of sins into a system of penances in which the various specie of payment involved type and length of fasts, prayers, and lashes. Concern was taken to establish exchange rates among the various punishments: "The equivalent of a special fast, one hundred psalms and one hundred genuflections, or the three 'fifties' and seven canticles." The Irish Canons, II *Of Equivalents*: c. 1, in McNeill and Gamer, *Medieval Handbooks of Penance* 122.

5. Punishment theorists insist that punishment as a general matter requires theoretical justification; see, for example, Waldron, "*Lex Talionis*," 28. Perhaps that is true as far as state-delivered systems of punishment go. I have never understood, though, why the burden to go first is upon those who would punish to formulate and justify a theory of punishment. It seems to me that those who would not punish harms have much harder accounting to do, given the way most if not all human societies have organized themselves to enforce norms. Do we need a theory justifying the obligation to repay a debt? Try to imagine a society in which there are no negative sanctions. It seems we have to punish whether or not we can come up with a theory any more sophisticated than it is just what we humans must do to live socially and to socialize children. Wonders Nozick, "Is it necessary, though, to offer any explanation at all of retributive punishment? Perhaps its appropriateness is just a fundamental fact, with nothing further underlying it. People who commit wrongs simply deserve to be punished" (*Philosophical Explanations* 366). Nonetheless, he feels obliged to give a justification. See also Mackie, "Morality and Retributive Emotions," 206–207. If the core of the problem lies in the distinction between criminal and civil sanction, between private and public enforcement of rights and duties, that too is seldom clarified.

6. The talion is the bête noire of much legal theoretical punishment literature. This literature – for whatever virtues it may have theoretically – is apocalyptically underinformed as an historical and philological matter. It is rare to find a writer in the tradition who has more than a cartoon view of revenge, largely abstracted from Elizabethan and Jacobean tragedy or the story of Michael Kohlhaus. Indeed the whole distinction this literature mobilizes between retribution and revenge is untenable given any serious account of revenge as actually instituted in revenge cultures. Invariably, revenge is caricatured as a crazy, imbalanced response to injury. No real revenge culture would put up with this kind of revenge for a second. I discuss this in more detail in a critique of Nozick's attempt (*Philosophical*

Explanations 366–368) to distinguish revenge and retribution in my "Clint Eastwood and Equity," 161–166. Another common error is to make the talion primarily a principle of punishment, which it is not in Exodus, Leviticus, or the Twelve Tables (the Deuteronomic talion marches to a bit of a different rhythm, where ideas of punition may trump ideas of compensation; see chapter 5, Deuteronomy's Artful Talionic Lesson) rather than a private law principle of compensation. Among the better performances in the punishment genre see Waldron, "*Lex Talionis.*" *Lex talionis* in this literature is either taken loosely, to indicate a general retributive proportionality principle, raising the standard issues of fit, of how much and for what (e.g., Davis, "Harm and Retribution"; Reiman, "Justice, Civilization, and the Death Penalty"; Waldron, "*Lex Talionis*"), or it is taken narrowly, as a straw man to be disposed of by Portia-like literalism, pointing out that even though the talion may be easy to apply in the case of an eye for an eye, what if the harmer has only one eye, or what if the crime is heterosexual rape – that is, by taking the talion to be a statement of literal identity of punishment and initial harm (Hart, *Punishment and Responsibility* 233; Reiman, "Justice, Civilization, and the Death Penalty," 127). I will ignore this literature, not as beside the point but as beside my points.

7. See, for example, Berlin and Brettler, *Jewish Study Bible* 154, and Douglas, *Leviticus as Literature* 212–213. Kerrigan, *Revenge Tragedy* 22, accepts this view of the biblical statement of the talion. It is one of the few places in his excellent book where he lets a solecism go unexposed.

8. Daube so argues, "*Lex Talionis,*" 105. See *Hammurabi* §230 and *Middle Assyrian Laws* §§15, 55. Vicarious and group liability, often a feature of bloodfeuding cultures, is a complex matter in practice, some of which I discuss in *Bloodtaking*. Different moral issues are raised when the group eligible to be hit is defined horizontally at a specific moment in time so that the people at risk are generally people close to and known by the actual wrongdoer, or when it is defined longitudinally through time, so that an unborn grandchild can be hit for the sins of his grandfather. In the latter case it is harder to justify the practice of group liability on utilitarian grounds of deterrence: there was not much the grandchild could do to restrain his sinful grandfather.

9. Paul, *Studies in the Book of the Covenant* 76; see also *Etz Hayim* 462; Plaut, *Torah* 572; Childs, *The Book of Exodus* 472.

10. Philo, *De Specialibus Legibus* 3.195–196.

11. *Hammurabi* §§196, 197, 200; §199.

12. Finkelstein, "Ammisaduqa's Edict," 98. Also in Childs, *The Book of Exodus* 472. Legal-historical attempts to impose our split between criminal and civil law on ancient polities is fraught with conceptual and historical difficulty and is best avoided, even if I commit the sin myself.

13. One can read the Stoical attacks on anger and revenge as its own form of revenge. Consider that if the person wronging you is Nero or Caligula

the only way to frustrate him is to cultivate complete passivity in the face of the horrors he inflicts. So, Nero, you think you can get a rise out of me? Not in the least. You can't get to me. In fact one can see Stoicism and the crazed cruelty of the Roman emperors as a system in which each side eggs the other on. Stoic passivity goads crazy emperors to ever more outlandish forms of cruelty just to see what in the end it will actually take to get a Stoic to bat an eyelash.

14. See Kerrigan, *Revenge Tragedy* ch. 1 on the natural affinity of revenge and drama.

15. On the proverb and its possible source in Martial see Foote, "Skömm er óhófs ævi."

16. See White, *Feuding and Peacemaking*; Miller, *Bloodtaking* ch. 6. On issues of timing in agonistic societies, see Bourdieu, "Sentiment of Honour in Kabyle Society" and *Outline of a Theory of Practice* 4–9.

17. See Westbrook, *Studies in Biblical and Cuneiform Law* 41–47.

18. On the talion as a rule of compensation see Daube, "*Lex Talionis.*" The amount of space and care he takes to argue, rightly, the compensatory aspect of revenge has to surprise a student of bloodfeud, especially of saga feud, because the idea that revenge was compensatory was obvious to the saga people and explicitly stated as such. I will return to the theme several times. On the nineteenth-century legal-historical views, see Whitman's excellent and informed discussion ("At the Origins of Law and the State"), which cuts across many of the themes of this book and to which I am greatly indebted. The view that compensation was a later reform and advance over talionic eyes for eyes is in part a Whiggish desire to see us progressing to softer modes of social control by turning a blind eye to the obviousness of the compensatory nature of revenge. The evolutionary view of revenge giving way to compensation cannot be maintained either as a conceptual rubric or as a matter of fact. For a bibliography of the various evolutionary models see Jackson, *Studies in the Semiotics of Biblical Law* 274n211; see Diamond, "An Eye for an Eye," for the opposed evolutionary view that compensation preceded corporal talionic punishment. Note too that early medieval kings were more than willing to let their underlings feud, to make a virtue of something they rarely had the power to prevent in any event. Given the high cost of maintaining armies, one way kings could devolve the cost of defense onto their subjects was to let them stay armed and feud with each other and then borrow their retinues for foreign campaigns; see Keen, "Warfare and the Middle Ages," 7.

19. Daube, "*Lex Talionis,*" 109; the relevant Talmudic passages are translated with very helpful commentary by Kraemer, *Reading the Rabbis*, 34–48.

20. The Icelandic laws some three thousand years later deal with many of the same issues as Hammurabi's concerning what people can actually pay over to satisfy debts denominated in silver. See *Hammurabi* §108, punishing the innkeeper who insists on silver rather than grain as a means of payment.

21. Bloch, "Natural Economy or Money Economy." There are more than a few Icelandic cases and laws that indicate the amount due in the standard ounce units of silver or ell units of cloth and then provide a separate stipulation as to how this is actually to be paid. See, for example, *Grágás* Ia 241: "That sum is to be paid out in refined silver or in new linen or in wax or in Icelandic trade goods or in livestock, and pay everything according to the standard values current at the place where it is to be paid out." See the stipulation regarding the precise means of payment in *Þorgils saga ok Hafliða* chs. 31–32.
22. *Ine* §54.1.
23. See *Grettir's saga*, ch. 24; Bourdieu, "Sentiment of Honour in Kabyle Society," 216. Joking that someone has gotten rich by taking wergeld for his dead kin got the joker killed in a well-known and powerfully told incident in Gregory of Tours, *History of the Franks* 9.19.
24. See generally Miller, *Bloodtaking*.
25. See *Æthelberht* §§43, 51, 54.3; it is not as if the biblical laws do not stipulate precise money compensations in other instances. Ex. 21.32, for example, requires 30 shekels compensation be paid the master of a slave gored by an ox.
26. Mary Douglas reads the Levitical talionic statement as demonstrating "the general principle of equivalence," *Leviticus as Literature* 208. Others have read the version of the talion in the Book of the Covenant in that way – for example, Sarna, *Torah Commentary* 126. Jackson, *Studies in the Semiotics of Biblical Law* 295–296, opposes these views on grounds I find strange – namely, that the cognitive structures for such abstract generality were not in place then; their mode of thinking was more case specific and part of a private system of ordering. The latter point about case-specific thinking is undeniable, but from such specifics they generated more than a few proverbial general precepts. Thus "an eye for an eye," which is a very telling way to capture the concern with, and the ideal of, balance in matters of negative reciprocity.
27. See Jackson, *Studies in the Semiotics of Biblical Law* 273n5, providing the bibliography. The location of the Exodus formula presents a multitude of interpretive problems; see further chapter 4, ns. 19–20.
28. Daube suggests that the last three members of the Exodus formula – burning, wound, and stripe – are late additions: "for they have regard not to definite limbs or organs lost but to various modes of hurting, hurting by burning, by wounding, by scourging," *"Lex Talionis,"* 112–113. See my discussion of commensurating pain in chapter 5.
29. Notice too that Ex. 21.26–27 – which deals with injuries to slaves and follows immediately upon the litany of life, eye, tooth, hand, foot, burn, wound, and stripe of the talion at 21.23–25 – mentions only the slave's eyes and teeth. Even the Exodus Covenant Code compiler felt there was something special about the eye and tooth distillation of the talion proverb. The blinding of the eye, the breaking of a bone, and the knocking out of

a tooth, in that order, get talionic treatment in *Hammurabi* §§196, 197, 200, but each in its own provision, thereby losing the terse force of the Hebrew version.

30. But compare the evidence of Josephus too readily dismissed by Daube; see chapter 4, n. 17.

31. Daube, "Eye for an Eye." The slap in the face in Jesus' time, as it was often to be elsewhere and later, was not meant to do physical damage or even to give physical pain; its purpose was to do moral damage to a person's honor.

32. Rousselle, *Porneia* 122–123. On the vogue of self-castration, see Brown, *Body and Society* 168–169; see further chapter 3, n. 13; examples of voluntary self-blinding are rare. The philosopher Democritus was rumored to have done so.

33. Philo, *De Specialibus Legibus* 3.195: "If, then, anyone has maliciously injured another in the best and lordliest of senses, sight, and is proved to have struck out his eye, he must in turn suffer the same, if the other is a free man, but not if he is a slave." The eyes of men and women within a status are equally valued. No distinction is made between the eyes of free men and women or between slave men and women, the crucial distinction being slave/free and not male/female in the Exodus version of the talion.

34. There is some suggestion in the formulation of the talion in Deuteronomy that punitive mutilation may be the desired goal, not as compensation to an injured party but as an end in itself. It is specially stated there that the person who is to be the object of the talion is to be made an object lesson to deter others from bearing false witness. That is not the case, however, with the formulations in Exodus and Leviticus. On the significance and practice of cutting off noses in fifteenth-and sixteenth-century Switzerland and south Germany, mostly but not solely of adulterous or loose women, see Groebner's fascinating discussion in *Defaced* ch. 3.

35. I owe this point to an anonymous outside reviewer who subsequently revealed herself to be Wendy Doniger. She also notes the expression, "I'd give my eye-teeth for that." Again the collocation of eye and tooth, with eye preceding the tooth, and again the two bound by some uncanny attraction to each other.

36. In 1997 *Lingua Franca*, sadly since defunct, published a lead article on whether reports of cannibalism from ancient times up to recent anthropological writing was so much fantasy of fearsome Otherness; see Osborne, "Does Man Eat Man?" The *Lingua Franca* article gave William Arens's book, *The Man-Eating Myth: Anthropology and Anthropophagy* (Oxford: Oxford UP, 1979), a wider audience than the small set of anthropologists who had noted it earlier. *Lingua Franca* was read by the trendy set who love revisionisms if they look to undo orthodoxies that "orientalize." In the end most of the truth of the prior orthodoxy survives, although there is indeed a certain value to clipping its wings a bit. See, for example, ns. 38–39 in this chapter. For a

Salon magazine piece that followed up on the *Lingua Franca* story, see http://archive.salon.com/may97/news/news970514.html.

37. *Iliad* 24.212; 22.346–347 (also 4.34–35).

38. The blood and flesh is to be of the herds of the enemies, but the image is still cannibalistic. See also Rousselle, *Porneia* 108–116, on accusations of cannibalism exchanged by Christian and pagan polemicists and the extent to which they may have been true. On the importance of food in funerary ritual, on the intimate connection of death and eating, see Burkert, *Homo Necans* 50–51. In *Beowulf* (vv. 1223, 3155) fire is figured as a swallower of corpses burning on pyres, and heaven as a swallower of the smoke that rises from them. There are also the beasts of battle – the raven, eagle, and wolf – which conventionally feast on the fallen in Old English battle poetry. On cooking up human corpses as food for the gods and other rituals of sacrifice associated with funerals, see Oestigaard, "Sacrifices of Raw, Cooked, and Burnt Humans." See also chapter 3, n. 45.

39. The Associated Press recently reported a Thyestian banquet at a wedding feast gone awry in the Philippines. See "Four Arrested for Eating Family Member," AP Online, Aug. 10, 2004.

40. God also promises the same auto-consumption for Israel's enemies (Is. 49.26). On the theme of eating one's children and its centrality not only to Greek tragedy but also to Renaissance tragedy and to Milton's God, see Braden, "Epic Anger."

Three. The Talionic Mint: Funny Money

1. One might argue that for law to promote efficient commerce the move must always be to substitute equivalence for identity. This is captured in the Roman law distinction between loans in which the specific thing loaned must be returned – *commodatum* – and loans of fungibles, in which the identical object need not be returned but objects of the same quantity and quality, the *mutuum*. See Daube, "Money and Justiciability," 10–14. This distinction finds itself maintained in the common law, too, in the forms of action of debt versus detinue; see Baker, *English Legal History* 321, 391. Eventually, it comes about that a money substance can substitute for fungible goods and finally for unique goods. See also Whitman's discussion of Hegel's view that the evolution of legal consciousness was largely about the development of the idea of value equivalence, of the idea that it is possible to put a price on things ("At the Origins of Law and the State," 59–60). Wise bloodfeuders seemed much more at home with ideas of value-equivalence than philosophers and legal historians are inclined to acknowledge. See Thormod's "everything is compensable," discussed in chapter 9.

2. Appadurai's useful formulation goes like this: In barter, A is exchanged for B where neither A nor B is money and the transaction is carried out with every effort to minimize transaction costs; this last qualification is

meant to distinguish it from gift exchange ("Commodities and the Politics of Value," 9).

3. In nineteenth-century American constitutional law, federal power over immigration was seen to derive from the commerce clause "due in part to the fact that many early immigrants to the United States came as indentured workers and slaves"; Cleveland, "Powers Inherent in Sovereignty," 99–100, 103; Bilder, "Indentured Servants, Slaves, and Articles of Commerce," 761–762.

4. See Einzig, *Primitive Money* 238–241.

5. *Iliad* 22.351; see also Laum, *Heiliges Geld* 137. Consider too the Kwakiutl copper plates of potlatch fame, where a plate was considered to be the equal of a human life; it could be sacrificed and "killed." See Graeber, *Toward an Anthropological Theory of Value* 206–208.

6. *Hittite Laws* §§1, 3.

7. See "Thorstein the Staffstruck"; also *Thorstein the White's saga* ch. 7; *Vápnfirðinga saga* ch. 18.

8. *New York Times*, Oct. 22, 1922, p. 14; cited in Zelizer, *Pricing the Priceless Child* 139. The dead girl's mother refused the offer.

9. See Westbrook, *Studies in Biblical and Cuneiform Law* 66–67; Oliver, *The Beginnings of English Law* 51, notes in her edition of the Kentish laws of Hloþhere and Eadric (late seventh century) §§1–2 that "the unfree killer is himself part of the payment. Should he escape, the owner must pay for him with equal value."

10. Ex. 21.21 has been discussed in light of *Hammurabi* §116, in which if a man kills his debt slave he loses the right to collect the debt and must pay 20 shekels to the original owner of the slave; see Houtman, *Das Bundesbuch* 153. Ex. 22.2 provides that a thief who cannot make restitution is to be sold to discharge his obligation.

11. Benveniste, *Indo-European Language and Society* 105–112, discussing Gr. *alphe*, Gmc. "sell" and "buy"; also Watkins, "New Parameters in Historical Linguistics," 789.

12. See Brown, *Body and Society* 168–169.

13. First Council of Nicea, Canon 1, text at http://www.intratext.com/IXT/ENG0425/_P4.HTM; see also Aquinas ST 2.2.Q65 A 1.

14. Odin's eye is called a *veð*, a wed, a security; *Voluspá* st. 28 in original, st. 20 in Terry, *Edda*. But the transaction does not envisage a day when Odin hands back the wisdom and gets his eye back. So in fact the eye is a purchase price rather than security for a loan.

15. *Gebetan*, literally "to make amends, to compensate," and its corresponding noun, *bót* (compensation, amends), still survive in the modern colloquial "to boot," meaning an added something to the good. According to Wormald *bót* slowly changes its sense in the Anglo-Saxon laws from indicating payments to the injured party in the eighth and ninth centuries as here, to indicating "a fine or penalty paid to God or the society at large"; see Wormald, "Inter Cetera Bona ... Genti Suae," 985. But the

earlier sense remains nonetheless, for the payment in the later laws is still intended to be compensatory, even though the recipient of the payment is the king or God. See, for example, 1 Æthelred §2.1, where the earlier meaning supplies the punch to the black humor of making the slave who fails the ordeal twice "not be able to make any amends (bót) except by his head."

16. Alf. §32; see also Alf. §6.1, where a thief is allowed to redeem the hand he is to lose upon a payment proportionate to his wergeld; 2 Æthelred 14.1, for the hand of a false moneyer.

17. Alf. §§52, 71; by the time of King Edgar, c. 975, the cost of redeeming a tongue guilty of bearing false witness was one's entire wergeld; 3 Edgar §4; likewise, 2 Canute §16; false moneyers were to lose a hand, which Canute denies them the right to repurchase "neither with gold nor with silver" (2 Canute §8.1).

18. Ceorl is ModE churl, but it bore no pejorative sense in Old English. It is often rendered simply as free man, commoner; Whitelock (English Historical Documents 392n3) feels "peasant proprietor" best captures the sense. In some contexts it means husband; see the discussion in Richards, "Dictionary of Old English and Old English Legal Terminology," 57–58.

19. Alf. §25.1.

20. The tough presumption is that the slave has no assets of value other than his body. Alfred's laws, however, contemplate a slave having some private property; slaves are allowed "to sell anything that anyone has given them out of charity or that they were able to earn during their free time" (Alf. §43); see also 4 Æthelstan 6.6–7, where slaves are fined three pennies.

21. Burkert notes how ancient funerary ritual emphasizes the parts of the body over the whole because the ceremony "often centers not so much on the corpse as on the bones from individual limbs" (Homo Necans 52).

22. It would be nice if excise, in the sense of a tax, were rooted in the idea of to cut off a part of the body, as when we say to excise a cyst, so that it could be made a member of a family of ideas that makes Hebrew neshekh, bite, mean usury. But such is not the case. Excise, the tax, takes its form from MDutch rendering of Lat. acensum, from census, a tax. Says the OED: "The notion of derivation from L. excisum 'something cut out' may have been the cause of the substitution of ex- for ac- in the MDutch form." Still, if the OED is right, though the idea of cutting was not at the origins of "excise" as a tax, it nonetheless led to the eventual "misspelling" of the word.

23. James Bennet, "Israeli Soldiers Search for Remains After Bomb Kills Six," New York Times, May 12, 2004, Section A, p. 10, col. 3. And as in the Iliad there is no end of revenge for those who desecrate bodies; within three months the Israelis successfully targeted and killed the man who had brandished the decapitated head of the Israeli soldier mentioned, alleging as justification his desecration of the corpse; see Los Angeles Times, July 24, 2004, Part A, p. 6.

24. Laum's views are important to Whitman's argument that ancient law was not about restraining private vengeance but about controlling the "magic" of prices and the value of things, including body parts. Whitman, "At the Origins of Law and the State," 83, although pursuing a rather different set of arguments than I am here, suggests at the conclusion of his penetrating study that there may be some intimate connection between the presence of mutilating punishments in the ancient law codes and their concern with price-setting. "Both mutilation and price-setting may in fact, at their origin, reveal a concern for maintaining proper cosmological order within a sacrifice-based religious system." My argument suggests that the idea connecting bodies and value was unavoidable, and that to the extent it was a feature of a magico-religious order, it was mostly so because it was also the stuff of buying and selling, and this meant that it was also the stuff of marrying and feuding, and doing justice. These were people for whom blood was a measure of value and a means of payment as a political, social, and legal matter, as well as a cosmological one.

25. Grimm's law identifies one of the defining sound changes that distinguished the Germanic languages as a distinct branch of general Indo-European as the change of IE p to Gmc f. Thus Latin *pisces, pater, pecus, pes/pedis, paucus*, Greek *pente, pteron* (wing) are cognate, respectively, with English *fish, father, fee, foot, few, five, feather*.

26. The *c* form comes from the Norman dialect, the *ch* form from Picard. Compare also the similar development of *canal* and *channel*.

27. I put aside money functioning as a store of value as not as theoretically interesting.

28. Laum, *Heiliges Geld* 27–29. Laum's work, to the extent that it deals with the history of religion, has been superseded; but his focus on the origins of money and value determination, and the fertile evocativeness of his exposition, provide a nice starting place for the points I am making about measurement and justice.

29. See Laum's discussion of *obolos, obelos, obeliskos (Heiliges Geld* 56–57).

30. Clendinnen, *Aztecs* 114.

31. Clendinnen distinguishes the Christian sacrifice of Jesus with its "'enormous symbolic weight' placed on the individual human body" from Aztec human sacrifice: "It is difficult indeed to entertain the possibility that Mexica might have killed humans with no particular regard for their individuality." Nonetheless the same ideas of debt-discharge and of blood obligation to appease angry gods underwrite Aztec justifications of the need for human sacrifice. It is hard to overstate the horror of the Aztec world; see *Aztecs* 73–75.

32. Freud, "War and Death," 293: "By the law of the talion," he claims, the sin that Christ is expiating must be a murder, because he is paying with his life. And to Freud that means the murder of the Father: "The original sin was an offense against God the Father, the primal crime of mankind must have been a parricide." Sacrificial substitutions seldom bear simple

one-to-one correspondences. Christ's sacrifice is not just paying a God for a God; Jesus is also Man the sacrificer, who owes atonement for his disobedience as Man. So it is Man for a Man, too, and to keep this from being an act of suicide, which it nearly is in the Gospel of John, we need to interpose the story of the trial. Or substitute a Lamb.

33. On lapses back into cannibalism and human sacrifice see Burkert, *Homo Necans* 45–46. I do not want to push my point too far; there is no denying that over the long durée in Jewish, Christian, and Indian ritual history the story is pretty much one of ever cheaper substitutions from human, to animal, to cakes and bread; see Doniger and Smith, "Sacrifice and Substitution." The Aztecs, however, seem to have moved to ever bloodier human sacrifice in the century before the arrival of the Spanish.

34. Consider Lev. 27.1–34, in which vows dedicating people, animals, and other things to the temple can be redeemed for a price, in effect, making substitution a basis for a kind of poll tax, which the priests administer. The Levitical statute sets a broad scale of prices for humans, based on age and gender, but if a person is too poor to pay the priest shall evaluate him according to his ability to pay (v. 8). The scale: for men twenty to sixty years old, 50 shekels; women in that age range, 30 shekels; for people five to twenty years old, 20 shekels for males, 10 for females; and for children one to five years old, 5 shekels for boys, 3 for girls. Subsequent provisions deal with land, animals, and so on. And lest someone of legalistic bent read these provisions as a warrant for wergeld to redeem people sentenced to death, that loophole is closed emphatically: "No one devoted, who is to be utterly destroyed from among men, shall be ransomed; he shall be put to death" (v. 29).

35. See Doniger and Smith, "Sacrifice and Substitution," 189–196, for the positions of various theorists of sacrifice.

36. The complexities of both believing and not believing that such substitutes are truly equal to the "real thing" are admirably treated using Vedic and Hindu evidence by Doniger and Smith, "Sacrifice and Substitution," 203–207: "On the one hand, the goat is not equal to the other *pasus*, on the other hand, the goat is said to be not only their equal but the best of all victims.... The inaccessibility of the original does not logically make the goat equal, let alone better, but it does make its use inevitable. And in order to justify this unavoidable reality, the texts simply *say* that the goat is just as good or ... even better" (203).

37. See generally Rubin, *Corpus Christi*.

38. Laum, *Heiliges Geld* 39; see too the history of English *yield* in OED s.v. yield, sb. 2. In OE (Old English) and OHG (Old High German) *geld* means payment or sacrifice; Benveniste, *Indo-European Language and Society* 57–61. Of some interest for Laum's thesis is that *sell* is pretty much in place in ON (Old Norse) and OE in the sense in which we use it now, but the Gothic form *saljan* does not mean "sell" but "to offer a sacrifice"; see Benveniste, 108. The idea supports the core of Laum's thesis that finds

mercantile-like behaviors emanating from the religious sphere, before they were normalized in the secular.

39. Laum, *Heiliges Geld* 64–67.
40. On the unquiet dead see Kerrigan, *Revenge Tragedy* ch. 2 and chapter 7 in this book. Even if wergeld payments in some settings were also accompanied by propitiary offerings to the gods, we are still in the world of paying and paying back. The offerings either are meant to compensate for a wrong done to the gods, thus to buy off their anger, or they are attempts, to the extent that they overpay for past wrongs, to predispose the gods to bring less misfortune in the future, in which case the offering is a kind of protection money.
41. Simmel, *Philosophy of Money* 355–356.
42. Grierson, "The Origins of Money," 12–19.
43. This understanding of "Man is the measure of value" is rather different from the sense Plato gives it, where Protagoras' "man is the measure of all things" stands for the proposition that perceptions of qualities differ from one person to the next. You think the room cold, while I think it warm; *Theaetetus* 152a–154b.
44. It is unclear to what extent Laum's thesis can withstand the discrediting of the once orthodox view that temple economies, in which the temple collected and distributed goods, preceded market economies. This view has lost most of its empirical support since Polanyi, its most estimable proponent, was writing. More archaeological and cuneiform information unavailable to the formulators of the temple economy theory has since been discovered or translated. See Curtin, *Cross-cultural Trade* 70, 87–88; and Silver, "Karl Polanyi and Markets in the Ancient Near East."
45. See Bynum's elegant discussion ("The Body of Christ in the Later Middle Ages") of the centrality of images of nourishment, eating and drinking, in the sacrifice of Christ, his blood serving as symbolic milk. On the prevalence of human body parts and slough and emissions in medical recipes and their eerie correspondence to food recipes, see Piero Camporesi's tour de force, *Incorruptible Flesh*, especially ch. 1. On the meaning of bread as flesh see Camporesi, *Bread of Dreams*; see also chapter 2, n. 38 and chapter 7, n. 14.
46. See Rubin, *Corpus Christi* 135–136; also Sinanoglou, "The Christ Child as Sacrifice."
47. *Hlafæta* appears only once in the OE corpus, and that is in the *Laws of Æthelberht* (early seventh century), portions of which will be discussed in chapter 8. To complete the array of "loafers": *lady* was originally *hlaf-dig*, loaf + *dig*, knead, cf. dough; she is the kneader of the loaf; see OED s.vv. lord, lady.
48. See Graeber, *Toward an Anthropological Theory of Value* 190, 198.
49. See Geary, "Sacred Commodities."

50. For a scandal involving an active trade in body parts excised from cadavers donated to UCLA, see John M. Broder, "UCLA Halts Donations of Cadavers for Research," *New York Times*, March 10, 2004, Section A, p. 14, col. 5.

51. Notice how the euphemism or synecdoche in English of "hand" for the whole of Michal's body makes one part of the body stand for the whole or for another more private part, thus serving as a symbolic money, and again recalls the body's partibility.

52. Milton, "Upon the Circumcision." See also the informative discussion of Christian anxieties and fantasies regarding circumcision and the Protestant exegesis of the relevant Pauline passages on circumcision in Shapiro, *Shakespeare and the Jews* 113–130.

53. Burkert, *Homo Necans* 35–36. Hebrew: *karat* Gen. 15.18: "On that day the Lord 'cut' [made] a covenant with Abram"; also Gen. 21.27, 32; 26.28.

54. 1 Sam. 11.2–3, 7; AV has Nahash answer, "On this condition will I make a covenant with you," but the Hebrew is terser, having only "on this condition I will cut it with you"; see further (chapter 7, n. 6 and the text at chapter 9, n. 7) the case of the Levite's concubine. The Dead Sea scrolls fill out the account to make Nahash's wit even nastier. It seems he had already gouged out the right eyes of the men of Gad and Rueben, a remnant of whom flee to Jabesh. When they sue Nahash for peace he gives his answer: "This is the way I cut a covenant...." (4QSam^a); Josephus backs the account in the Dead Sea scrolls, to which he adds the telling detail that Nahash cut out the right eyes of the Jews who lived east of the Jordan because with a good left eye they would still make useful slaves, but would be rendered totally unfit as soldiers because their shields would cover their left eyes (*Antiquities* 6.5.69–71).

55. In the Jewish liturgy this passage from Jeremiah provides the additional reading for the week that the Book of the Covenant, the home of the Exodus talion, is scheduled as the weekly portion from the Torah.

Four. The Proper Price of Property in an Eye

1. The fantasy is of mutilation run amok, not just an eye here and a tooth there but a tearing to pieces: the *locus classicus* is Euripides, *Bacchantes*, or the Orpheus myths.

2. See Grossberg, *Governing the Hearth* 262, discussing the right of a master to assign his apprentice to another: "Apprentices had even been listed among the assets of bankrupts in colonial America, used as payment for debts and considered as part of estates." Compare dependents in medieval Iceland, who are valued as liabilities on a sliding scale according to their degree of kinship with the head of household; *Grágás* Ib 5–6; see Dennis, et al., *Grágás* II p. 31n19.

3. The Bible does show, however, talionic retribution involving the severance of body parts in war. Thus Adoni-bezek: "Threescore and ten kings, having their thumbs and their great toes cut off, gathered their meat under my table: as I have done, so God hath requited me" (Judg. 1.7).

4. *Twelve Tables* 3 c. 6. The problem is in interpreting *tertiis nundinis partis secanto* ("on the third market day creditors shall cut pieces"). Pieces of what? Roman writers thought it meant the body, but more squeamish modern commentators have sought to interpret it to mean dividing the debtor's property; see *Twelve Tables* 440. I am inclined to favor the bloodier interpretation as being more in tune with the role the body plays generally in ancient law as a security device.

5. It is clear in the Twelve Tables, and it should also be in the biblical case, that these rules are part of legal and social practices that contemplate bargaining, negotiating, and arbitrating compromises. In the biblical setting see Jackson, *Studies in the Semiotics of Biblical Law* 281, who though not quite a lone voice is remarkable for seeing what should have been obvious to others. It is extraordinary that biblical scholars, among the most learned as a general matter in the scholarly enterprise, should only lately be discovering what was standard fare in the anthropological and legal literature from the 1930s through the 1970s. The rule embodied in most laws is a default rule only. In other words, the outcome declared by the rule may in fact be the outcome least selected by the people involved, who bargained to a different outcome; people bargained in the shadow of the rules, with the rules less defining a specific outcome than providing ammunition for various bargaining positions.

6. On passing before the debtor see Maimonides, *Book of Civil Laws* 3.1.3; exemption of tools, 3.1.7; widows, 3.3.1; on the court's representative not being able to enter the home of the debtor, 3.3.4.

7. Maimonides, *Book of Civil Laws* 3.3.5. There is also a strict prohibition against usury among Jews, and the rabbis were remarkably astute at piercing through any sham transactions that might disguise an interest component, such as purchase and leasebacks (3.5.15) and what were called iron sheep contracts (3.8.12). With such unfavorable rules to creditors, credit markets dried up. Certain concessions were then made to creditors, one crucial one allowed a debt to survive the sabbatical year because people were refusing to lend in years 5 and 6 (3.2.2). Deuteronomy was already aware of this problem. Thus: "Beware that there be not a thought in thy wicked heart, saying, The seventh year, the year of release, is at hand; and thine eye be evil against thy poor brother, and thou givest him nought; and he cry unto the Lord against thee, and it be sin unto thee" (Deut. 15.9). On loopholes to avoid the effect of the sabbatical year's cancellation of debt, see Maimonides, *Book of Agriculture* 7.9.6–19, discussing Hillel's instituting the *prosbul* "in order that debts might not be cancelled and people might continue to grant loans" (7.9.16).

8. He could be an accidental or an intentional wrongdoer. That would make a difference in some settings but not for our purposes here.
9. Calabresi and Melamed, "Property Rules, Liability Rules."
10. We make our eyes inalienable, that is, not voluntarily transferable at any price. But put that aside in the interests of our eye-for-an-eye hypothetical.
11. The valuation problem is significantly easier if the thief is still in possession of the thing stolen, in which case the actual object will be restored to the owner and the decision maker need not bother to price the thing taken, although he would still have to determine the rental value of the asset for the time the thief had it.
12. Westbrook, alone among biblical commentators I have read, notes that such a right would enable the poor to enrich themselves at the expense of wrongdoers, but he does not generalize the insight; *Studies in Biblical and Cuneiform Law* 74.
13. Clendinnen, *Aztecs* 61.
14. With a slightly different twist, the modern Hebrew phrase for "specific performance of a contract" – that is, when conventional money damages are not acceptable to compensate for breach and only carrying out the letter of the promise will do – is "performed in the eye" (*bitzuah b'eyin*), where the eye serves as an image of high-stakes seriousness. Compare too the standard Hebrew expression for "actually," which is literally "in the bone" (*b'etzem*). Not a stone, but the bone. The idea seems to be that real reality must not only be hard as a rock but also must have the capacity to feel pain.
15. On mutilation of corpses and accusations of cannibalism in the aftermath of late medieval battle, see Groebner's interesting discussion, *Defaced* 139–146. Given that the dead were quickly stripped of their clothing (one needs to be reminded how valuable a change of clothes was before the automation of cloth production) and so not identifiable as to the side they had fought on, the mutilation of corpses might not have been confined to enemy corpses, but might well have included those of the buddy of your buddy.
16. *Guðmundar saga dýra* 26:212; see Miller, *Bloodtaking* 2. In one Norse story, clearly folkloric, a two-eyed man falsely accused by a one-eyed man of stealing his eye offers to settle the matter by ordeal: each of them is to remove an eye and place them on a scale. If they weigh the same then the accuser makes his proof. Needless to say the one-eyed accuser forgoes the challenge; see *Hróa þáttr heimska* in *Flateyjarbók*, II. 73–80. Talionic bargaining makes for good tales.
17. Josephus, *Antiquities* 4.8.35.280. Also discussed and dismissed in Daube, "Eye for an Eye," 178, as being out of step with contemporary Jewish practice at the time of Christ. See Jackson, *Studies in the Semiotics of Biblical Law* 281, disputing Daube; I too would not be so hasty to reject Josephus' authority; buy-out was always an option, if not officially then privately. See further n. 19 in this chapter.

NOTES TO PAGES 53–57

18. See the case of Jon Loftsson setting aside Sturla's excessive self-judged award; *Sturlu saga* chs. 33–34. See my discussion of the Norse custom of "self-judgment," in which one party grants the other the right to be the judge in his own dispute. It was understood that the "judge" was to play fair (*Bloodtaking* 285–289). Some of the best saga stories are about over-reaching self-judged awards. In another saga case, the defendant paid the excessive sum without cavil and thereby took home all the honor in the case (*Þorgils saga ok Hafliða* chs. 31–32) in much the same way that Gudmund captures it here by being willing himself to pay the excessive damages he adjudged. See also my discussion of forgiveness in *Faking It* 90–94.

19. Daube, "*Lex Talionis*," 108. Daube, 117, discussing 1 Kings 20.39– "Keep this man; if by any means he be missing, then shall thy life be for his life, or else thou shalt pay a talent of silver" – finds the "or else thou shalt pay a talent of silver" to be a later interpolation, but why? His own argument is not undone if the contrary were the case. See also n. 17 in this chapter. Authorities also disagree as to whether the attack on the wife in Ex. 21.22 is deliberate or accidental. Deliberate: Daube, "*Lex Talionis*," 108; Paul, *Studies in the Book of the Covenant* 68, 74; unintentional with fatal consequence: Otto, "Town and Rural Countryside in Ancient Israelite Law," 16. Unintentional miscarriage: Jackson, in "*Lex Talionis*: Revisting Daube's Classic"; Sprinkle, "Interpretation of Exodus 21.22–25." But the passage commonly rendered "as the judges shall determine" is notoriously difficult. See the discussion in Houtman, *Das Bundesbuch* 158 and the various translations: "He must also pay for the abortion," Houtman, 155; "The payment to be based on a reckoning," Paul, *Studies in the Book of the Covenant* 70 and the JPS translation; AV, "And he shall pay as the judges determine," also RSV; Westbrook, *Studies in Biblical and Cuneiform Law*, 69, translates, "He alone shall pay." I try to make some sense of the AV rendering in the text to which this note is appended.

20. The statement of the Exodus talion that follows hard upon the italicized clause quoted in the text could then be understood in this way: that the oddman would be without power to keep V from taking an eye "if any mischief follow," but perhaps we would still see the oddman intervene if V decided to sell his right to W's eye back to W for a sum beyond all reason, even though he could simply take the eye. Perhaps, as with the Vikings, there was a general distrust of those who were too willing to use their own injuries to enrich themselves with sheep and silver, rather than just take blood.

21. Miller, *Bloodtaking* 61–68.

22. In Roth, *Law Collections from Mesopotamia* 16–17.

23. Thanks to Kyle Logue for this and many more points but to whom I am denying the last word here.

Five. Teaching a Lesson: Pain and Poetic Justice

1. In fact the rabbis in the Mishna made the verse of burning for burning, wound for wound, stripe for stripe the textual warrant for assessing damages for pain, in addition to the other four categories of compensable damage: for the actual damage – as for the loss of a limb – for the loss of time at work, for the cost of healing, and for the insult; see the discussion in Daube, "Eye for an Eye."

2. See Nietzsche, *Genealogy of Morals* 2.7; Améry, *At the Mind's Limits* 37–38; Pernick, *A Calculus of Suffering.*

3. "Kel" is a contraction of kettle. As with the tripods of Greek epic, the amount of wealth that went into making a kettle made "kettle" an honorific suitable for a person's name.

4. Couvade provides an interesting instance of the ritual substitutions needed to make up for the fact that another's pain mostly eludes us; see Broude, "Rethinking the Couvade."

5. See Daube, "Law in the Narratives," 39–62, discussing *go'el,* redeemer, avenger.

6. Notice too how Thorgeir blames old Thorbjorn's "accident" as an intentional act of revenge taking, but on an inappropriate target: "I didn't kill his son; he shouldn't be seeking revenge on me."

7. Thorkel does an encore later in the saga, where he justifies the torture doled out to the uneven Hrafnkel as a lesson in fellow-feeling (ch. 13): "We have heard that you have been very little inclined to go easy on your enemies, and it is fitting now, that you should experience the same today."

8. On their and even our mistrust of claims of accident see my *Faking It* 77–95.

9. The Hebrew in Deuteronomy changes the preposition translated as "for" from the iterations in Exodus and Leviticus. For the *tachat* (*tof-chet-tof*) of Exodus and Leviticus, Deuteronomy has *b* (*bet*); see Daube, "Lex Talionis," 110–115, 129–130. See also Paul, *Studies in the Book of the Covenant* 74n5. The *b* in Deuteronomy lessens the compensatory force of the talionic formulations in Exodus and Leviticus. The *tachat* formula more forcefully suggests actual substitution of an identical object for the one lost. See too Carmichael's reading of the Deut. talionic provisions as a stricture governing the mutilation of a criminal's corpse, arising as a gloss on Naboth's murder by Jezebel; *The Spirit of Biblical Law* ch. 6.

10. There are varying views as to what makes an instance of justice qualify as poetic. Lewis, "The Punishment that Leaves Something to Chance," 60: "Making the punishment fit the crime, Mikado fashion, is *poetic* justice." Nozick would find the poetry in poetic justice when the appropriate punishment occurs but without being produced or intended as a punishment (*Philosophical Explanations* 370). But that does not exhaust all the poetry, for it misses the fact that many authorities tried to make intended

punishment share in the panache of having a kind of aesthetic perfection that made it qualify as "poetic." And the punishment's poetry was not the least affected by the fact that it was imposed intentionally.

11. Thus Kant, *Metaphysics of Morals* 332. On the biblical commitment to make retribution mirror the offense in remarkably subtle ways, thus poetizing the justice, see Carmichael, *The Spirit of Biblical Law* 142–161, especially the discussion of the two accounts of Saul's death, 143–149. The idea of a special domain of the aesthetic independent of the moral is a rather late development by most accounts. Yet the Greeks, for whom beauty was moral, knew of poetic theory independent from the moral (even this is arguable), if not the moral independent of the aesthetic.

12. *Hamlet* 5.2.331; *Revenger's Tragedy* 3.4; on revenge and the comic see Kerrigan, *Revenge Tragedy* ch. 8.

13. Westbrook, *Studies in Biblical and Cuneiform Law* 56. Westbrook cites also 2 Sam. 12.13–15, where David's punishment for having Uriah killed is commuted from death to the death of the child David fathered on Uriah's wife. The narrative is explicit that the punishment is being mitigated: "And Nathan said unto David, The Lord also hath put away thy sin; thou shalt not die. Howbeit because by this deed thou hast given great occasion to the enemies of the Lord to blaspheme, the child also that is born unto thee shall surely die." David prays for the child to survive the illness that afflicts him, but he does not ask that God take him, David, instead; David asks only that God remit the sentence against the child. David's case does not raise the issue of artful talionic symmetry that the Hammurabic one does. Still the justice is poetic. The fruit of the illicit intercourse is killed.

14. Waldron, "*Lex Talionis*," 44; also Lewis, "The Punishment that Leaves Something to Chance," 60, discussing the virtues and vices of having a penal lottery for punishing attempts: because what the criminal did was to create an unlawful risk, why not put him at risk? "The point we want to dramatize, both to the criminal and to the public, is that what we think of the crime is just like what the criminal thinks of his punishment. If it's a risk for a risk, how can anybody miss the point?" (60). In this light see Jackson's discussion of two styles of biblical statement of the talion, the classic talionic *tachat* formula, which he says demands quantitative exactitude: eye for an eye versus the *ka-asher*, or the "as-so" formula of qualitative reciprocity; thus Samson gives as his justification for smiting the Philistines hip and thigh for having burned his wife and father-in-law: "*As* they did unto me *so* have I done unto them" (Judg. 15.11); *Studies in the Semiotics of Biblical Law* 271–280.

15. See my "Clint Eastwood and Equity," 164–170, for a fuller discussion of these metaphors.

16. *Njál's saga* ch. 44.

17. "Sayings of the High One," st. 45, in Terry, *Edda*.

18. Xenophon, *Anabasis* 1.9.11, Warner tr., p. 92.

Six. A Pound of Flesh

1. Hazlitt, *A View of the English Stage* 188.
2. "Smug" is Shylock's term for Antonio (3.1.41); it still bears there its nonpejorative sense of spruce, sleek, well-groomed, but one suspects it is already showing hints of indicating a kind of culpable complacent self-satisfaction.
3. See Patterson, "The Bankruptcy of Homoerotic Amity in Shakespeare's *Merchant of Venice*," 10n3, for bibliography, and his article in general. The 2004 movie rendition of the play strongly suggests a homosexual bond between Antonio and Bassanio, to no discernible elucidation of character or motive.
4. On Antonio as usurer see Shell, "The Wether and the Ewe," 74–75; also Engle's astute observation discussing Antonio's comment, "Mark you this Bassanio, / The devil can cite Scripture for his purpose": "What the scene illustrates is the diabolism forced on Shylock by Antonio's near-hysterical resistance to any formal acceptance of the nature of the economic system he lives in" ("Thrift is Blessing," 32). The Jewish presence in Elizabethan England was negligible, they having been expelled in the reign of Edward I and not readmitted until the Protectorate. Much of the moneylending in England was handled by the local parson, and a prominent role in local credit markets was played by widows; see Jones, *God and the Moneylenders* 71–72, and Holderness, "The Clergy as Money-Lenders" and "Widows in Pre-industrial Society," 435–442.
5. And Shylock is not just given to irrational revenge; as W. Cohen, "*The Merchant of Venice* and the Possibilities of Historical Criticism," 769, points out, "His desire for revenge is both motivated by economics and possessed of a large degree of economic logic (e.g., 1.3.39–40; and 3.1.49, and 117–118)."
6. This is a regular trope that begins any number of critical essays on the play; see Lewalski, "Biblical Allusion and Allegory in *The Merchant of Venice*," 327; W. Cohen, "*The Merchant of Venice* and the Possibilities of Historical Criticism," 767.
7. Lewalski ("Biblical Allusion and Allegory in *The Merchant of Venice*," 329, 343) suggests that Bassanio's spendthrift habits are in fact moral. She is not arguing the virtues of trickle-down economics or Mandevillian private vices producing public benefits; rather, her good Christian Bassanio gives all for love and trusts to Providence; he is considering the lilies of the field.
8. The word *incarnation* is played upon almost blasphemously by Launcelot Gobbo in one of his many malapropisms: "Certainly the Jew is the very devil incarnation" (2.2.26).
9. Lev. 25.36–37. On the general theme of Jews in Shakespearean England see Shapiro, who nicely relates the images of feasting and dining in the play with fears of Jews as blood drinkers and cannibals (*Shakespeare and the*

Jews 109–111); also Harris, *Sick Economies* 78–79; contrast Whigham, who in discussing images of the alimentary tract in Renaissance drama sees *The Merchant of Venice* solely in terms of anality, not mouths, but compaction, money, feces ("Reading Social Conflict in the Alimentary Tract," 336–339). His discussion is clever but not convincing.

10. Michal, David's wife, makes an effigy of him using goat's hair for its head to make it look to Saul's messengers as if David is sick in bed (1 Sam. 20.13).

11. Clendinnen, *Aztecs* 47–48.

12. See Rawson, *God, Gulliver, and Genocide* 12, discussing the language of punitive castigation such as in "exterminate the brutes" as involving a "volatile combination of 'meaning it,' not meaning it, and not not meaning it."

13. It is a commonplace of the antiusury argument taken from Aristotle that it is "unnatural" for money to breed its like, to have offspring that resemble it, *Politics* I.10, 1258b1–8. In his view money's only use is for purposes of exchange, not to produce more of itself directly; when it facilitates exchange it is realizing its proper end, when it generates more of itself directly, it is not realizing its proper end.

14. Thus too Jacob's making Laban's single-colored sheep produce particolored sheep in Shylock's account (1.3.76–90) of Gen. 31.37–42; the ewes would not recognize their lambs. Note that Jessica by taking her father's money, and running to her new faith launders it of its Jewish taint. It will no longer earn interest like Jewish money; it will be squandered in hedonic pursuits like proper Belmontian money.

15. When Shylock "layest in [his] unhallowed dam" he was infused with the spirit of a wolf who had been hanged for killing a human (4.1.134–136).

16. As W. Cohen points out, ("The crisis of the play arises not from [Shylock's] insistence on usury, but from his refusal of it" ("*The Merchant of Venice* and the Possibilities of Historical Criticism," 769). On the history of late medieval and early-modern usury prohibitions, see Jones, *God and the Moneylenders*.

17. See Shell, "The Wether and the Ewe," 49–50.

18. The Synagogue in conventional medieval and Renaissance iconography is often depicted blindfolded; for an image from the south transept portal of Strasbourg cathedral, see http://www.kfki.hu/~arthp/html/zgothic/gothic/1/index.html.

19. Stones are a common term for testicles. See Shapiro's discussion on circumcision, *Shakespeare and the Jews* 126–130.

20. Harris, *Sick Economies* 77–78, links the tainted Antonio to the particolored lambs of Jacob. In each case, Antonio's and Laban's sheep, flesh is transformed into interest.

21. Thus Coverdale's translation of Gen. 17:11: "Thus shall my couenaunt be in youre flesh for an euerlastinge couenaunt. And yf there shalbe any manchilde vncircumcided in the foreskinne of his flesh, his

soule shalbe roted out from his people, because he hath broken my couenaunt."

22. Note too how Milton plays with the idea of circumcision and real piercing of the heart in the poem quoted earlier at chapter 3, n. 52.

23. Law does not have this meaning for Jesus in the Sermon on the Mount, who in that sermon is an observant and respectful Jew and urges fulfillment of the Law; see Matt. 5.18–21.

24. "Satisfice" is Herbert Simon's term for a level of acceptability less than optimal though "good enough," which we might think of as one step better than "making do" (*Models of Man* 205).

25. *Twelve Tables* III c. 6.

26. Lewalski, "Biblical Allusion and Allegory in *The Merchant of Venice*," 341: "His brief 'I am content' suggests, I believe, not mean-spiritedness but weary acknowledgement of the fact that he can no longer make his stand upon the discredited Law." Oh my. Also Coghill, "The Governing Idea," 16, who notes that "from Antonio's point of view Shylock has his chance of eternal joy, and it is he who has given it to him."

27. Hazlitt, *Characters of Shakespeare's Plays*, 213, 215. Also: "Portia is not a very great favourite with us … Portia has a certain degree of affectation and pedantry about her, which is very unusual in Shakespear's women, but which perhaps was a proper qualification for the office of a 'civil doctor,' which she undertakes and executes so successfully."

28. Luxon, "A Second Daniel," 3: "An audience that warms to Portia's mercy speech would regard Shylock's carnal humanism – revenge for revenge – as something very low indeed." See also Lewalski, "Biblical Allusion and Allegory in *The Merchant of Venice*," 330–331.

29. And unlike the diction of debt, the teaching-a-lesson metaphor does not work to capture the obligation to return good favors.

30. Those who believe that revenge is hardwired might wish to argue that Shylock has not broken the litany of bodily needs at all, but merely continued them. Some argue that revenge is in some respects a bodily need and interpret certain psychological experiments to indicate that, with culture either further elaborating and reinforcing it, or working desperately to repress it. See chapter 10, n. 11.

31. Montaigne, "Apology for Raymond Sebond," *Essays* 2.12, p. 495.

32. The rabbis were hardly pro-blood-revenge, having interpreted the talion to be satisfied by compensation payment and not body parts; see Daube, "*Lex Talionis*," 107–109. The requirement to forgive those who offend is very strong; see Maimonides, "Laws of Repentence," 2.9–20, *Book of Knowledge* 81b, and "Law Relating to Moral Dispositions," 7.7, ibid., 56b: "He who takes revenge, violates a prohibition." Nonetheless there are exceptions; see, for example, "Laws Concerning the Study of Torah," 7.12, ibid., 65a, where a scholar who has been reviled in public is not allowed to forgive the offense. To do so would be to show contempt for the Torah.

Seven. Remember Me: Mnemonics, Debts (of Blood), and the Making of the Person

1. Nietzsche, *Genealogy of Morals* 2.3.
2. *Genealogy of Morals* 2.2; Nietzsche's delight in metaphors of violence and cruelty to construct the genealogy of guilt and the creation of conscience should be compared with the gentler conventional rational-choice metaphor for making credible commitments: Odysseus having himself bound to the mast; see Elster, *Ulysses and the Sirens*. It is nearly impossible to get the rough-and-tumble out of stories of commitment; see, for example, Schelling's classic *The Strategy of Conflict* chs. 1–3.
3. See Miller, "Choosing the Avenger."
4. *Eyrbyggja saga* ch. 27.
5. *Njál's saga* ch. 116.
6. Cf. also 1 Sam. 11.7 and see further the text at chapter 9, n. 7.
7. For some telling tales see Hyams, *Rancor and Reconciliation* 119–127, who reveals the more complex attitude monastic Christian culture had toward revenge, because monks found themselves praying *for* it so often; for a particularly subtle account of saintly vengeance see White, "Garsinde v. Saint Foy."
8. For an especially interesting example from southern Italy in which memory creation is precisely the issue, see Lewis, *Naples '44* 65.
9. See Daube, "*Lex Talionis*," 116; see also the case of the woman of Tekoa, 2 Sam. 14.7.
10. Eiland, "Heidegger's Etymological Web," 49; see OED s.v., plight sb.1; and Huizinga's discussion, *Homo Ludens* 38–41.
11. On plighting troth and putting in plight, see Burrow, *Gestures and Looks* 14–15.
12. See Miller, *Humiliation* 5; also my *Mystery of Courage* ch. 9, and Herdt, "Sambia Nosebleeding Rites." Herdt demonstrates the extraordinarily intense and intrusive socialization work that must be undertaken to maintain a culture of violence in the face of fear, risk aversion, prudence, and desires for ease and relaxation.
13. Consider too that the word "to tell," like "to account," operates both in the world of moneyed numbers and in the world of storytelling. To count is both to tell a story and to count out. The bank "teller" still bears witness. This association is more than an Indo-European phenomenon. In Hebrew, too, to count numbers and to tell stories share the same root: *s-p-r*.
14. Jesus' reference to his body as bread is richer in its suggestiveness in Semitic languages. The Arabic cognate of Hebrew *lechem* (bread) means meat, flesh. In Hebrew too *lechem* can mean food in general and in one instance at least refers clearly to meat; Lev. 3.11. There is thus more force in Jesus' Aramaic to the suggestion that this bread is his flesh. My lack of Greek prevents me from knowing whether the fleshly suggestiveness

of Semitic *lechem* is borne by Greek words for bread. See also chapter 3, n. 45.

15. 8 *Æthelred* §35.

16. These forms of sublime recallings of oneself are brilliantly discussed and made a central concern of Braden's *Renaissance Tragedy and the Senecan Tradition* 68.

17. There are critics who desperately seek to back Hamlet's concern that the ghost may be a "damned ghost" or a "devil" as if that would resolve the claim made on Hamlet to take revenge; see Prosser, *Hamlet and Revenge*; also McGee, *The Elizabethan Hamlet*. But this need not detain us, for the discourse of remembrance and revenge would be the same whether voiced by a devil or a poor unfortunate soul hoping someone will properly remember him.

18. Kerrigan, in Hamlet's case, opposes remembering to revenge (*Revenge Tragedy* 182–186). It should be clear that I do not think they are opposed terms in vengeance cultures. Kerrigan underestimates, I think, the obligation-creating aspect of remembrance. It is of some interest that the Hebrew root *p-k-d* is used to mean both to remember (1 Sam. 15.2) and to revenge, punish, visit upon (e.g., Jer. 9.8; AV 9.9).

19. Herodotus, *Histories* I.33, p. 53. See too Aristotle, *Nicomachean Ethics* I.x–xi.

20. Montaigne, "That we should not be deemed happy till after our death," *Essays* 1.19.

21. *Grettir's saga* ch. 93; cf. *Gísli's saga* ch. 22. The revenge for Grettir's death was not lawful, because he was killed legitimately as an outlaw. But because it was held that Grettir's killers had behaved contemptibly in how they went about killing him there was considerable popular support for taking revenge on his behalf.

22. *Grettir's saga* ch. 86.

23. See my "Deep Inner Lives, Individualism, and People of Honour."

24. *Egil's saga* ch. 24.

25. Rosaldo, *Knowledge and Passion* 157–158; the emotions have become something of a fad in a variety of disciplines. The work varies enormously in quality and sophistication. For a model on the social and political uses and stagings of anger, see White, "The Politics of Anger in Medieval France."

26. See, for example, *Ine* §70; the 600-shilling man is not known outside the codes of Ine and Alfred, but there are numerous references in several codes to 200- and 1200-men.

27. Unless, that is, the king or royal officials took an interest in the case.

28. *Geþyncðo* c. 2, cc. 6–7, in Liebermann, *Gesetze* 1.456, 458; 5 *Æthelred* §9.1; 6 *Æthelred* §5.3; 8 *Æthelred* §28.

29. *Njál's saga* ch. 37.

30. Recall Daube's reading in chapter 2, n. 31: Jesus' counsel to turn the other cheek is to recommend forgoing money compensation for injuries

to honor. Maybe Jesus had concerns about the kinds of problematic incentives such money might give rise to.

31. *Gulathing law* §186.
32. *Njál's saga* ch. 37.
33. See especially *Njál's saga* chs. 69–70, 72, 74.
34. Miller, *Bloodtaking* 271–284.
35. See Black-Michaud, *Feuding Societies* 12, 78–80, 110, 116.

Eight. Dismemberment and Price Lists

1. *Að* §1, in Liebermann, *Gesetze* 1.464; Whitelock *EHD* 470; numbers written out are written out in the manuscript; Arabic numerals are in Roman in the manuscript. The provision comes from a group of texts authored by Archbishop Wulfstan of York (d. 1023). They appear to be in the nature of restatements of the law. On the Wulfstan texts, see Wormald, *The Making of English Law* 391–394.
2. *Wer* §1, in Liebermann, *Gesetze* 1.392. For a discussion of this anonymous text see Wormald, *The Making of English Law* 374–378.
3. *Ine* §28.2; cf. §§45, 48; 2 *Æthelstan* §2.2.
4. For example, *Ine* §§19, 52, 53, 54; *Alf.* §11.4; see Liebermann, "Die Eideshufen"; also Chadwick, *Studies on Anglo-Saxon Institutions* 134–153.
5. *Alf.* §4.
6. 3 *Edgar* §4.
7. 1 *Æthelred* §1.5; 5 *Æthelred* §§28, 31; 1 *Canute* §2.4; 2 *Canute* §§29, 36, 52.
8. *Hammurabi* §§215–216.
9. Clendinnen, *Aztecs* 38.
10. *Ine* §11; see also Icelandic provisions prohibiting selling poor kin abroad; exceptions were made for getting rid of defectives, *Grágás* Ib 21; defects are not to be counted against a person until age sixteen. Dennis et al., *Grágás* II, p. 46n104, note the specific defects listed in the laws of the Gulathing (Norway) and Gotland: epilepsy, bedwetting, bone pains, sucking cows' udders. The problem of selling people abroad in England seemed to be an enduring one: Archbishop Wulfstan complains some three centuries later than Ine that "poor men are... sold far and wide out of this country into the power of foreigners, although quite innocent; and children in the cradle are enslaved for petty theft" (Whitelock, *EHD* 930).
11. Simmel argues that wergeld began purely as a means of compensating economic losses before it ultimately became a status marker, divorced from the economic. Thus the refusal to extend wergeld to slaves (*Philosophy of Money* 358).
12. *Grágás* Ib 35. Men no less than women had to measure up to the slave standard of value; see *Grágás* Ib 21–22.

13. Note the negotiability of the boundary between slave and free in *Ine* §74.1. (c. 700). It provides that a Welsh slave who kills an Englishman is either to be handed over by his owner to the dead Englishman's kin or to be redeemed for 60 shillings instead. But if the slave owner declines either to hand him over or buy him back for 60 shillings then he must free the slave. The obligation to pay the wergeld of the dead Englishman now falls to the murderous ex-slave's free kinsmen. But should he have no free kin, "his enemies can deal with him." The slave earns his freedom – his freedom to get whacked – by becoming a killer. This gives a perverse twist to the notion that with freedom comes responsibility. As a slave, the killer was a 60-shilling liability to his owner; as a free man he is a 200-shilling liability to his kin, who will no doubt be strongly tempted to hand him over to his enemies anyway.

14. The Icelandic example is not quite apt in the Anglo-Saxon context because the Icelandic practice did not provide for fixed wergeld payments. Wergelds were up for negotiation, thereby generating their own set of anxieties, although in fact, as noted in chapter 1, the payments for corpses tended to cluster around certain customary prices; see Guðmundsson, "Manngjöld-hundrað."

15. See the essays in Algazi, Groebner, and Jussen, eds., *Negotiating the Gift*; see also my *Humiliation* ch. 1 and *Bloodtaking* ch. 3.

16. *Primitive* is a word we have come to use with trepidation, but nonetheless the case can be made for thus characterizing Æthelberht's laws; Wormald and Oliver argue the appropriateness of the term, offering as grounds the "utter simplicity" of its syntax, but also substantively, there being "no statements of principle whence certain consequences must follow"; Wormald, *The Making of English Law* 95; Oliver, *The Beginnings of English Law* 34. The laws have recently been subjected to sophisticated and very fruitful linguistic analysis by Schwyter, "Syntax and Style in the Anglo-Saxon Law-Codes"; see also his *Old English Legal Language*.

17. The conventional editorial practice distinguishes ninety provisions or laws in Æthelberht's code. Oliver, in her recent edition of the code, argues persuasively for renumbering the provisions, reducing some sections to subsections and elevating others. I feel guilty for reproducing the old divisions, which are without manuscript authority anyway, but all references in the literature until 2002 employ that enumeration and are likely to do for some time because of the force of Liebermann's edition of the corpus of Anglo-Saxon law. In any event, Oliver takes care to provide the old numbering along with her presentation of the new.

18. In seventh-century Kent the *sceatt* was 1/20th of a shilling; see Oliver, *The Beginnings of English Law* 82–83. As in note 1 in this chapter Arabic numerals are Roman in the manuscript, those written out are written out in the manuscript.

19. No one knows what is being referred to here; see ibid., 101–102.

20. Again, it is not clear what is being referred to; see ibid.
21. A word seems to be missing; the piercing of the nose already was dealt with in §45; Liebermann guesses "throat" (*Gesetze* 3:11); see Oliver, *The Beginnings of English Law* 71.
22. OE *dynt*, yielding ModE *dint, dent*; variously glossed as bruise or blow.
23. See Oliver's discussion, *The Beginnings of English Law* 73.
24. The sum of 30 sceattas on top of what he received for the blow.
25. In Old English *friends* means kin and was extended to those who were obliged to you as if they were kin; see Oliver, *The Beginnings of English Law* 75, note e. Evidently the 12 shillings was a fixed payment no matter how the bone healed. The amount of damage commensurate with the disability is left for arbitration and negotiation when the consequences of the injury are finally known; see ibid., 49.
26. See Whitman, "At the Origins of Law and the State," on the essential nexus between price lists, mutilation, and the idea of primitive legislation itself. He would, following von Amira, argue the connection of mutilation with the sacral. These provisions, however, look remarkably unsacral; they have as much aura of the uncanny as a worker's comp schedule. The sacred does play a part in this code, but it is embedded obscurely in the notion of *mund*, of which more anon.
27. See, for example, Cal. Labor Code §§4662–4664 (2004).
28. I cannot agree with Oliver, *The Beginnings of English Law* 107, that "fraud" refers to the bride's virginal status. I would guess, in accordance with the Icelandic law cited earlier, that the fraud goes more to matters of her health, or maybe her legal status, which would be compromised had she, say, already been promised to another.
29. See the discussion ibid., 36–38.
30. See Oliver's comment, ibid., 73.
31. Not that such a well-connected thief couldn't be brought to justice. There is the case of a certain Helmstan, a thieving thegn, who loses his property, though he still has the law twisted a bit in his favor by the support of powerful benefactors; see Keynes, "The Fonthill Letter"; also Wormald, *The Making of English Law* 144–148. One can see in the Anglo-Saxon laws of the tenth century an intense anxiety regarding the kinless, judgment-proof, loner on the one hand – the thief – and the thieving lord, who with his kin and retainers is anything but a loner, on the other. One was a concern because he was alone, the other because he wasn't.
32. One of the best short stories in world literature, "Thorstein the Staffstruck," has its initial fillip in the shame of receiving a facial wound, and hence a visible mark that bears witness to its not having been properly avenged; see Miller, *Bloodtaking* ch. 2.
33. Above all Liebermann's massive edition (*Gesetze*) and Wormald's recent magisterial work, *The Making of English Law*, among many others.
34. *Hlophere and Eadric* §§12–14; see also *Ine* §6.

35. See the compensation Gunnar is assessed to pay even though he had an absolute defense of self-defense; *Njál's saga* chs. 66, 74; Miller, *Bloodtaking* 282–283.
36. Beyerle, *Rechtsgang* 44–45, assumes offsets in Frankish and other continental settings, citing saga evidence.
37. *Njál's saga* chs. 72, 139.
38. See *Njál's saga* chs. 64–66; see Miller, *Bloodtaking* 277–283.
39. See Gregory of Tours, *History of the Franks* 7.47.
40. *Þorgils saga ok Hafliða* ch. 31. Icelandic body parts were not scheduled as they were in Kent and Wessex.
41. See further chapter 11.
42. Liebermann, *Gesetze* 3.11.
43. Keynes, "The Fonthill Letter," 76: presumably the money is not to bribe the judge, though one can never be sure, but represents an offer to compensate or actual compensation paid to the other side to settle the dispute.
44. *Ine* §55; see also §§58–59.
45. Montaigne, "On thumbs," *Essays* 2.26.
46. The equal value of hand, eye, and foot is something of a commonplace in the barbarian codes; see Wormald, *The Making of English Law* 281. Alfred, recall, adds the tongue to this trinity; see chapter 3, n. 17.
47. 3 *Edmund* §4; Liebermann, *Gesetze* s.v. Finger, 2.402.
48. *Leges Henrici Primi* §93.15–19. Alfred does not rank the middle finger – *impudicus* – the lowest; it is one step above the little finger in his schedule, which from thumb to little finger is as follows: 30-15-12-17-9. In his scheme the decorative value of the ring finger trumps any functional value attributable to the others except for the thumb; *Alf.* §§56–60.
49. There is evidence in classical sources that gesturing with the middle finger had "dirty" meanings; see, for example, Martial, *Epigrams* 2.28, where it appears to indicate anal penetration of a male; also Suetonius, *Twelve Caesars* Life of Augustus, c. 45: Augustus expelled an actor named Pylades from Italy for "making an obscene movement of his middle finger" to a spectator who hissed at his performance. Wilda, *Strafrecht* 768, conveniently charts the values of the various fingers in all the Germanic codes in which they are priced. The middle is the lowest, or tied for lowest with the ring finger, in the Alamannic, Bavarian, Frisian, and Rotharian codes. The middle finger in these codes is blandly referred to as the middle, or the longest, or the third, and not as *impudicus*. Yet the low value of the finger in a significant number of the codes suggests a possible independent Germanic taboo associated with the middle finger.
50. *Kormak's saga* ch. 3, v. 7.
51. The literature on fetishization of female body parts is enormous. For a piece a cut above the usual fare see Vickers's informative discussion of those Renaissance poetic catalogues of praise, sincere or faux, of body parts, the *blazons anatomique* ("Members Only: Marot's Anatomical Blazons").

52. *Grettir's saga* chs. 2, 10–11.
53. Grettir's death scene recalls Onund's stump. Grettir must fight his last battle from his knees because one of his legs is badly infected from an accident hewing wood. Grettir thus dies a "treefoot" of sorts.

Nine. Of Hands, Hospitality, Personal Space, and Holiness

1. Kant, *Groundwork for the Metaphysics of Morals* 52 [Ak 4.434].
2. *Þórðar saga kakala* ch. 14.
3. *Mund* is Latinized in several of the continental Germanic law codes as *mundium*. It appears five times in *Beowulf* as a simplex meaning hand, twice in a compound meaning protector, and five times compounded with *grip*; *hand*, however, appears more than thirty times and also in five different compounds. However, *mund* in the sense of hand occurs only once in OE prose. *Mund* pretty much dies out in English in all its senses by the thirteenth century, although fourteenth-century romances still employ it in an alliterative phrase: "muchel mound," great worth, strength. See MED, s.v. mound, n.1. The philology of *mund* is rather complex; see Stanley's treatment of the word, "Words for the Dictionary of Old English," 39–47.
4. *Æthelberht* §§8, 15, 75; the *mund* of an eorl can be deduced from other provisions to be 12 shillings; see §§13–14.
5. The great Rechtsschule scholars of the nineteenth century have discussed this ad nauseam. I mean to go at it in a less strictly legal way than they do.
6. *Mund* covers ground similar to notions like *grið* (quarter or sanctuary), *frið* (peace), and *borh* (surety), but this would get us into technical legal matters beyond my present needs; see my discussion of *grið* and the sense of the inviolate home in "Homelessness in the Middle of Nowhere." See Liebermann, *Gesetze* 2 s.vv. *grið*, *frið*, *borh*, Frieden, and Schutz.
7. See Dresch, *Tribes, Government, and History in Yemen* 62, discussing *mund* equivalents ("something like personal sovereignty or jurisdiction") among the Yemeni tribes.
8. See also Gen. 19.8, where Lot offers his virgin daughters to the men of Sodom.
9. A related point from the Old Norse world: Carol Clover notes that Old Norse had no separate word for vagina that could not also be used for anus. She suggests that the male anus is primary in the Old Norse world and that the vagina is understood merely as a variant of it; see Clover, "Regardless of Sex," 375–378. Her point seems to be even more starkly appropriate to the stories of Lot and the men of Sodom and of the Levite's concubine and the base fellows of the tribe of Benjamin.
10. Thus it is that the special sense that *mund* came to have in Old Norse, unlike the other Germanic languages, was narrower and had to do with legitimizing sexual relations. It was the name given to the payment a groom was to make the bride that was to become her property as soon as they

were properly bedded. It was a purchase of her "hospitality," *Grágás* Ia 222. (I am brushing over a small problem in that ON *mundr* is masculine, whereas the OE *mund* we have been talking about is a feminine noun. ON has a feminine *mund* also, meaning hand. The two forms are related, but exactly how is not clear.)

11. Statutes enabling the incorporation of business firms in the nineteenth century gave corporations the "right" to be sued. That business interests would fight for such a right mystifies law students, until it is explained that the right to be held liable means that people will be willing to do business with you. To be capable of being held liable, to be blamable, is the surest sign of legal personhood; and of moral personhood too.

12. *Hlophere and Eadric* §15.

13. See OED s.v. guest, sb.; and chapter 1, n. 35.

14. We still retain certain ritual practices that hearken back to *mund*: thus the bottle of wine presented almost simultaneously with crossing the threshold into the dinner host's domain. Graeber contrasts the casual entry and exit into and out of college dorm rooms with the gift of wine that formalizes relations of adults in a way "that makes spontaneity more difficult; [the wine] is as much a bar to sociality as an expression of it" (*Toward an Anthropological Theory of Value* 221). I am not sure he is right: the bottle of wine does not make for the formality; it is the invitation that is delivered more than a day in advance that does that.

15. In Iceland she would also have a claim in her own right, although for her effectively to bring it her master would have to act on her behalf.

16. See *Hlophere and Eadric* §§11–13. Something less than the full value of the *mund* is assessed, but §14 makes it clear that it is still a violation of the *mund* that is being compensated; the amount is lowered if the offense does not involve blood. Note too that for us and them the misbehavior need not be in your house for it to violate your *mund*; it would be no different were the incident to occur at a restaurant, as long as the dinner there was understood to be under your auspices.

17. See Goffman, *Relations in Public* ch. 2. Ethological studies of critical distance of the fight-or-flight reflex have some primitive connection with *mund*.

18. I do not want to get into the *Rechtsschule* debates on the origins of the king's peace. Goebel takes the view that the king's *mund* was there as a concept to be employed by kings opportunistically to justify expansions of their power (*Felony and Misdemeanor* 49).

19. To be within the *word* of the king has the same protective qualities as to be within his *mund* or hand; see Goebel's discussion in *Felony and Misdemeanor* 47–53. See also the case of the girl taken into the *verbum regis*, the king's protection, after she killed her would-be rapist as he slept in Gregory of Tours, *History of the Franks* 9.27; also *Lex Salica* §14.5 (*Pactus* §13.6).

20. *Helgi* thus pretty much takes over the conceptual substance of *mund*.

21. In one respect the Icelandic laws grant a slave greater rights than a free man and the laws explicitly make mention of that very fact: "A slave has more right than a free man in one respect. A slave has the right to kill on account of his wife even though she is a bondwoman but a free man has no right to kill on account of his bondwoman even though she is his wife," *Grágás* Ia 191. The unfree wife of a slave can be avenged in blood. The unfree wife of a free man is not free game, however, but is protected by a liability rule payable in nonblood compensation.

22. Josephus, *The Jewish War* 1.13.9 (1.276); his account in *Antiquities* 14.13.10 is less cannibalistic: "He cut off his ears."

Ten. Satisfaction Not Guaranteed

1. Various catharsis models of emotions, especially regarding aggression, are constantly being "disproved" by psychological experiments, and much to the chagrin of the psychologists doing the disproving we still insist on thinking in terms of letting off steam and in all passion being spent. See the lament of Bushman, "Does Venting Anger Feed or Extinguish the Flame?"

2. Chaucer, *Canterbury Tales* 3.152–157.

3. In sexual matters there is concern that the parties get about equal levels of pleasure, or there will be dissatisfaction, and revenge. The Wyf, however, has no fear that she will come out on top in her debt relations. She will give her husband so much satisfaction as to make a hell of his heaven. The connection between sex, satisfaction, and debt discharge runs deep. German *befrieden, Befriedung* runs the same range, from dry-as-dust satisfaction of a legal claim, to the feeling states following upon the fulfillment of desire. German even goes somewhat further than English, so that *sich befriedigt* is a conventional way to talk about masturbation.

4. See my *Anatomy of Disgust*, especially chs. 6, 8.

5. Among the Kwakiutl vomit is sacred; see Walens, *Feasting with Cannibals* 146–148.

6. Paris Psalter 77.29 (AV 78.29); see Krapp, *The Anglo-Saxon Poetic Records* 5.41.

7. MED s.v. sad, adj. 5.

8. Auden, *The Enchafed Flood or the Romantic Iconography of the Sea* 113–114; cited with discussion in Kerrigan, *Revenge Tragedy* 279.

9. Frustration with imperfect satisfaction is the standard stuff of folk wisdom, the standard stuff about the constant striving to recover a lost satisfying unity of being, from rich proverbs about sour grapes or greener grass or Tantalean torments to the various mystifying Lacanian formulations of the same old stuff.

10. Montaigne, "On cowardice, the mother of cruelty," *Essays* 2.27, p. 791; Billacois, *The Duel* 63–64.

11. *Iliad* 18.109; Aristotle, *Rhetoric* 1370b; recent work in psychology suggests that revenge is processed in the same part of the brain that some pleasure is. So science is now telling us that Aristotle and Homer had it right all along. Revenge *is* sweet. See Harmon-Jones and Sigelman, "State Anger and Prefrontal Brain Activity"; Bushman, "Does Venting Anger Feed or Extinguish the Flame?" See also n. 19, this chapter. The frustrating aspect of the psychology literature, no different from the literature on punishment, is that it has such an unnuanced view of revenge. It makes no allowance for the politics of it, the norms of timing and of waiting years sometimes to even up the score. Experiments testing the anger response of undergrads to insults have not much to tell us about *cultures* of revenge. See too the discussion in Solomon, *A Passion for Justice* ch. 3, for a critique of the flatness of ideas of motivation in much of the scientific literature.

12. Boehm, *Blood Revenge* 54.

13. On the distinction between remorse and regret and how it plays out in apology rituals, see my *Faking It* 77–95.

14. The connection is even more obvious in German, where *Schuld* means both guilt and debt.

15. In fact the film nicely puts the matter of remorse in issue with the authentic contrition of Davey, one of the cowboys involved in the scarring of the prostitute. He tried to make amends to the woman but was thwarted by her workmates.

16. The originator of this thought refuses acknowledgement, but it would not be right for me to claim it as my own.

17. Nietzsche, *Genealogy of Morals* 2.14–15.

18. Nozick, *Philosophical Explanations* 368–370; French, *The Virtues of Vengeance* 69; cf. Kafka's *The Penal Colony,* where the offender has his crime written in needles on his body. Many forms of early punishment were meant to make the wrongdoer bear the sign of his or her wrong; examples are legion from the handlessness of thieves to Hester Prynne's *A.*

19. Berkowitz, "Experimental Investigations of Hostility Catharsis," 6; later work supports the same position; see Harmon-Jones and Sigelman, "State Anger and Prefrontal Brain Activity." See n. 11, this chapter.

20. *Grettir's saga* ch. 86; examples abound of glorious revenges in which the target did not know what hit him; see, for example, Montaigne, "Fortune is often found in reason's train," *Essays* 1.34.

21. Macbeth must surely die for the play to end properly, although Macduff is more than willing to keep him alive to have him mocked and hooted at (5.8.23–7). It is Macbeth who decides that death is preferable.

22. On the Stoic frustrating his opponent by refusing to admit he has been touched as a conscious strategy of vengefulness and striving for honor, see Braden, *Renaissance Tragedy and the Senecan Tradition* 18–19; see further chapter 2, n. 13.

23. Wharton, *House of Mirth* Bk. 1, ch. 12.

24. Or does revenge give rise to its own particular passion, which Hobbes called revengefulness? He defines anger as "sudden courage" (*Human Nature* 9.5), characterized mainly by its quick onset and its rapid decay rate; it does not have the staying power to carry revenge through to its conclusion; revengefulness endures longer.

25. Hobbes, *Human Nature* 9.6.

26. See Nietzsche, *The Wanderer and His Shadow*, no. 33, distinguishing the blows to defend oneself in a fight from revenge.

27. *Grettir's saga* ch. 15.

28. *Hrafnkel's saga* problematizes precisely this issue.

29. "Everyone knows that there is... more contempt in making him bow his head than in making him die... Killing is all right for preventing some future offence but not for avenging one already done. It is a deed more of fear than of bravery; it is an act of caution rather than of courage; of defense rather than of attack." The "mercy" of letting your target live is hardly funded by sweetness of soul (Montaigne, "On cowardice, the mother of cruelty," *Essays* 2.27, p. 787); thus too Hobbes, as noted in n. 25, this chapter.

30. This trope of villainy is of ancient pedigree; see Montaigne's discussion of the dilemma of tyrants who draw out the deaths of their enemies ("On cowardice, the mother of cruelty," *Essays* 2.27, p. 794.)

31. "Hatred, hatred is the only thing that keeps us together," sings Ray Davies, of The Kinks, in "Hatred (A Duet)," sung with his brother Dave, with whom he has warred incessantly to the point of frequent fist fights on stage. The knowledge that enmity and hatred give a mutual sense of purpose is as old as the hills. When old Sturla discovers that his inveterate enemy, Thorbjorg, has died, a woman who had tried to gouge out his eye when Sturla was embroiled with her husband in a complicated lawsuit, he takes to his bed in depression, complaining that much of his purpose in living, the tormenting of her and her sons, has died along with her; *Sturlu saga* ch. 36.

32. See Sassoon, *Memoirs of an Infantry Officer* 176–177, and his poem, "Blighters"; see also Fussell's discussion, *The Great War* 86–87; from World War II, J. Glenn Gray observes that "a civilian far removed from the battle area is nearly certain to be more bloodthirsty than the front-line soldier whose hatred has to be responsible" (*The Warriors* 135).

33. Hazlitt, *Characters of Shakespeare's Plays* 83; there are significant variations among the several editions of Hazlitt's text. Some have, "He declines it altogether," others, "He misses it altogether."

Eleven. Comparing Values and the Ranking Game

1. Thus Joseph Raz, Elizabeth Anderson, Donald Regan, Ruth Chang, and Martha Nussbaum, among others. In 1998 the *University of Pennsylvania Law Review* devoted a lengthy symposium volume to "Law and

Commensurabity." It is not as if the commensurability question wasn't an object of contention before, it is just that in the 1980s–1990s it became a position on which many left-liberals felt it necessary to draw a line in the sand, mostly for the reasons I suggest in the text.

2. Often, what precisely is meant by values and by incommensurability varies from author to author. Some take incommensurability to mean strictly requiring a single scalar metric such as dollars; others argue that the issue is not scalar metrics but whether rational comparisons can be made. Comparisons require only that we be able to declare something greater than, equal to, or less than another thing with respect to some value in some context. Other confusions: some seem to be arguing against the marketability of certain things, like love, babies, art; others are simply against ranking things hierarchically in some kind of esteem regime. For attempts at clarification see Chang, "Introduction."

3. See Raz, *The Morality of Freedom* 332, who argues that we can rationally eliminate many options and reduce the choice situation to a smaller group of options that satisfy an eligibility requirement. At that point choice becomes a matter of wanting and willing, not reasoning and evaluating. See Regan's answer to Raz's notion of want, arguing that wanting is itself intimately involved with ranking reasons and not merely a reflex of raw desire; Regan, "Value, Comparability, and Choice," 138–144.

4. Two articles, to which I am much indebted, by philosopher/law professor, Donald Regan, make a compelling case for the commensuralist position and offer a strong critique of Raz's version of the incommensuralist position. See Regan, "Authority and Value," 1056–1075; and Regan, "Value, Comparability and Choice." Among Regan's points: the apples-and-oranges people do not specify with adequate detail the choice situation. One doesn't just compare the life of a lawyer against the life of a clarinetist. There are many possible such lives, and if we have a more detailed picture the choice becomes more justifiable on a reasoned basis and ever the less a matter of apples and oranges. Why also, if there is supposedly no rational basis for making the right choice, do we agonize over the choice in precisely those settings where the incommensuralist says there is no point in doing so? Why not flip a coin? Even incommensuralists, in other words, don't act as their views predict they should. Incommensuralists, Regan also shows, often claim impossibility for what is merely difficult.

5. See Miller, "Of Outlaws, Christians, Horsemeat"; the story is a remarkable one for revealing the noteworthy genius of Thorgeir, who decided the case.

6. Margaret Radin's "Market-Inalienability," an often-cited piece in legal scholarship, articulates the benefits of a strong principle of market inalienability regarding matters that go to core dignity values. In that piece she sticks to the issue of the propriety of market transactions and feels no need to take a position on incommensurability. In her later *Contested*

Commodities 9, however, she identifies herself as committed to the incommensuralist position, which she now understands to be "central to [her] critiques of universal commodification." I see no reason that the attack on universal commodification need seek a foundation in incommensurability.

7. Anderson, *Value in Ethics and Economics* 57. Nussbaum taxes Plato for his commitment to commensurability (*The Fragility of Goodness* 106–117). Plato even seems to joke about it, claiming in the *Republic* that the philosopher king is happier for being a just king, exactly 729 times happier than the tyrant (*Republic* 9.587).

8. See Zelizer's *Morals and Markets* 46.

9. The shaming of the slacker is actually more complexly motivated. Shaming is the very sanction employed to kick him out of the game if the shamers are third parties or his second-party opponent. But that same shaming also might work to motivate the shamed one to avenge his shame; a second-party shamer may thus come to regret that he provoked his opponent into crawling back onto the field of honor. But it was often the case that the most aggressive shaming the shamed person would have to face was from his own kin – his wife or mother; most of the time they had only to gain by the reassertion of his honor.

10. I should say that the apples-and-oranges position I am using as my argumentative Other is a composite, abstracted not only from the writings of the academics who have defended these positions and whom I have cited, but also from a kind of baseline apples-and-orangesism that permeates the halls of certain wings of the law schools and every wing of humanities departments, where it is a set of commitments that are opposed to the pro-market types on one hand, and to the few remaining cultural conservatives on the other. But manifestly, not all people who identify themselves as liberals or left-liberal are fully committed incommensuralists.

11. I am barely caricaturing the law and economics literature on social norms. See, for example, Eric Posner, "Altruism, Status, and Trust," 579–581, 584, 590–591. For a penetrating critique of the theory of economic rationality that informs this and other rational choice positions in political and moral theory, see Herzog, *Cunning*.

12. Practical reason does not confront us with choice problems between things or values that it makes no sense to rank; see Chang, "Introduction," 29; Regan, "Authority and Value," 1061. We simply are not called on to determine which insurance policy tastes best.

13. Anderson, "Practical Reason and Incommensurable Goods," 99–100.

14. For the powerful influence Dante's poem had in establishing the general understanding of Purgatory, and for an examination of the relation of ideas of justice to the ways different sins are classified and ranked, see Le Goff, *The Birth of Purgatory* 334–355.

15. See Regan's discussion of wanting, n. 3 in this chapter.

16. Q/Mojo: Special Limited Edition: *The 150 Greatest Rock Lists Ever* (London: EMAP Metro, 2004), 12.

17. See Clover, "The Germanic Context of the Unferð Episode."
18. See, for example, *Heiðarviga saga* ch. 37.
19. *Eyrbyggja saga* ch. 37.
20. *Guðmundar saga dýra* ch. 16, my trans.
21. For an especially good example see *Ljósvetninga saga* ch. 21.
22. *Njál's saga* ch. 35.
23. Montaigne, "On the most excellent of men," *Essays* 2.36.
24. Schauer, "Instrumental Commensurability," 1227–1228; see also Anderson, "Practical Reason and Incommensurable Goods," 108. See Calabresi and Bobbitt, *Tragic Choices* 135, who discuss the virtues of disguising the low dollar value that is placed on lives. The degree to which we should allow a certain elite in the culture to know the truth and to deny it to others has a complex history; see generally Herzog, *Poisoning*, especially chs. 2–3.
25. *Iliad* Bk. 23; see, for example, *Egils saga* chs. 44, 49, 71.
26. Incommensurability, as distinguished from incomparability, is generally understood to require a uniform scalable metric; incommensurability is merely a subset, raising purely technical matters, of the larger central conceptual issue of comparability; see Chang, "Introduction," 1–2. None of my points hinges on the difference, and the difference largely evaporates, for if in any comparison situation we can always answer the greater, equal, or less than question, we can get by without a universal scalar metric just fine.
27. See chapter 3, n. 7.

Twelve. Filthy Lucre and Holy Dollars

1. *Njál's saga* ch. 27.
2. The risk of making certain desired objects inalienable is that black and gray markets often arise to fill the void.
3. Zelizer, *Pricing the Priceless Child* 151.
4. Simmel, *Philosophy of Money* 406.
5. http://www.nytimes.com/2004/05/06/arts/design/06auction.html?ex= 1090555200&en=f0ce844205b6d6e8ei=5070.
6. See Appadurai's discussion of what he calls tournaments of value in "Commodities and the Politics of Value," 20–21. The Mercian law provides that the king's wergeld "is to be that of six thegns," Mircna Laga §2 in Liebermann, *Gesetze* 1.462.
7. For a little more punch, the second line of the sign adds fifteen years. The $7,500 is independent of what the dead worker's estate or family might collect civilly, but the criminal fine does not even come close to approaching respectability and is noted by motorists not as a threat to scare them into careful driving but as an insult to the road workers.
8. *Iliad* 6.232–236.
9. See Curtin's classic work on trade diasporas, *Cross-cultural Trade*.

239

10. Mandeville, *Fable of the Bees*; see Appadurai's discussion of Sombart, *Luxury and Capitalism*, in "Commodities and the Politics of Value," 36–39.

11. Simmel, *Philosophy of Money* 367, makes this point and notes further that there seems to be a conservation in the way money and people are commoditized. As money becomes more commoditized it becomes less proper to do so with people: "The concepts of money and of man move continuously in exactly opposite directions." He was writing when life insurance was not quite the phenomenon it is today or when certain forms of utilitarianism had not yet run amok; see Zelizer, *Morals and Markets*.

12. Bohannan, "The Impact of Money on an African Subsistence Economy." See also the discussion of the extraordinarily complex classifications of property in the Talmud as a consequence of various divine liens that were imposed on human property; Kochen, *Beyond Gift and Commodity*.

13. Kopytoff, "The Cultural Biography of Things," 65.

14. I am here indebted to the work of Appadurai and Kopytoff.

15. We, on the other hand, redescribe the sphere of redemption and call it insurance, or tort.

16. In Anglo-American law, relief will be denied if the damages are too remote or too uncertain to measure. This, however, is not a statement of apples and oranges, but a reflection rather that the likelihood of error in mismeasuring is greater than the harm suffered by the plaintiff.

17. See Radin's "Market-Inalienability" for the case for limiting the range of markets. Some of her points are anticipated by Calabresi and Melamed, "Property Rules, Liability Rules" and Calebresi and Bobbitt, *Tragic Choices*.

18. See Simmel, *Philosophy of Money* 376–384.

19. R. Posner, *Economic Analysis of the Law* 170, hints at this.

20. See chapter 11, n. 24.

21. See Calabresi and Bobbitt, *Tragic Choices* 135 *passim*, arguing the benefits of maintaining a good show for a "priceless" life valuation in a few select areas even though it must come at the expense of other areas: "Since many other values depend on valuing life as an incommensurable and since these values are constantly being eroded by decisions which, in fact, place a low value on human life, substantial benefits accrue from any demonstration by society of its devotion to life's pricelessness."

22. Rawls, *Theory of Justice* 132; Anderson, *Value in Ethics* 67, acknowledges these concessions, an admission that seems to me to give away the shop on the commensurability issue, though not on the seemliness and marketability issues.

23. Carlin and Sandy, "Estimating the Implicit Value of a Young Child's Life," who "describe a method for calculating the implicit value of a young child's life to his or her mother as revealed by her decisions about child car safety seat usage . . . We present a first-ever 'willingness to pay' estimate of this evaluation . . . A second reason for interest in a parent's valuation of his or

her child's life is to assess public policy with respect to the regulation of parents' child-safety behavior and the provision of public-good safety for children" (186–187). It is not as if extraordinarily sophisticated attempts have not been made by utilitarian philosophers to get at how best to weigh quality of lives. The economists' "willingness to pay" handle on this issue though, is fraught with all kinds of problems, only some of them moral; see Broome's critique of "willingness to pay" (*Weighing Lives* 262–264).

24. See Elster, *Alchemies* ch. 5, for the argument that talking a certain way constrains us to behave as we have talked to avoid being seen as hypocritical; see also my *Faking It* on the powerful effects of paying lip service.

25. "Moral menials" is a term I used once to describe those who carry out socially necessary but morally suspect tasks, such as lawyers, politicians, and hangmen, and now to which I add actuaries and debt collectors; Miller, *Anatomy of Disgust* 184–186.

26. It is an often-noted perception that the law-and-econ people who take this view frequently coauthor articles, are generous with helping younger academics in the field, get along well with staff, and make the best of institutional citizens, whereas those voicing the properly pious views are, well, you fill in the blanks. But the marketeers catch a break, for when they do not live up to their professed positions, rather than getting blamed as hypocrites they are honored as decent human beings, but when the pious-dignity people fail to live up to their preaching they get tarred as hypocrites and selfish careerists. Could the economists have figured this into their personal utility curves? Best to create low moral expectations, you can hear one economist say to another, and pleasantly surprise others; our good deeds will get noticed and their bad deeds will get noticed because each will fly in the face of the professed views. And because we will get a lot more credit for our good deeds than they will get for their good deeds, we won't even have to do as many of them. Moreover, we can rely on them to publicize our good deeds because they will claim that our very decency disproves our theories, that not even an economist can live as an economist says we live.

Works Cited

Æthelberht, Laws of. See Attenborough, ed., 1–17.

Æthelred, Laws of. See Robertson, ed., 45–133.

Æthelstan, Laws of. See Attenborough, ed., 122–169.

Aijmer, Karin. *English Discourse Particles.* Amsterdam: John Benjamins, 2002.

Alfred, Laws of. See Attenborough, ed., 62–93.

Algazi, Gadi, Valentin Groebner, and Bernhard Jussen, eds. *Negotiating the Gift: Pre-Modern Figurations of Exchange.* Veröffentlichungen des Max-Planck-Instituts für Geschichte, 188. Göttingen: Vandenhoeck and Ruprecht, 2003.

Améry, Jean. *At the Mind's Limits: Contemplations by a Survivor on Auschwitz and Its Realities.* Translated by Sidney and Stella P. Rosenfeld. 1976. New York: Schocken, 1986.

Anderson, Elizabeth. *Value in Ethics and Economics.* Cambridge, Mass.: Harvard University Press, 1993.

Anderson, Elizabeth. "Practical Reason and Incommensurable Goods." In Chang, ed., 90–109.

Appadurai, Arjun, ed. *The Social Life of Things: Commodities in Cultural Perspective.* Cambridge: Cambridge University Press, 1986.

Appadurai, Arjun. "Introduction: Commodities and the Politics of Value." In Appadurai, ed., 3–63.

Aquinas, St. Thomas. *Summa Theologiæ.* Blackfriars edition. New York: McGraw-Hill, 1964.

Aristotle. *Nicomachean Ethics.* Translated by W. D. Ross. Revised by J. O. Urmson. In *The Complete Works of Aristotle.* Edited by Jonathan Barnes. Princeton, N. J.: Princeton University Press, 1984. Vol. 2: 1729–1867.

Aristotle. *Politics.* Translated by Benjamin Jowett. In *The Complete Works of Aristotle.* Edited by Jonathan Barnes. Vol. 2: 1986–2129.

Aristotle. *Rhetoric.* Translated by W. Rhys Roberts. In *The Complete Works of Aristotle.* Edited by Jonathan Barnes. Vol. 2: 2152–2269.

Attenborough, F. L., ed. and trans. *The Laws of the Earliest English Kings.* 1922. Rpt. New York: Russell and Russell, 1963.

Auden, W. H. *The Enchafèd Flood or the Romantic Iconography of the Sea.* New York: Random House, 1950.

Baker, J. H. *An Introduction to English Legal History.* 4th ed. London: Butterworths, 2002.

Benveniste, Emile. *Indo-European Language and Society.* Translated by Elizabeth Palmer. London: Faber, 1973.

Beowulf and the Fight at Finnsburg. Edited by Friedrich Klaeber. 3rd ed. Boston: Heath, 1950.

Berkowitz, Leonard. "Experimental Investigations of Hostility Catharsis." *Journal of Consulting and Clinical Psychology* 35 (1970), 1–7.

Berlin, Adele, and Marc Zvi Brettler, eds. *The Jewish Study Bible.* Oxford: Oxford University Press, 2004.

Beyerle, Franz. *Das Entwicklungsproblem im germanishen Rechtsgang.* Deutschrechtliche Beiträge, X. Heidelberg: Carl Winter, 1915.

Bianchi, Herman. "The Scales of Justice as Represented in Engraving, Emblems, Reliefs, and Sculptures in Early Modern Europe." In *Images and représentations de la justice du xvi au xix siècle.* Edited by G. Lamoine. Actes du colloque de l'association internationale des historiens du crime et de la justice criminelle. Toulouse, 1983.

Bilder, Mary S. "The Struggle over Immigration: Indentured Servants, Slaves, and Articles of Commerce." *Missouri Law Review* 61 (1996), 743–822.

Billacois, François. *The Duel: Its Rise and Fall in Early Modern France.* Translated by Trista Selous. New Haven, Conn.: Yale University Press, 1990.

Black-Michaud, Jacob. *Cohesive Force.* 1975. Paperback published as *Feuding Societies.* Oxford: Basil Blackwell, 1980.

Bloch, Marc. "Natural Economy or Money Economy: A Pseudo-Dilemma." In *Land and Work in the Middle Ages: Selected Papers by Marc Bloch.* Translated by J. E. Anderson. London: Routledge and Kegan Paul, 1967. 230–243.

Boehm, Christopher. *Blood Revenge: The Anthropology of Feuding in Montenegro.* Lawrence: University Press of Kansas, 1984.

Bohannan, Paul. "The Impact of Money on an African Subsistence Economy." *Journal of Economic History* 19 (1959), 491–503.

Bourdieu, Pierre. *Outline of a Theory of Practice.* Translated by Richard Nice. Cambridge: Cambridge University Press, 1977.

Bourdieu, Pierre. "The Sentiment of Honour in Kabyle Society." In Peristiany, ed., 191–242.

Braden, Gordon. "Epic Anger." *Milton Quarterly* 23 (1989), 28–34.

Braden, Gordon. *Renaissance Tragedy and the Senecan Tradition: Anger's Privilege.* New Haven, Conn.: Yale University Press, 1985.

Broome, John. *Weighing Lives.* Oxford: Oxford University Press, 2004.

Broude, Gwen J. "Rethinking the Couvade: Cross-Cultural Evidence." *American Anthropologist* 90 (1988), 902–911.

Brown, Peter. *The Body and Society: Men, Women, and Sexual Renunciation in Early Christianity.* New York: Columbia University Press, 1988.

Burkert, Walter. *Homo Necans: The Anthropology of Ancient Greek Sacrificial Ritual and Myth*. Translated by Peter Bing. Berkeley: University of California Press, 1983.

Burnett, Anne Pippin. *Revenge in Attic and Later Tragedy*. Berkeley: University of California Press, 1998.

Burrow, J. A. *Gestures and Looks in Medieval Narrative*. Cambridge: Cambridge University Press, 2002.

Bushman, B. J. "Does Venting Anger Feed or Extinguish the Flame? Catharsis, Rumination, Distraction, Anger, and Aggressive Responding." *Personality and Social Psychology Bulletin* 28 (2002), 724–731.

Bynum, Caroline Walker. "The Body of Christ in the Later Middle Ages: A Reply to Leo Steinberg." In Bynum, *Fragmentation and Redemption: Essays on Gender and the Human Body in Medieval Religion*. New York: Zone, 1992. 79–117.

Calabresi, Guido, and Philip Bobbitt. *Tragic Choices*. New York: Norton, 1978.

Calabresi, Guido, and A. Douglas Melamed. "Property Rules, Liability Rules, and Inalienability: One View of the Cathedral." *Harvard Law Review* 85 (1972), 1089–1128.

Camporesi, Piero. *Bread of Dreams: Food and Fantasy in Early Modern Europe*. Translated by David Gentilcore. Rpt. Chicago: University of Chicago Press, 1996.

Camporesi, Piero. *The Incorruptible Flesh: Bodily Mutation and Mortification in Religion and Folklore*. Translated by Tania Croft-Murray and Helen Elsom. Cambridge: Cambridge University Press, 1988.

Canute, Laws of. See Robertson, ed., 135–219.

Carlin, Paul S. and Robert Sandy. "Estimating the Implicit Value of a Young Child's Life." *Southern Economic Journal* 58 (1991), 186–202.

Carmichael, Calum. *The Spirit of Biblical Law*. Athens: University of Georgia Press, 1996.

Chadwick, H. M. *Studies on Anglo-Saxon Institutions*. Cambridge: Cambridge University Press, 1905.

Chang, Ruth, ed. *Incommensurability, Incomparability, and Practical Reason*. Cambridge, Mass.: Harvard University Press, 1997.

Chang, Ruth. "Introduction." In Chang, ed., 1–34.

Chaucer, Geoffrey. *The Works of Geoffrey Chaucer*. 2nd ed. Edited by F. N. Robinson. Boston: Houghton Mifflin, 1957.

Childs, Brevard S. *The Book of Exodus: A Critical, Theological Commentary*. Philadelphia: Westminster Press, 1974.

Christiansen, Eric. *The Norsemen in the Viking Age*. Oxford: Blackwell, 2002.

Clendinnen, Inge. *Aztecs: An Interpretation*. Cambridge: Cambridge University Press, 1991.

Cleveland, Sarah. "Powers Inherent in Sovereignty." *Texas Law Review* 81 (2002), 1–284.

Clover, Carol J. "The Germanic Context of the Unferð Episode." *Speculum* 55 (1980), 444–468.

Clover, Carol J. "Regardless of Sex: Men, Women, and Power in Early Northern Europe." *Speculum* 68 (1993), 363–388.

Coghill, Nevill. "The Governing Idea: Essays in Stage-Interpretation of Shakespeare." *Shakespeare Quarterly* 1 (1948), 9–17.

Cohen, David. *Law, Violence and Community in Classical Athens.* Cambridge: Cambridge University Press, 1995.

Cohen, Walter. "*The Merchant of Venice* and the Possibilities of Historical Criticism." *ELH* 49 (1982), 765–789.

Curtin, Philip D. *Cross-cultural Trade in World History.* Cambridge: Cambridge University Press, 1984.

Daube, David. "Eye for an Eye." In *New Testament Judaism: Collected Works of David Daube.* Vol. 2. Edited by Calum Carmichael. Berkeley: Robbins Collection, 2000. 177–186.

Daube, David. "Law in the Narratives." In Daube, *Studies in Biblical Law.* Cambridge: Cambridge University Press, 1947. 1–73.

Daube, David. "*Lex Talionis.*" In Daube, *Studies in Biblical Law.* Cambridge: Cambridge University Press, 1947. 102–153.

Daube, David. "Money and Justiciability." *Zeitschrift der Savigny-Stiftung für Rechtsgeschichte* 96 (1979), 1–16.

Daube, David. "The Scales of Justice." *The Juridical Review* 63 (1951), 109–129.

Davis, Michael. "Harm and Retribution." *Philosophy and Public Affairs* 15 (1986), 236–266.

Diamond, A. S. "An Eye for an Eye." *Iraq* 19 (1957), 151–155.

Doniger, Wendy, and Brian K. Smith. "Sacrifice and Substitution: Ritual Mystification and Mythical Demystification." *Numen* 36 (1989), 189–224.

Douglas, Mary. *Leviticus as Literature.* New York: Oxford University Press, 1999.

Dresch, Paul. *Tribes, Government, and History in Yemen.* Oxford: Clarendon Press, 1989.

Edgar, Laws of. See Robertson, ed., 16–39.

Edmund, Laws of. See Robertson, ed., 3–15.

Egil's saga. Translated by Hermann Pálsson and Paul Edwards. Harmondsworth: Penguin, 1976.

Eiland, Howard. "Heidegger's Etymological Web." *Boundary* 2 10 (1982), 39–58.

Einzig, Paul. *Primitive Money: In Its Ethnological, Historical and Economic Aspects.* 2nd ed. Oxford: Pergamon Press, 1966.

Elster, Jon. *Alchemies of the Mind: Rationality and the Emotions.* Cambridge: Cambridge University Press, 1999.

Elster, Jon. *Ulysses and the Sirens: Studies in Rationality and Irrationality.* Rev. ed. Cambridge: Cambridge University Press, 1984.

Engle, Lars. "'Thrift is Blessing': Exchange and Explanation in *The Merchant of Venice*." *Shakespeare Quarterly* 37 (1986), 20–37.

Etz Hayim: Torah and Commentary. Edited by David Lieber. New York: Jewish Publication Society, 2001.

Evans, Michael. "Two Sources for Maimed Justice." *Source: Notes in the History of Art* 2 (1982), 11–15.

Eyrbyggja saga. Translated by Hermann Pálsson and Paul Edwards. Harmondsworth: Penguin, 1989.

Finkelstein, J. J. "Ammisaduqa's Edict and Babylonian 'Law Codes.'" *Journal of Cuneiform Studies* 15 (1961), 91–104.

Foote, Peter. "Skömm er óhófs ævi: On Glaucia, Hrafnkell and Others." In *Idee, Gestalt, Geschichte: Festschrift Klaus von See*. Edited by Gerd Wolfgang Weber. Odense: Odense University Press, 1988. 285–298.

Fraser, Bruce. "What Are Discourse Markers?" *Journal of Pragmatics* 31 (1999), 931–952.

French, Peter A. *The Virtues of Vengeance*. Lawrence: University Press of Kansas, 2001.

Freud, Sigmund. "Thoughts for the Times on War and Death." 1915. In *The Standard Edition of the Complete Psychological Works of Sigmund Freud*. Edited by James Strachey. London: Hogarth Press, 1953–1974. Vol. 14: 273–302.

Fussell, Paul. *The Great War and Modern Memory*. Oxford: Oxford University Press, 1975.

Geary, Patrick. "Sacred Commodities: The Circulation of Medieval Relics." In Appadurai, ed., 169–191.

Gísli's saga. The Saga of Gísli the Outlaw. Translated by George Johnston. Toronto: University of Toronto Press, 1963.

Goebel, Julius, Jr. *Felony and Misdemeanor: A Study in the History of Criminal Law*. 1937. Philadelphia: University of Pennsylvania Press, 1976.

Goffman, Erving. *Relations in Public*. New York: Basic Books, 1971.

Graeber, David. *Toward an Anthropological Theory of Value: The False Coin of Our Own Desire*. New York: Palgrave, 2001.

Grágás Ia 1-Ia 217. In *Laws of Early Iceland: Grágás. The Codex Regius of Grágás with Material from Other Manuscripts*. Vol. I. Translated and edited by Andrew Dennis, Peter Foote, and Richard Perkins. Winnipeg: University of Manitoba Press, 1980.

Grágás Ia 218-Ib 218. *Laws of Early Iceland: Grágás. The Codex Regius of Grágás*. Vol. II. Translated and edited by Andrew Dennis, Peter Foote, and Richard Perkins. Winnipeg: University of Manitoba Press, 2000.

Gray, J. Glenn. *The Warriors: Reflections on Men in Battle*. New York: Harper and Row, 1967.

Gregory of Tours. *History of the Franks*. Translated by Lewis Thorpe. Harmondsworth: Penguin, 1974.

Grettir's saga. Translated by Denton Fox and Hermann Pálsson. Toronto: University of Toronto Press, 1974.

Grierson, Philip. "The Origins of Money." *Research in Economic Anthropology* 1 (1978), 1–35.

Groebner, Valentin. *Defaced: The Visual Culture of Violence in the Late Middle Ages*. Translated by Pamela Selwyn. New York: Zone, 2004.

Groebner, Valentin. *Liquid Assets, Dangerous Gifts: Presents and Politics at the End of the Middle Ages*. Translated by Pamela Selwyn. Philadelphia: University of Pennsylvania Press, 2000.

Grossberg, Michael. *Governing the Hearth: Law and the Family in Nineteenth-Century America*. Chapel Hill: University of North Carolina Press, 1985.

Gulathing, Laws of the. In *The Earliest Norwegian Law, Being the Gulathing Law and the Frostathing Law*. Edited and translated by Laurence M. Larson. New York: Columbia University Press, 1935.

Guðmundar saga dýra. Translated by Julia H. McGrew and R. George Thomas. In *Sturlunga saga*. 2 vols. New York: Twayne, 1970–74. 2: 145–206.

Guðmundsson, Valtýr. "Manngjöld-hundrað." In *Germanistische Abhand. zum 70 Geburtstag Konrad von Maurers*. Edited by Oscar Brenner. Göttingen, 1893. 523–554.

Hammurabi, Laws of. See Roth, ed., 71–142.

Harmon-Jones, E., and J. Sigelman. "State Anger and Prefrontal Brain Activity: Evidence That Insult-Related Relative Left Prefrontal Activation Is Associated with Experienced Anger and Aggression." *Journal of Personality and Social Psychology* 80 (2001), 797–803.

Harris, Jonathan Gil. *Sick Economies: Drama, Mercantilism, and Disease in Shakespeare's England*. Philadelphia: University of Pennsylvania Press, 2004.

Hart, H. L. A. *Punishment and Responsibility: Essays in the Philosophy of Law*. Oxford: Clarendon Press, 1968.

Hazlitt, William. *Characters of Shakespeare's Plays*. 2nd ed. 1818. London: Oxford University Press, 1955.

Hazlitt, William. *A View of the English Stage*. Edited by W. Spencer Jackson. London: George Bell, 1906.

Heiðarviga saga. The Saga of the Slayings on the Heath. In *The Complete Sagas of Icelanders*. Edited by Viðar Hreinsson. Reykjavík: Leifur Eiríksson, 1997. Vol. 4: 67–130.

Herdt, Gilbert. "Sambia Nosebleeding Rites and Male Proximity to Women." In *Cultural Psychology: Essays on Comparative Human Development*. Edited by James W. Stigler, Richard A. Shweder, and Gilbert Herdt. Cambridge: Cambridge University Press, 1990. 366–400.

Herodotus. *The Histories*. Translated by Aubrey de Sélincourt. Harmondsworth: Penguin, 1972.

Herzog, Don. *Cunning*. Princeton, N. J.: Princeton University Press. In press.

Herzog, Don. *Poisoning the Minds of the Lower Orders*. Princeton, N. J.: Princeton University Press, 1998.

Hittite Laws. See Roth, ed., 211–247.

Hlophere and Eadric, Laws of. See Attenborough, ed., 18–23.

Hobbes, Thomas. *Human Nature.* 1650. In *British Moralists 1650–1800.* Vol. 1. Edited by D. D. Raphael. 1969. Rpt. Indianapolis: Hackett, 1991. 1–17.

Holderness, B. A. "The Clergy as Money-Lenders in England, 1550–1700." In *Princes and Paupers in the English Church, 1500–1800.* Edited by R. O'Day and F. Heal. Leicester: Leicester University Press, 1981. 185–209.

Holderness, B. A. "Widows in Pre-industrial Society: An Essay upon Their Economic Functions." In *Land, Kinship, and Life-cycle.* Edited by R. M. Smith. Cambridge: Cambridge University Press, 1984. 423–442.

Houtman, Cornelius. *Das Bundesbuch: Ein Kommentar.* Leiden: Brill, 1997.

Hrafnkel's saga. In *Hrafnkel's Saga and Other Stories.* Translated by Hermann Pálsson. Harmondsworth: Penguin, 1971. 35–71.

Homer. *The Iliad.* Translated by Martin Hammond. Harmondsworth: Penguin, 1987.

Homer. *The Odyssey.* Translated by A. T. Murray. 2 vols. 2nd ed., rpt. with corrections. Loeb Classical Library. Cambridge, Mass.: Harvard University Press, 1998.

Huizinga, Johan. *Homo Ludens.* Boston: Beacon Press, 1950.

Hróa þáttr heimska. In *Flateyjarbók: En Samling af norske kongesagaer med indskudte mindre fortællinger ombegivenheder i og udenfor Norge samt annaler.* Edited by Guðbrandr Vigfusson and C. R. Unger. Christania [Oslo]: P. T. Mallings forlagsboghandel. 3 vols. 1860-1868. English translation (1875) by Eirikr Magnússon and William Morris, http://www.northvegr.org/lore/love/00501.php.

Hyams, Paul R. *Rancor and Reconciliation in Medieval England.* Ithaca, N. Y.: Cornell University Press, 2003.

Ine, Laws of. See Attenborough, ed., 36–61.

Jackson, Bernard S. "*Lex Talionis*: Revisiting Daube's Classic." 2001. http://www.law2.byu.edu/Biblical_Law/papers/jackson_bs_lex_talionis.pdf.

Jackson, Bernard S. *Studies in the Semiotics of Biblical Law. Journal for the Study of the Old Testament.* Supplement Series 314. Sheffield: Sheffield Academic Press, 2000.

Jacob, Robert. *Images de la justice: Essai sur l'iconographie judiciaire du Moyen Âge à l'âge classique.* Paris: Léopard d'Or, 1994.

Jay, Martin. "Must Justice Be Blind?" In *Law and the Image: The Authority of Art and the Aesthetics of Law.* Edited by Costas Douzinas and Lynda Nead. Chicago: University of Chicago Press, 1999. 19–35.

Jones, Norman L. *God and the Moneylenders: Usury and the Law in Early Modern England.* Oxford: Blackwell, 1989.

Josephus. *Jewish Antiquities.* Book IV. Translated by H. St. J. Thackeray. Loeb Classical Library. Cambridge, Mass.: Harvard University Press, 1930.

Josephus. *The Jewish War.* Translated by G. A. Williamson. Rev. ed. Harmondsworth: Penguin, 1970.

Kane, Pandurang V. *History of Dharmasastra: Ancient and Medieval Religious and Civil Law.* 2nd ed. 5 vols. Poona: Bhandarkar Oriental Research Institute, 1973.

Kant, Immanuel. *Groundwork for the Metaphysics of Morals.* 1785. Translated by Allen W. Wood. New Haven, Conn.: Yale University Press, 2002.

Kant, Immanuel. *Metaphysics of Morals.* 1797–1798. Translated by Mary Gregor. Cambridge: Cambridge University Press, 1991.

Kay, Paul. "Even." *Linguistics and Philosophy* 13 (1990), 59–111.

Keen, Maurice. "Introduction: Warfare and the Middle Ages." In *Medieval Warfare: A History.* Edited by Maurice Keen. Oxford: Oxford University Press, 1999. 1–9.

Kerrigan, John. *Revenge Tragedy: Aeschylus to Armageddon.* Oxford: Clarendon Press, 1996.

Keynes, Simon. "The Fonthill Letter." *In Words, Texts and Manuscripts: Studies in Anglo-Saxon Culture Presented to Helmut Gneuss on the Occasion of his Sixty-Fifth Birthday.* Edited by Michael Korhammer et al. Cambridge: D. S. Brewer, 1992. 53–97.

Kisch, Bruno. *Scales and Weights: A Historical Outline.* New Haven, Conn.: Yale University Press, 1965.

Kissel, Otto Rudolf. *Die Justitia: Reflexionen über ein Symbol und seine Darstellung in der bildenden Kunst.* München: Beck, 1984.

Klein, Ernest. *A Comprehensive Etymological Dictionary of the Hebrew Language for Readers of English.* New York: Macmillan, 1987.

Kochen, Madeline. *Beyond Gift and Commodity: A Theory of the Economy of the Sacred in Jewish Law.* Dissertation. Department of Government and Department of Near Eastern Languages. Harvard University, 2004.

Kopytoff, Igor. "The Cultural Biography of Things: Commoditization as Process." In Appadurai, ed., 64–94.

Kormak's saga. Translated by Rory McTurk. In *Sagas of the Warrior-Poets.* Harmondsworth: Penguin, 2002. 3–67.

Kraemer, David. *Reading the Rabbis: The Talmud as Literature.* New York: Oxford University Press, 1996.

Krapp, G. P. ed. *The Anglo-Saxon Poetic Records.* Vol 5. New York: Columbia University Press, 1933.

Langland, William. *The Vision of Piers Plowman.* Edited by A. V. C. Schmidt. A Critical edition of the B-text based on Trinity College Cambridge MS B.15.17. London: Dent, 1978.

Laum, Bernhard. *Heiliges Geld: eine historische Untersuchung über den sakralen Ursprung des Geldes.* Tübingen: Mohr, 1924.

Lee, David. "Categories in the Description of *Just.*" *Lingua* 83 (1991), 43–66.

Lee, David. "The Semantics of *Just.*" *Journal of Pragmatics* 11 (1987), 377–398.

Leges Henrici Primi. Edited and translated by L. J. Downer. Oxford: Clarendon Press, 1972.

Le Goff, Jacques. *The Birth of Purgatory*. Translated by Arthur Goldhammer. Chicago: University of Chicago Press, 1984.

Lewalski, Barbara K. "Biblical Allusion and Allegory in *The Merchant of Venice*." *Shakespeare Quarterly* 13 (1962), 327–343.

Lewis, David. "The Punishment That Leaves Something to Chance." *Philosophy and Public Affairs* 18 (1989), 53–67.

Lewis, Norman. *Naples '44: An Intelligence Officer in the Italian Labyrinth*. 1978. London: Eland, 1983.

Lex Salica. Edited by Karl August Eckhardt. Weimar: Hermann Böhlaus, 1953.

Liebermann, Felix. "Die Eideshufen bei den Angelsachsen." In *Historische Aussätze: Karl Zeumer Festgabe*. Weimar: Hermann Böhlaus, 1910. 1–9.

Liebermann, Felix. *Die Gesetze der Angelsachsen*. 3 vols. Halle: Niemeyer, 1903–1916.

Ljósvetninga saga. Translated by Theodore M. Anderson and William Ian Miller. In *Law and Literature in Medieval Iceland*. Stanford, Calif.: Stanford University Press, 1989. 119–255.

Luxon, Thomas H. "A Second Daniel: The Jew and the 'True Jew' in *The Merchant of Venice*." *Early Modern Literary Studies* 4.3 (1999), 1–37.

Mackie, J. L. "Morality and Retributive Emotions." In J. L. Mackie, *Persons and Values*. Edited by Joan Mackie. Oxford: Clarendon Press, 1985. 206–219.

Maimonides, Moses. *Mishneh Torah: The Book of Knowledge*. Vol 1. Translated by Moses Hyamson. New York: Feldheim Publishers, 1981.

Maimonides, Moses. *Mishneh Torah. The Code of Maimonides: The Book of Agriculture*. Book 7. Translated by Isaac Klein. New Haven, Conn.: Yale University Press, 1979.

Maimonides, Moses. *Mishneh Torah. The Code of Maimonides: The Book of Civil Laws*. Book 13. Translated by Jacob J. Rabinowitz. New Haven, Conn.: Yale University Press, 1949.

Mandeville, Bernard. *The Fable of the Bees or Private Vices, Publick Benefits*. 1732. 6th ed. Edited by F. B. Kaye. 2 vols. Oxford: Clarendon Press, 1924. Rpr. Liberty Press, 1988.

Martial. Epigrams. Vol. 1. Edited and translated by D. R. Shackleton Bailey. Loeb Classical Library. Cambridge, Mass.: Harvard University Press, 1993.

McGee, Arthur. *The Elizabethan Hamlet*. New Haven, Conn.: Yale University Press, 1987.

McNeill, John T., and Helena M. Gamer. *Medieval Handbooks of Penance: A translation of the principal "libri poenitentiale" and selections from related documents*. 1938. Rpt. New York: Columbia University Press, 1990.

MED. *Middle English Dictionary*. http://ets.umdl.umich.edu/m/med/.

Middle Assyrian Laws. See Roth, ed., 151–194.

Miller, William Ian. *The Anatomy of Disgust*. Cambridge, Mass.: Harvard University Press, 1997.

Miller, William Ian. *Bloodtaking and Peacemaking: Feud, Law, and Society in Saga Iceland*. Chicago: University of Chicago Press, 1990.

Miller, William Ian. "Choosing the Avenger: Some Aspects of the Bloodfeud in Medieval Iceland and England." *Law and History Review* 1 (1983), 159–204.

Miller, William Ian. "Clint Eastwood and Equity: The Virtues of Revenge and the Shortcomings of Law in Popular Culture." In *Law in the Domains of Culture*. Edited by Austin Sarat and Thomas Kearns. Ann Arbor: University of Michigan Press, 1998. 161–202.

Miller, William Ian. "Deep Inner Lives, Individualism, and People of Honour." *History of Political Thought* 16 (1995), 190–207.

Miller, William Ian. *Faking It*. Cambridge: Cambridge University Press, 2003.

Miller, William Ian. "Home and Homelessness in the Middle of Nowhere." In *Home and Homelessness in the Medieval and Renaissance World*. Edited by Nicholas Howe. Notre Dame, Ind.: University of Notre Dame Press, 2004. 125–142.

Miller, William Ian. *Humiliation: And Other Essays on Honor, Social Discomfort, and Violence*. Ithaca, N. Y.: Cornell University Press, 1993.

Miller, William Ian. *The Mystery of Courage*. Cambridge, Mass.: Harvard University Press, 2000.

Miller, William Ian. "Of Outlaws, Christians, Horsemeat, and Writing: Uniform Laws and Saga Iceland." *Michigan Law Review* 89 (1991), 2081–2095.

Milton, John. *John Milton: Complete Poems and Major Prose*. Edited by Merritt Y. Hughes. New York: Odyssey Press, 1957.

Montaigne. *Michel de Montaigne: The Complete Essays*. Translated by M. A. Screech. Harmondsworth: Penguin, 1991.

Nevalainen, Terttu. *But, Only, Just: Focusing Adverbial Change in Modern English, 1500–1800*. Helsinki: Société Néophilogique, 1991.

Nietzsche, Friedrich. *On the Genealogy of Morals*. 1887. Translated by Walter Kaufmann and R. J. Hollingdale. New York: Vintage, 1967.

Nietzsche, Friedrich. *The Wanderer and His Shadow*. In *Human, All Too Human*. Translated by R. J. Hollingdale. Cambridge: Cambridge University Press, 1996. 301–395.

Njál's saga. Translated by Magnus Magnusson and Hermann Pálsson. Baltimore: Penguin Books, 1960.

Nozick, Robert. *Philosophical Explanations*. Cambridge, Mass.: Harvard University Press, 1981.

Nussbaum, Martha C. *The Fragility of Goodness: Luck and Ethics in Greek Tragedy and Philosophy*. 1986. Rev. ed. Cambridge: Cambridge University Press, 2001.

OED. *Oxford English Dictionary*. 2nd ed. Prepared by J. A. Simpson and E. S. C. Weiner. Oxford: Clarendon Press, 1989.

Oestigaard, Terje. "Sacrifices of Raw, Cooked, and Burnt Humans." *Norwegian Archaeological Review* 33 (2000), 41–58.

Oliver, Lisi. *The Beginnings of English Law*. Toronto: University of Toronto Press, 2002.

Osborne, Lawrence. "Does Man Eat Man? Inside the Great Cannibalism Controversy." *Lingua Franca* 7 No. 4 (April/May, 1997), 28–38.

Otto, Eckart. "Town and Rural Countryside in Ancient Israelite Law: Reception and Redaction in Cuneiform and Israelite Law." *Journal for the Study of the Old Testament* 57 (1993), 3–22.

Patterson, Steve. "The Bankruptcy of Homoerotic Amity in Shakespeare's *Merchant of Venice*." *Shakespeare Quarterly* 50 (1999), 9–32.

Paul, Shalom M. *Studies in the Book of the Covenant in the Light of Cuneiform and Biblical Law*. Leiden: E. J. Brill, 1970.

Peristiany, J. G., ed. *Honour and Shame: The Values of Mediterranean Society*. Chicago: University of Chicago Press, 1966.

Pernick, Martin S. *A Calculus of Suffering: Pain, Professionalism, and Anesthesia in Nineteenth-Century America*. New York: Columbia University Press, 1985.

Philo. *De Specialibus Legibus*. In *Philo*. Vol. VII. Translated by F. H. Colson. Loeb Classical Library. Cambridge, Mass.: Harvard University Press, 1937.

Plato. *Republic*. Translated by Paul Shorey. In the *Collected Dialogues of Plato*. Edited by Edith Hamilton and Huntington Cairns. Bollingen Series LXXI. New York: Pantheon, 1961. 575–844.

Plato. *Theaetetus*. Translated by F. M. Cornford. In the *Collected Dialogues of Plato*. 845–919.

Plaut, W. Gunther, ed. *The Torah: A Modern Commentary*. New York: Union of American Hebrew Congregations, 1981.

Poe, Edgar Allan. *Poe: Essays and Reviews*. Edited by G. R. Thompson. New York: Library of America, 1984.

Posner, Eric. "Altruism, Status, and Trust in the Law of Gifts and Gratuitous Promises." *Wisconsin Law Review* (1997), 579–81.

Posner, Richard. *Economic Analysis of the Law*. 5th ed. New York: Aspen, 1998.

Prosser, Eleanor. *Hamlet and Revenge*. 2nd ed. Stanford, Calif.: Stanford University Press, 1971.

Radin, Margaret Jane. *Contested Commodities*. Cambridge, Mass.: Harvard University Press, 1996.

Radin, Margaret Jane. "Market-Inalienability." *Harvard Law Review* 100 (1987), 1089–1937.

Rawls, John. *A Theory of Justice*. 1972. Rev. ed. Cambridge, Mass.: Harvard University Press, 1999.

Rawson, Claude Julien. *God, Gulliver, and Genocide: Barbarism and the European Imagination, 1492–1945*. New York: Oxford University Press, 2001.

Raz, Joseph. *The Morality of Freedom*. Oxford: Clarendon Press, 1986.

Regan, Donald. "Authority and Value: Reflections on Raz's *Morality of Freedom*." *Southern California Law Review* 62 (1989), 995–1095.

Regan, Donald. "Value, Comparability, and Choice." In Chang, ed., 129–150.

Reiman, Jeffrey H. "Justice, Civilization, and the Death Penalty: Answering van den Haag." *Philosophy and Public Affairs* 14 (1985), 115–148.

Revenger's Tragedy. Cyril Tourneur? [Thomas Middleton]. Edited by Brian Gibbons. The New Mermaids. New York: Hill and Wang, 1967.

Richards, Mary. "The Dictionary of Old English and Old English Legal Terminology." *Subsidia* 26 (1998), 57–61.

Robertson, A. J., ed. and trans. *The Laws of the Kings of England from Edmund to Henry I.* Cambridge: Cambridge University Press, 1925.

Rosaldo, Michelle. *Knowledge and Passion: Ilongot Notions of Self and Social Life.* Cambridge: Cambridge University Press, 1980.

Roth, Martha T., ed. and trans. *Law Collections from Mesopotamia and Asia Minor.* 2nd ed. Atlanta: Scholar's Press, 1997.

Rousselle, Aline. *Porneia: On Desire and the Body in Antiquity.* Translated by Felicia Pheasant. New York: Barnes and Noble, 1996.

Rubin, Miri. *Corpus Christi: The Eucharist in Late Medieval Culture.* Cambridge: Cambridge University Press, 1991.

Sarna, Nahum M. *The JPS Torah Commentary: Exodus.* Philadelphia: The Jewish Publication Society, 1991.

Sassoon, Siegfried. *Memoirs of an Infantry Officer.* London: Faber and Faber, 1930.

Schauer, Frederick. "Instrumental Commensurability." *University of Pennsylvania Law Review* 146 (1998), 1215–1234.

Schelling, Thomas C. *The Strategy of Conflict.* Cambridge, Mass.: Harvard University Press, 1960.

Schourup, Lawrence. "Discourse Markers: A Tutorial Overview." *Lingua* 107 (1999), 227–265.

Schwyter, J. R. *Old English Legal Language: The Lexical Field of Theft.* Odense: Odense University Press, 1996.

Schwyter, J. R. "Syntax and Style in the Anglo-Saxon Law-Codes." In *Verschriftung und Verschriftlichung: Aspekte des Medienweschsels in verschiedenen Kulturen und Epochen.* Edited by Christine Ehler and Ursula Schaefer. Tübingen: Gunter Narr, 1998. 189–231.

Shakespeare, William. *Hamlet.* Edited by Harold Jenkins. The Arden Shakespeare. New York: Methuen, 1982.

Shakespeare, William. *King Richard II.* Edited by Charles R. Forker. The Arden Shakespeare. London: Thomson, 2002.

Shakespeare, William. *The Merchant of Venice.* Edited by John Russell Brown. The Arden Shakespeare. New York: Methuen, 1955.

Shakespeare, William, *Othello.* Edited by E. A. J. Honigmann. The Arden Shakespeare. London: Thomson, 1999.

Shapiro, James. *Shakespeare and the Jews.* New York: Columbia University Press, 1996.

Shell, Marc. "The Wether and the Ewe: Verbal Usury in *The Merchant of Venice.*" In Shell, *Money, Language, and Thought: Literary and Philosophic Economies from the Medieval to the Modern Era.* 1982. Rpt. Baltimore: Johns Hopkins University Press, 1993. 47–83.

Silver, Morris. "Karl Polanyi and Markets in the Ancient Near East: The Challenge of the Evidence." *Journal of Economic History* 43 (1983), 795–829.

Simmel, Georg. *The Philosophy of Money.* Edited by David Frisby. Translated by Tom Bottomore and David Frisby. 2nd enlarged ed. London: Routledge, 1990.

Simon, Herbert. *Models of Man.* New York: John Wiley, 1957.

Sinanoglou, Leah. "The Christ Child as Sacrifice: A Medieval Tradition and the Corpus Christi Plays." *Speculum* 48 (1973), 491–509.

Solomon, Robert C. *A Passion for Justice: Emotions and the Origins of the Social Contract.* Reading, Mass.: Addison-Wesley, 1990.

Sombart, Werner. *Luxury and Capitalism.* 1922. Translated by W. R. Dittmar. Ann Arbor: University of Michigan Press, 1967.

Sprinkle, Joe M. "The Interpretation of Exodus 21.22–25 (*Lex Talionis*) and Abortion." *Westminster Theological Journal* 55 (1993), 233–253.

Stalsberg, Anne. "Women as Actors in North European Viking Age Trade." In *Social Approaches to Viking Studies.* Edited by Ross Samson. Glasgow: Cruithne Press, 1991. 75–86.

Stanley, E. G. "Words for the Dictionary of Old English." *Subsidia* 26 (1998), 33–56.

Sturlu saga. The Saga of Hvamm-Sturla. Translated by Julia H. McGrew and R. George Thomas. In *Sturlunga saga.* 2 vols. New York: Twayne, 1970–74. 1: 59–113.

Suetonius. *The Twelve Caesars.* Translated by Robert Graves. 1957. Rev. ed. Harmondsworth: Penguin, 1979.

Terry, Patricia, trans. *Poems of the Elder Edda.* Philadelphia: University of Pennsylvania Press, 1990.

Þórðar saga kakala. Translated by Julia H. McGrew and R. George Thomas. In *Sturlunga saga.* 2 vols. New York: Twayne, 1970–74. 2: 227–322.

Þorgils saga ok Hafliða. Translated by Julia H. McGrew and R. George Thomas. In *Sturlunga saga.* 2 vols. New York: Twayne, 1970–74. 2: 25–70.

"Thorstein the Staffstruck." In *Hrafnkel's Saga and Other Stories.* Translated by Hermann Pálsson. Harmondsworth: Penguin, 1971. 72–81.

Thorstein the White's saga. In *The Complete Sagas of Icelanders.* Edited by Viðar Hreinsson. Reykjavík: Leifur Eiríksson, 1997. Vol. 4: 303–313.

Thucydides. *History of the Peloponnesian War.* Translated by Rex Warner. Rev. ed. Harmondsworth: Penguin, 1972.

Twelve Tables. In *Remains of Old Latin.* Vol. III. Translated by E. H. Warmington. Loeb Classical Library. Cambridge, Mass.: Harvard University Press, 1938.

Ur-Namma, Laws of. See Roth, ed. 13–22.

Vápnfirðinga saga. The Saga of the People of Vopnafjord. In *The Complete Sagas of Icelanders.* Edited by Viðar Hreinsson. Reykjavík: Leifur Eiríksson, 1997. Vol. 4: 313–334.

Vickers, Nancy J. "Members Only: Marot's Anatomical Blazons." In *The Body in Parts: Fantasies of Corporeality in Early Modern Europe.* Edited by David Hillman and Carla Mazzio. New York: Routledge, 1997. 3–21.

Vlastos, Gregory. "Equality and Justice in Early Greek Cosmologies." *Classical Philology* 42 (1947), 156–178.

Vlastos, Gregory. "Socrates' Contribution to the Greek Sense of Justice." *Archaionosia* 1 (1980), 301–323.

Waldron, Jeremy. *"Lex Talionis." Arizona Law Review* (1992), 25–51.

Walens, Stanley. *Feasting with Cannibals: An Essay on Kwakiutl Cosmology.* Princeton, N. J.: Princeton University Press, 1981.

Watkins, Calvert. "New Parameters in Historical Linguistics, Philology, and Culture History." *Language* 65 (1989), 783–799.

Weil, Simone. *Simone Weil: An Anthology.* Edited by Siân Miles. New York: Weidenfeld and Nicolson, 1986.

Westbrook, Raymond. *Studies in Biblical and Cuneiform Law.* Cahiers de la Revue Biblique. Vol. 26. Paris: J. Gabalda, 1988.

Wharton, Edith. *House of Mirth.* 1905. New York: Library of America, 1985.

Whigham, Frank. "Reading Social Conflict in the Alimentary Tract: More on the Body in Renaissance Drama." *ELH* 55 (1988), 333–350.

White, Stephen D. *Feuding and Peacemaking in Eleventh-Century France.* Variorum Reprints Series. Aldershot, Hampshire: Ashgate Press, 2005.

White, Stephen D. "Garsinde v. Saint Foy: Argument, Threat, and Vengeance in Eleventh-Century Monastic Litigation." In *Religious and Laity in Western Europe, 1000–1300: Interaction, Negotiation and Power.* Edited by Janet Burton and Emilia Jamroziak. Tournhout: Brepols. In press.

White, Stephen D. "The Politics of Anger in Medieval France." In *Anger's Past: The Social Uses of an Emotion in the Middle Ages.* Edited by Barbara H. Rosenwein. Ithaca, N. Y.: Cornell University Press, 1998. 127–52.

Whitelock, Dorothy, ed. *English Historical Documents, Vol.1, c. 500–1042.* 2nd ed. London: Eyre Methuen, 1979.

Whitman, James Q. "At the Origins of Law and the State: Monopolization of Violence, Mutilation of Bodies, or Setting of Prices?" *Chicago-Kent Law Review* 71 (1995), 41–84.

Wierzbicka, Anna. *Cross-Cultural Pragmatics: The Semantics of Human Interaction.* Berlin: Mouton de Gruyter, 1991.

Wilda, Wilhelm Eduard. *Das Strafrecht der Germanen.* Halle: C. A. Schwetschke, 1842.

Wormald, Patrick. *"Inter Cetera Bona . . . Genti Suae:* Law-making and Peace-keeping in the Earliest English Kingdoms." *La Guistizia nell'alto Medioevo* 2 (1995), 963–993.

Wormald, Patrick. *The Making of English Law: King Alfred to the Twelfth Century. Vol. 1: Legislation and Its Limits.* Oxford: Blackwell, 1999.

Xenophon, *Anabasis. The Persian Expedition.* Translated by Rex Warner. 1949. Harmondsworth: Penguin, 1972.

Zelizer, Viviana A. *Morals and Markets: The Development of Life Insurance in the United States.* New York: Columbia University Press, 1979.

Zelizer, Viviana A. *Pricing the Priceless Child: The Changing Value of Children.* 1985. Princeton, N. J.: Princeton University Press, 1994.

Index

just, 82
  as discourse particle, 11,
    12–13
justice, 81
  corrective, 4, 182
  distributive, 16
  iconography of, 1, 191
  measuring, 160
  poetic, 7, 63, 65, 120, 144,
    221n10
  remedial, 5
  rough, 160

Kant, Immanuel, 18, 130
Kerrigan, John, 204n13, 207n7,
  208n14, 227n18
King Æthelberht, 9, 113, 132. *See
  also* Æthelberht, laws of
King Æthelred, 97, 106. *See also*
  Æthelred, laws of
King Alfred, 9, 34. *See also* Alfred,
  laws of
King Edmund, 124
King Ine, 26. *See also* Ine, laws of
Kings Hloþhere and Eadric. *See*
  Hloþhere and Eadric, laws of
Kohlhaus, Michael, 206n6
Kopytoff, Igor, 189

Lady Aequitas, 1
Lady Justice, 1, 3–4, 5, 6
  Portia as, 72
  Shylock as parody of, 79
Lamech, 24
Last Supper, 42. *See also* Eucharist
Laum, Bernhard, 36–39, 42
law, flexibility of, 81–82
  Portia making ass of, 80
  primal form of, 116
Leges Henrici Primi, 124
Levite's concubine, 92, 133–134
Lex Salica, 127
liability
  group, 150, 207n8
  vicarious, 65, 66, 207n8

liability rules, 49, 51
liberal pluralism, 162
Liebermann, Felix, 121
literalism, 80
lord, etymology of, 42
Lydia, 26

Maat, 1, 3, 5
Maimonides, 48, 218n7
Mandeville, Bernard, 186
man-evening, 174–176
mannjafnaðr. See man-evening
man-price. *See* wergeld
Marvel, Andrew, 127
measure of value
  man as, 41, 216n43
measuring
  commensurability and, 161–165
  See also value, measuring
memory, 89–91, 95, 128
  misremembering, 101, 103
mercy, 79, 83, 84, 152–153
mere, merely, 13–14
mete. *See* measuring; value,
  measuring
Middle Assyrian Laws, 66, 207n8
mitigation, 66
money, 70, 74
  blood as, 104–108
  body parts as, 31
  origins of, 36–38, 41
  special use, 20, 108, 188
Montaigne, Michel de, 88, 100, 123,
  156, 176
Montoya, Inigo, 143
mund, 132–138
mutilation, of corpses, 219n15

neshekh "bite," interest, 75
Newton's third law of motion,
  10
Nietzsche, Friedrich, 90, 91, 97, 99,
  150
Njál's saga, 69, 107, 120
no-harm principle, 23, 138

546-60

122-26, 130-3, Miller-416-57